THE NEW ATLAS OF AFRICAN HISTORY

THE NEW ATLAS OF AFRICAN HISTORY

G. S. P. FREEMAN-GRENVILLE

(Greville Stewart Parker)

SIMON & SCHUSTER

A Paramount Communications Company

New York   London   Toronto   Sydney   Tokyo   Singapore

Cartography: Lorraine Kessel
Designed and produced by Carta, Jerusalem
Printed in Israel

Academic Reference Division
Simon and Schuster
15 Columbus Circle, New York, NY 10023

A Paramount Communications Company

Library of Congress Cataloging-in-Publication Data
Freeman-Grenville, G. S. P. (Greville Stewart Parker)
    The new atlas of African history / G.S.P. Freeman-Grenville.
        p.   cm.
    Includes index.
    ISBN 0-13-612151-9
    1. Africa--Historical geography--Maps.   I. Title. Atlas of
African history.
32446.S1F73 1991   G&M
911 ′6--dc20
                                                            90-47195
                                                                CIP
                                                                MAP

PREFACE

The purpose of this atlas, with 103 maps facing sixty-four pages of commentary, is to illustrate the history of the African continent from prehistoric times to 1990. Africa is too varied and diffuse in its peoples and languages to be regarded as a cultural entity, any more than the kaleidoscope of Europe or that of the Americas are cultural entities. Laplanders and Greeks are both Europeans; Bantu, Berbers, and Boers are all Africans. But other than that these peoples have their respective continents in common, they have little similarity. Not less fallacious than "European" and "African" are terms like "black" and "white."

There are various determinants of human history. Ibn Khaldun was the first to perceive the relations between history and physical geography. In the following pages almost all the maps show relief, because desert, mountain, and river systems, along with bush and rain forest, are among the principal determinants in Africa. The most mysterious event in African history, the Bantu expansion and dispersion, can only be understood in the context of physical geography. Geography also determines trade routes, and these likewise the commerce of ideas, whether of religion or of politics.

The spelling of place names is a perpetual problem in atlases. Here, as far as possible, the most ordinary conventional spellings have been used such as were in vogue at the period under discussion. Systems of diacritical marks such as are used for transliterating Amharic, Arabic, and other languages have been ignored; they are intelligible only to specialists, and not to the ordinary intelligent reader. Where countries or areas have had changes of name, these are cross-referenced in the index. A typical example of renaming is Tanzania, an area which has had five different names during the twentieth century alone.

I have not included a bibliography. The *Cambridge History of Africa* contains lengthy bibliographies, as do many encyclopaedias. Specialized periodicals such as the *Journal of African History* keep such bibliographies up to date with critical reviews. Finally, the *Index Islamicus* is invaluable.

In some areas I am dependent on work in progress by other scholars. In particular I am indebted to Doctors Claude Allibert, Mark Horton, and Stuart Munro-Hay. I must also thank Professors Eric Axelson and Richard Gray for their valuable criticism of earlier work, and Father William Burridge, W.F., and Father Kenneth Campbell, O.F.M., for information concerning missions. Likewise the librarians in the School of Oriental and African Studies, London, and in York University Library have shown me invariable kindness. Once again I am most grateful to Lorraine Kessel who, now in yet a third atlas, has been so elegant and perceptive an interpreter of what I have had in mind.

Sheriff Hutton, York
October 1990

G. S. P. F.-G.

TABLE OF CONTENTS

AFRICA, PHYSICAL

Africa, a continent second only to Asia in size, lies astride the Equator, with its northern and southern limits at almost identical latitudes, 37°N and 35°S. It is roughly pear-shaped, with the northern portion twice the size of the southern. Between these extremes are a remarkable series of differing features and environments, bounded by Mediterranean-type climates.

The greater part of the continent is an elevated plateau, bounded on the east by the mountains of eastern Africa. From north to south it is cut by the river Nile, and then by the Great Rift Valley, with its series of lakes. There are also depressions, the Qattara sand sea of Egypt, the desert region of the Afar (Danakil), and others. In the north and in the Cape there are high mountainous ranges. The Sahara Desert bisects the whole continent, stretching from the Red Sea to the Atlantic. South of it, by contrast, are the huge tropical forests of western and equatorial Africa, with their heavy rainfalls.

The political divisions of Africa are largely the result of the colonial period, and reflect little of geographic diversity. The colonial powers largely ignored both natural and ethnic boundaries as well as economic and commercial ones, and in some cases united hitherto separated peoples whose traditions and cultures had little or nothing in common.

Ten zones may be arbitrarily defined.

I NORTHERN AFRICA This zone comprises the temperate seaboards of Morocco, Algeria, and Tunisia, with the coast of Cyrenaica and Egypt, all historically linked with Europe.

II THE SAHARA BELT Mauritania, the southern parts of Morocco, Algeria, Tunisia, Libya, and the Nile Valley as far as the Sudd marshes make up the Saharan Belt. Save for oases and the Nile Valley, this is a naked desert of sand, erg, and rock, presently inhabited only by nomads.

III THE SAHEL The Sahel includes southern Mauritania, Senegal, The Gambia, Guinea, Guiné, northern Sierra Leone, Ivory Coast, and Ghana; Burkina Faso, the greatest part of Mali, southern Niger, Chad, and Sudan; and northern Togo, Benin, Nigeria, and Cameroon. All these lands are closely linked with the Saharan Belt by ancient trade connections as far as the Mediterranean and have had a succession of great empires, with Islam as a uniting factor.

IV THE GUINEA COASTLANDS These coastlands extend from Sierra Leone as far south as Zaïre, and far inland; the predominant feature is tropical forest. On the coast principally, this area has been exposed more than any other to European contacts since the fifteenth century, by which time it had already developed its own traditions of kingship.

V CENTRAL EQUATORIAL AFRICA The Central African Republic, southern Cameroon, Chad, Gabon, Congo and northern Zaïre, with Equatorial Guinea, unlike other areas, did not develop states of any extent or significance before colonial times.

VI EASTERN AFRICA The southern Sudan has more in common with Uganda than the rest of the Sudan. With its proximity to Arabia, its Semitic tradition in language and political outlook, and its link to Egypt (since the fourth century) by Coptic Christianity, Ethiopia has a unique place in African history. Its mountains adjoin those of Uganda, Kenya and northern Tanzania, which are inhabited chiefly by Bantu-speaking peoples. The Somali deserts, with shade temperatures as high as 150° in the Rift Valley, are an exception. A slender littoral from the Horn merges with the Swahili coastlands as far as Mozambique; largely united by Islam and the Swahili language, it forms a subzone of its own.

VII SOUTH CENTRAL AFRICA The savannah countries of Angola, Zambia, Zimbabwe, and Mozambique had evolved traditions of kingship and already traded from coast to coast by the sixteenth century.

VIII SOUTHERN AFRICA The Republic of South Africa, Namibia, Botswana, Swaziland, and Lesotho are marked by the arrivals, for the most part comparatively recent, of Bantu-speaking peoples moving down the eastern side of the zone and by European settlement, initially Dutch, from the southwest.

IX MADAGASCAR AND THE COMOROS These islands belong as much to the Indian Ocean as to Africa. On the mainland Malagasy, a non-African language, is the principal tongue. The Comoros are an outpost of the Islamic culture of the Swahili coast, which also has historic links with northwestern Madagascar.

□

1 AFRICA, PHYSICAL

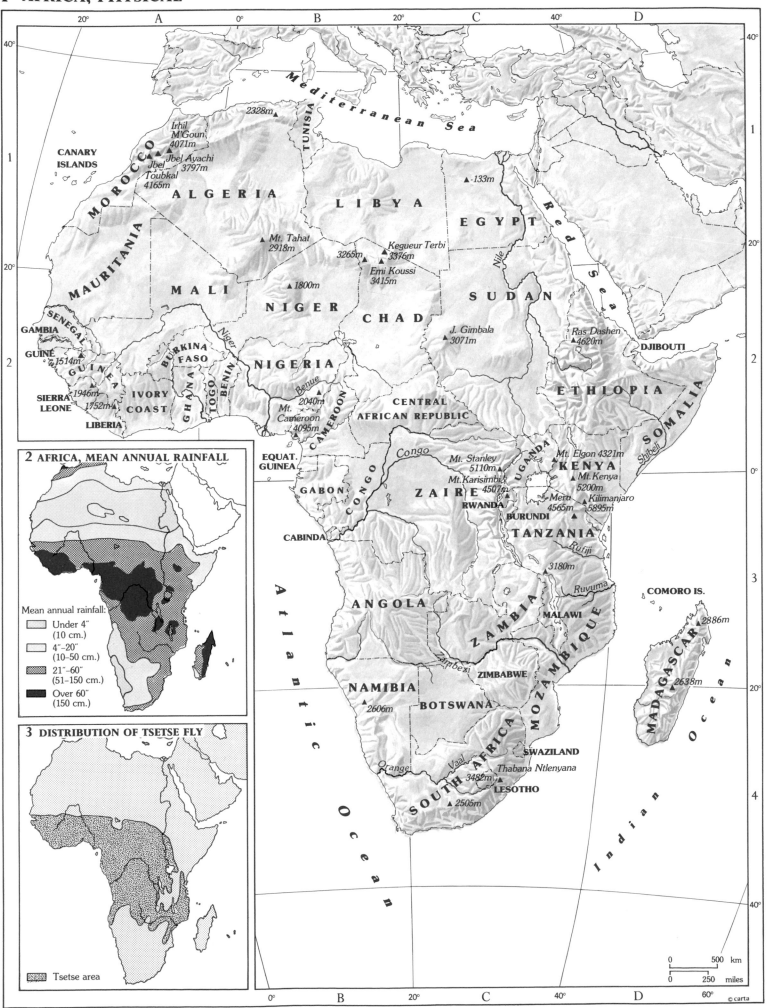

20° A 0° B 20° C 40° D
40° 20° 0° 20° 40°
1 2 3 4
Mediterranean Sea
MOROCCO
CANARY ISLANDS
Irhil M'Goun 4071m
Jbel Ayachi 3797m
Jbel Toubkal 4165m
2328m
TUNISIA
ALGERIA
LIBYA
EGYPT
-133m
Red Sea
Nile
Mt. Tahat 2918m
Kegueur Terbi 3376m
3265m
Emi Koussi 3415m
1800m
MAURITANIA
MALI
NIGER
CHAD
SUDAN
J. Gimbala 3071m
Ras Dashen 4620m
DJIBOUTI
SENEGAL
GAMBIA
GUINÉ
1514m
GUINEA
Niger
BURKINA FASO
NIGERIA
Benue
SIERRA LEONE
1946m
1752m
LIBERIA
IVORY COAST
GHANA
TOGO
BENIN
2040m
Mt. Cameroon 4095m
CAMEROON
CENTRAL AFRICAN REPUBLIC
ETHIOPIA
SOMALIA
Shibeli
EQUAT. GUINEA
GABON
CONGO
Congo
ZAIRE
Mt. Stanley 5110m
Mt. Karisimbi 4507m
UGANDA
Mt. Elgon 4321m
KENYA
Mt. Kenya 5200m
Meru 4565m
Kilimanjaro 5895m
RWANDA
BURUNDI
TANZANIA
Rufiji
CABINDA
3180m
Ruvuma
COMORO IS.
ANGOLA
ZAMBIA
MALAWI
MOZAMBIQUE
2886m
MADAGASCAR
2638m
Zambezi
ZIMBABWE
NAMIBIA
2606m
BOTSWANA
SOUTH AFRICA
SWAZILAND
Orange
Vaal
Thabana Ntlenyana 3482m
LESOTHO
2505m
Atlantic Ocean
Indian Ocean
0 500 km
0 250 miles
0° B 20° C 40° D 60°
© carta
2 AFRICA, MEAN ANNUAL RAINFALL
Mean annual rainfall:
Under 4″ (10 cm.)
4″–20″ (10–50 cm.)
21″–60″ (51–150 cm.)
Over 60″ (150 cm.)
3 DISTRIBUTION OF TSETSE FLY
Tsetse area

THE EARLY STONE AGE

On the present evidence it seems almost certain that Africa was the birthplace of the human race. First argued more than a hundred years ago by Charles Darwin, this view has since then been confirmed by new evidence, chiefly from eastern and southern Africa; but sites in Algeria, Chad, and Morocco, suggest that further evidence may yet be found elsewhere in Africa. The view generally accepted was that humans evolved from apes (pongoids) into Australopithecines, or near-humans, over a period of several million years. But in Kenya in 1963 a creature provisionally called *Kenyapithecus wickeri* was identified as belonging to the family of Hominids dating back some twelve million years, a superfamily which would have been ancestral both to apes and to humankind.

The most famous site is the Olduvai Gorge in Tanzania, near the Kenyan border and close to the game reserves of Serengeti and Ngorongoro. The gorge is part of the Rift Valley, a fault in the earth's surface which extends all the way from the Jordan to Lake Malawi. Olduvai lies in wild, waterless country. The cutting brought about by a volcanic upheaval many thousands of years ago exposed neatly stratified layers of ancient settlement. Here L. S. B. Leakey found Nutcracker Man (*Zinjanthropus boisei*), dating 1.7 million years back, together with quantities of rough stone implements assumed to have been his tools. Use of tools, to Leakey, represents the essential difference between "humans" and "near-humans", or between *Zinjanthropus* and the Australopithecines familiar at the sites in South Africa.

In 1960, however, Leakey conducted further excavations at Olduvai, where he found further Hominid remains of a different species. He named it *Homo habilis*, Toolmaking Man. *Homo habilis* had a larger brainpan than *Zinjanthropus* and teeth that indicated that he ate meat as well as vegetables.

It was thought, therefore, that *Homo habilis* was more likely to have been the maker of the stone tools, because they would have been of use to him to smash animal bones in order to extract the marrow, whereas no such tool could have been of value to a vegetarian such as Zinjanthropus.

On present evidence it is not possible to distinguish the changes or progress that would have been made during approximately one million years of Oldowan culture. But the change from vegetarian habits to hunting as well as gathering must have been a revolutionary one. The nails and teeth of humans are not adapted to tearing or cutting the skin of wild animals, not even the smallest antelopes or pigs. The human who hit upon the idea of using a stone tool was as much an inventor as the later discoverers of fire, electricity, or nuclear energy. The discovery would have provided greater strength and chances of survival, and it is not simply by chance that tools of this culture have been found in Morocco, Algeria, and Chad in the north, in Ethiopia on the river Awash, and at three sites in South Africa: clearly the human population was now increasing and expanding. During the second half of this long period rather more sophisticated tools appear, along with evidence that larger animals (including the elephant) were being hunted and human beings had learned to join together in hunting expeditions and thus in social organization.

Leakey's definition of humans as creatures "capable of making tools to a set and regular pattern" is not satisfactory, because this ability is possessed also to a limited degree by chimpanzees, and because the definition ignores the human being's capabilities of abstract reasoning and spiritual perception, as evidenced already by the careful burial of the dead, which would argue for early belief in an afterlife.

□

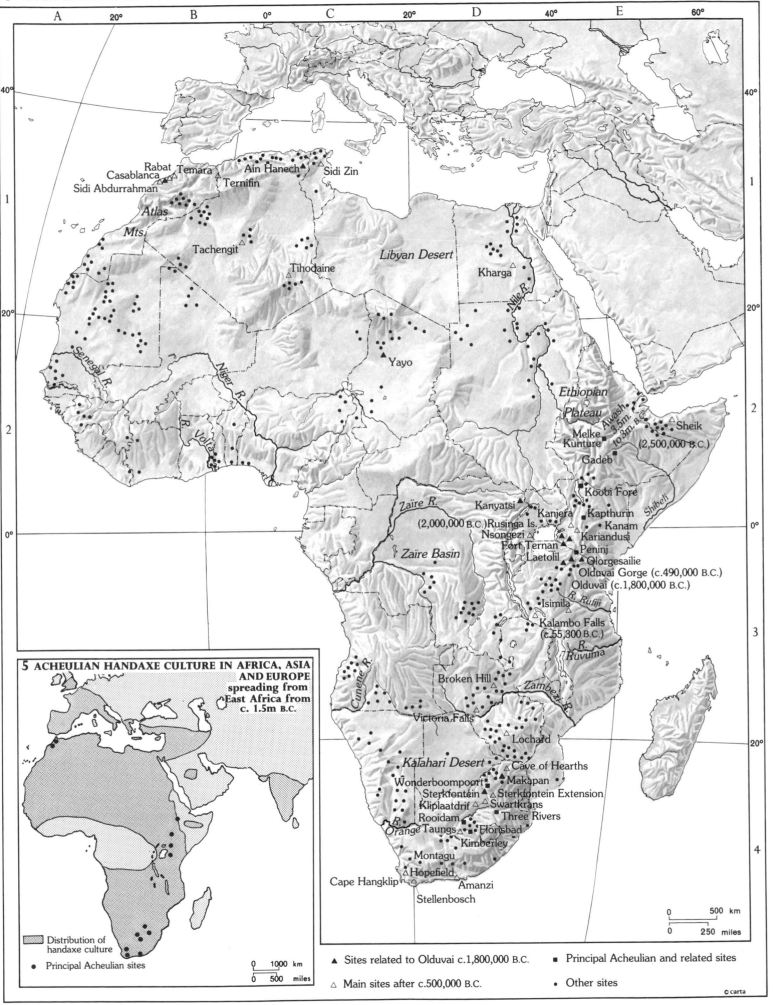

4 THE EARLY STONE AGE

Casablanca
Rabat
Temara
Sidi Abdurrahman
Ain Hanech
Sidi Zin
Ternifin
Atlas
Mts.
Tachengit
Tihodaine
Libyan Desert
Kharga
Nile R.
Yayo
Senegal R.
Niger R.
Volta R.
Ethiopian Plateau
Awash
3.5m. to 3m. B.C.
Melke Kunture
Gadeb
Sheik
(2,500,000 B.C.)
Shibeli
Koobi Fora
Kanyatsi
(2,000,000 B.C.)
Kanjera
Rusinga Is.
Nsongezi
Fort Ternan
Laetolil
Kapthurin
Kanam
Kariandusi
Peninj
Olorgesailie
Olduvai Gorge (c.490,000 B.C.)
Olduvai (c.1,800,000 B.C.)
Zaïre R.
Zaïre Basin
Isimila
R. Rufiji
Kalambo Falls
(c.55,300 B.C.)
R. Ruvuma
Broken Hill
Zambezi R.
Victoria Falls
Cunene R.
Lochard
Kalahari Desert
Cave of Hearths
Wonderboompoort
Makapan
Sterkfontein
Sterkfontein Extension
Kliplaatdrif
Swartkrans
Rooidam
Three Rivers
Orange R.
Taungs
Florisbad
Kimberley
Montagu
Hopefield
Cape Hangklip
Amanzi
Stellenbosch

5 ACHEULIAN HANDAXE CULTURE IN AFRICA, ASIA AND EUROPE
spreading from East Africa from c. 1.5m B.C.

Distribution of handaxe culture
• Principal Acheulian sites

0   1000 km
0   500 miles

▲ Sites related to Olduvai c.1,800,000 B.C.   ■ Principal Acheulian and related sites

△ Main sites after c.500,000 B.C.   • Other sites

0   500 km
0   250 miles

© carta

11

THE LATER STONE AGE

Definitions in archaeology are fraught with danger, and can only be taken generally. The Early Stone Age (Paleolithic) extends from the emergence of human beings to the end of the last Ice Age (c. 10,000 B.C.). Around 1,500,000 B.C. the Acheulian Handaxe culture emerged in Africa from an epicenter at present unlocated. It spread throughout the African continent and much of Europe and Asia. In Africa it survived longest, perhaps up until one hundred thousand years ago. The development was by no means uniform.

At some as yet undetermined time tools became more refined. Microliths (tiny stone tools) fitted with wooden hafts began to appear and to be greatly diversified. Human being were still hunter-gatherers, but their circumstances became more sophisticated. Luxury articles began to appear: beads, pendants and cosmetics are depicted in rock paintings.

About forty thousand years ago the Sahara became uninhabitable. Fishing settlements crowded toward the Nile. About 8000 B.C. bone was used for harpoons and stone rings and weights for fishing nets were introduced. The manufacture of pottery began. Similar developments occurred in Ethiopia and Kenya and as far as Timbuktu and Bamako. By then some differentiation had taken place in human stock (see map 7).

Grindstones dating to around 18,000 B.C. survive in Upper Egypt and Nubia, showing that human beings were then eating cereals. The cultivation of wheat, barley, and flax is attested at around 6000 B.C. Other than maize (Indian corn) and manioc (cassava), which are known to have been introduced from the Americas after A.D. 1500, with bananas somewhat earlier from India, most crops now available in Africa were already being cultivated as early as 6000 B.C. The domestication of animals is much more difficult to date, for only after selective breeding has begun is it possible to demonstrate the difference between wild and domestic stock. There are no wild prototypes of African sheep or goats, and it is difficult to differentiate them on the basis of bone survival.

By 6000 B.C. trade movements were visible. From Nubia ivory and skins traveled northward to Egypt, making their way upriver along with stone vessels, copper tools, palettes, and amulets. By 3000 B.C. houses were being built, but perhaps only for the elite. Flocks of sheep and goats provided wool for cloth.

Elsewhere developments were slower. In North Africa pottery began to be made during the sixth millennium, and small animals were domesticated at the same time. Large cattle were not domesticated before the third millennium. Attempts were made to domesticate wild animals such as the giraffe and antelope, as is seen in rock art; unfortunately there is no way to date this practice. Near lakes barley and sorghum were cultivated, and grindstones survive.

In western and central Africa indigenous food crops were cultivated, and pottery and refined stone implements appear in the fourth millennium. In Ethiopia too, local grains — noog, teff, ensete, and perhaps finger millet — were cultivated. There were long-horned cattle, shown in rock paintings. About 3000 B.C. camels first appeared in small numbers in nearby Kenya. Essentially, the inhabitants were herders. Unlike anywhere else, they practiced cremation, burying the ashes along with a stone bowl, pestle, and mortar. Other eastern African areas were less sophisticated but were based primarily on herding. Farther south hunting and gathering remained the principal occupations.

□

6 THE LATER STONE AGE

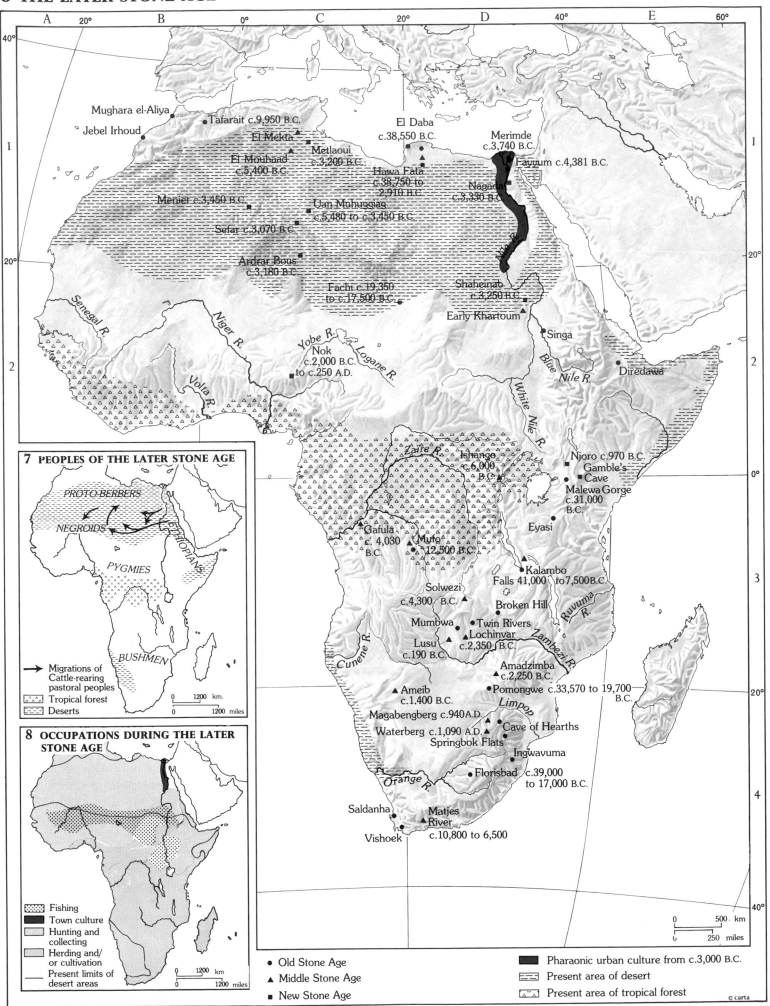

Mughara el-Aliya
Jebel Irhoud
Tafarait c.9,950 B.C.
El Mekta
El Mouhaad c.5,400 B.C.
Metlaoui c.3,200 B.C.
El Daba c.38,550 B.C.
Merimde c.3,740 B.C.
Fayyum c.4,381 B.C.
Hawa Fata c.38,750 to 2,910 B.C.
Nagada c.3,330 B.C.
Meniet c.3,450 B.C.
Uan Muhuggiag c.5,480 to c.3,450 B.C.
Sefar c.3,070 B.C.
Ardrar Bous c.3,180 B.C.
Fachi c.19,350 to c.17,500 B.C.
Shaheinab c.3,250 B.C.
Early Khartoum
Singa
Nok c.2,000 B.C. to c.250 A.D.
Diredawa
Njoro c.970 B.C.
Gamble's Cave
Malewa Gorge c.31,000 B.C.
Ishango c.6,000 B.C.
Eyasi
Gafula c.4,030 B.C.
Mufo c.12,500 B.C.
Kalambo Falls 41,000 to 7,500 B.C.
Solwezi c.4,300 B.C.
Broken Hill
Mumbwa
Twin Rivers
Lochinvar c.2,350 B.C.
Lusu c.190 B.C.
Amadzimba c.2,250 B.C.
Ameib c.1,400 B.C.
Pomongwe c.33,570 to 19,700 B.C.
Magabengberg c.940 A.D.
Cave of Hearths
Waterberg c.1,090 A.D.
Springbok Flats
Ingwavuma
Florisbad c.39,000 to 17,000 B.C.
Saldanha
Matjes River c.10,800 to 6,500
Vishoek

7 PEOPLES OF THE LATER STONE AGE

PROTO BERBERS
NEGROIDS
ETHIOPIANS
PYGMIES
BUSHMEN

→ Migrations of Cattle-rearing pastoral peoples
△ Tropical forest
Deserts

0   1200 km.
0   1200 miles

8 OCCUPATIONS DURING THE LATER STONE AGE

Fishing
Town culture
Hunting and collecting
Herding and/ or cultivation
Present limits of desert areas

0   1200 km
0   1200 miles

• Old Stone Age
▲ Middle Stone Age
■ New Stone Age

Pharaonic urban culture from c.3,000 B.C.
Present area of desert
Present area of tropical forest

© carta

0   500 km
0   250 miles

13

MOVEMENT OF PEOPLES IN NORTHERN AFRICA BETWEEN c. 3500 AND c. 500 B.C.

By the time of earliest recorded history in Egypt (c. 3100) numerous villages of fishermen and agriculturalists already existed in what is now desert between the seventeenth and twenty-first parallels. About the same time in Ténéré, in what is now inaccessible desert, villagers dwelt in stone houses. Near Khartoum, in the Fayyum, and in the present-day Sahara fishermen used flints and bones to make harpoons.

During the third millennium the Sahara desiccated sharply, causing the inhabitants to emigrate southward in search of water as far as the present Benin, Nigeria, Mali and Chad. Among them were ancestors of those who were to develop the neolithic Nok culture in the first millennium. Farmers in Mali who were the ancestors of the founders of the ancient African empire of Ghana grew millet, African rice (*oryza glaberrima*) and other crops.

Pastoralists inhabited the Sahara throughout this period. In the Tassili 'n-Ajjer region they have left a remarkable series of cave paintings. Their culture reached as far as Gao on the Niger bend and the Senegal valley, and across the whole Sudanic belt. Physical antropologists have demonstrated a remarkable stability of human types in these areas, as can be seen even today among the peoples of northern Africa. □

PROBABLE MIGRATIONS OF THE BANTU FROM c. 500 B.C.

The name *Bantu* was coined in 1862 by the linguist W. H. Bleek, from *ntu* (a common phoneme denoting "humankind") and *ba* (a plural indicator), to represent the remarkably close relationship of all the African languages from the Cameroon Mountains across the whole of Africa to south of Ethiopia as far as the Cape. There are also descendants of some earlier linguistic groups, who are non-Bantu, of which obvious examples are the *Iraqw* in Tanzania and the Khoi-San (Bushmen and Hottentot) people in South Africa. There are some 350 Bantu languages in which a complex series of prefixes, infixes, and suffixes revolve around unchanging roots. This linguistic hypothesis is sustained by evidence from pottery and later from metal.

The epicenter of the populations which led to the migration of these peoples appears to have been in the Cameroon Mountains, with a secondary epicenter in what is now southern Zaïre. Other groups also appear to have moved westward as far as the Bauchi plateau in Nigeria. There is no evidence for what might be described as tribal migrations. Rather it seems that the Bantu movement was that of a slow trickle of families seeking land in well-watered areas and that these groups later developed into tribal agglomerations. □

MOVEMENT OF INDONESIAN PEOPLES INTO MADAGASCAR, c. 500 B.C. TO A.D. 250

The origins and history of the peoples of Madagascar have been much debated, but it is not disputed that the principal language, Malagasy, is of Indonesian origin. The languages of the two areas are as strikingly close in vocabulary and phonetics as are the Romance languages of Europe or the Bantu languages of Africa. However, the archaeology of Madagascar is still in its infancy and there is no firm evidence to date as to when the migration from Indonesia took place, or precisely why.

Map 11 shows the currents that cross the ocean from east to west, and thus indicates how the long-distance journey would have been achieved. In fact, Indonesia, Madagascar, and the eastern African coast are the only parts of the world where outrigger canoes (Swahili, *ngalawa*) are known. Outrigger canoes are recorded in the *Periplus of the Erythraean Sea* (c. A.D. 50), but the movement would have begun long before that date. Migration would have ended no later than the second century, since it was shortly thereafter that Hinduism spread to Indonesia.

Even today most Malagasy have Indonesian physical characteristics, although immigrants of Bantu origin are found on the western side of the island, with those of Arab descent residing in the northwest. The influence of these layers of different peoples is also evident in Malagasy society, religion, and culture. □

9 MOVEMENT OF PEOPLES IN NORTHERN AFRICA BETWEEN c.3500 AND c.500 B.C.

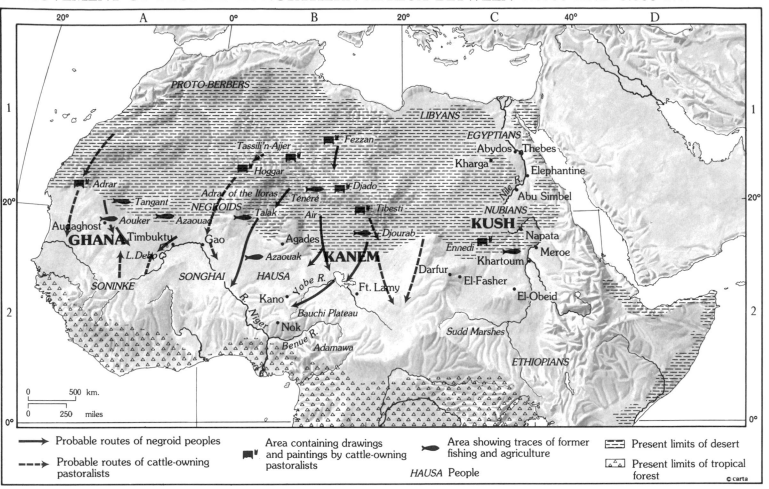

Probable routes of negroid peoples

Probable routes of cattle-owning pastoralists

Area containing drawings and paintings by cattle-owning pastoralists

Area showing traces of former fishing and agriculture

HAUSA People

Present limits of desert

Present limits of tropical forest

© carta

10 PROBABLE MIGRATIONS OF THE BANTU FROM c.500 B.C.

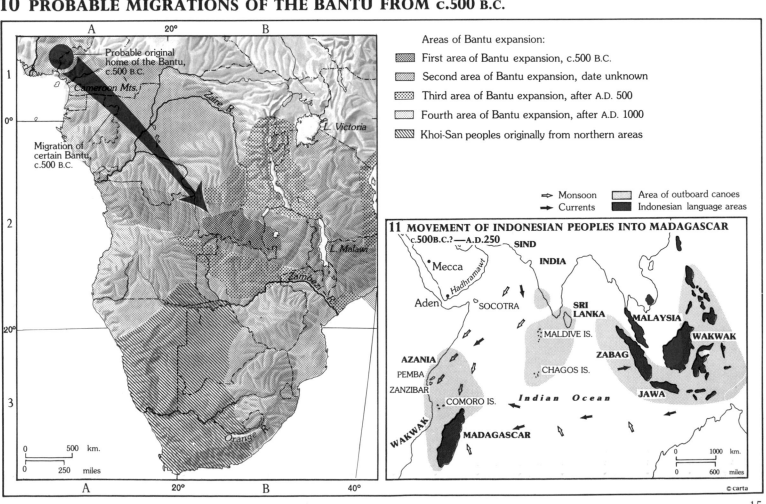

Areas of Bantu expansion:

First area of Bantu expansion, c.500 B.C.

Second area of Bantu expansion, date unknown

Third area of Bantu expansion, after A.D. 500

Fourth area of Bantu expansion, after A.D. 1000

Khoi-San peoples originally from northern areas

Monsoon

Currents

Area of outboard canoes

Indonesian language areas

11 MOVEMENT OF INDONESIAN PEOPLES INTO MADAGASCAR

c.500 B.C.? — A.D.250

© carta

EGYPT UNDER THE PHARAOHS

As the population grew beside the Nile following the desiccation of the Sahara and was compressed into the valley, the domestication of animals and the cultivation of edible plants progressed. Between 5000 B.C. and 3000 B.C. kingdoms emerged in Lower Egypt — in the rich agricultural land of the Delta — as well as in Upper Egypt, partly because of its wealth in gold and other minerals. Shortly before 3000, Narmer unified the two states; it fell to his son Menes to build a capital at Memphis, near modern Cairo. To do this he diverted the Nile, a great feat of engineering equaled only around 2650 B.C., when the Pyramids began to be built as part of an elaborate religious cult. The theological elaboration proceeded side by side with an ever-increasing sophistication in engineering, medicine, agriculture, and art, and the emergence of a privileged aristocracy.

Thiry-one dynasties succeeded one another in turn over the next three millennia, sometimes in conflict with competing dynasties established by provincial governors. Whether in the Delta or upstream in Upper Egypt, the maintenance of Egyptian society depended on the effective control and distribution of the annual flooding of the Nile, with the waters and silt that washed down from Ethiopia and faraway Lake Victoria. In the second millennium B.C. Egyptian rule was extended to Nubia, a conquest completed under Sesostris III (1878–1841). His fortresses near the Second Cataract still partly survive.

In 1674 B.C. the Hyksos, a people with Palestinian antecedents, seized Egypt. They had light, two-wheeled chariots and a composite bow. Their military prowess was at first unchallengeable, but they controlled only the Delta. Upper Egypt soon learned the skills of its enemies and, under Amasis I (1552–1527) reconquered Egypt, expelling the Hyksos.

Now a period of imperial expansion began, beyond the Fourth Cataract to the south, and then, under Thutmose I (1506–1494), into Palestine and Syria as far as Mesopotamia. The city states of Syria were not easily held, and, save for the Damascus region, did not extend for long east of the Jordan and the Orontes. For this a standing army was needed of both volunteers and conscripts, which in fact offered a promising career to ambitious peasants.

The Tell el-Amarna tablets, the state archive of the pharaoh Akhenaton (1364–1347), present a vivid picture of what was now a declining administration. Turbulent cities had grown up, owing only a nominal allegiance to Egypt, which now faced a new threat in the north from the Hittites. Nevertheless it was the peak of commercial prosperity and long-distance trade from the mines of Nubia as far as the uplands of Syria and beyond. This was the age of the building of the great temples of Karnak and Luxor, and the carving of colossal statuary. The furnishings and jewelry of the tomb of Tutankhamen (1347–1337) are unsurpassed in luxury, taste, and extravagance.

Under Tutankhamen's successors territory that had been lost on the Orontes was regained, and the Hittites were finally defeated at Qadesh (1286 B.C.). Shortly thereafter Egypt was surrounded by enemies: Libya on the west, Assyria to the east. For two centuries (945-715) Libyan monarchs held sway, followed by a century under a Nubian dynasty (to 656 B.C.). Already by 671 B.C. Egypt was paying tribute to Assyria. Following an attempt to refuse tribute, the Assyrians attacked and pillaged the country. In 525 Cambyses of Persia conquered Egypt, and Darius I had dug a forerunner of the Suez Canal, linking the Nile to the Red Sea.

In 332 B.C. Alexander the Great conquered Egypt and made it part of the vast empire that was broken up among his generals on his death in 323 B.C. A new dynasty was founded with its capital at Alexandria by Ptolemy I (Ptolemy Soter). This Greco-Egyptian city, with its heavy Greek and Jewish population, soon became not only the commercial capital of the world but the intellectual center of Greek culture, renowned for its library. After the death of Cleopatra, the last of the Ptolemaic dynasty, in 31 B.C. Egypt fell to Rome. Nevertheless, outside the hellenized capital, the essential Egyptian characteristics of a civilization that had endured the vicissitudes of three thousand years remained unchanged. □

12 EGYPT UNDER THE PHARAOHS

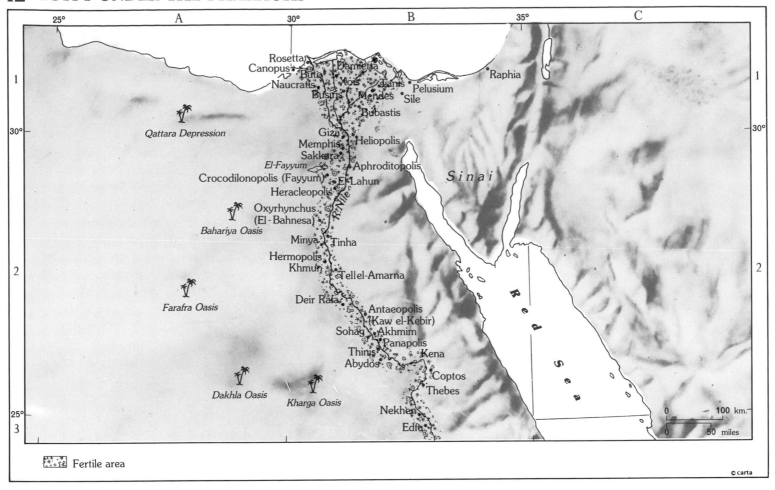

Fertile area

13 EGYPT AND THE NEAR EAST IN PHARAONIC TIMES

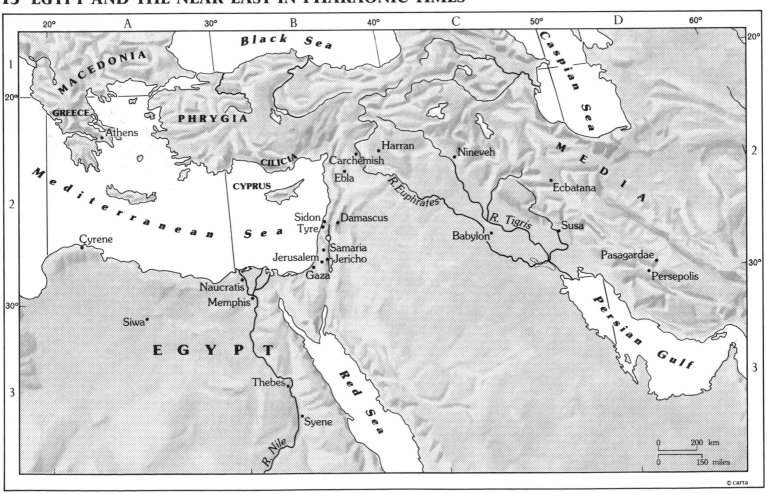

NUBIA AND THE SUDAN IN THE TIME OF THE PHARAOHS

The lands south of Egypt are frequently referred to as Ethiopia, a blanket term used by the Greeks for all those with "burned faces" who lived beyond the First Cataract. In the time of the Old Kingdom (c. 2500 B.C.) this was the southern frontier of Egypt, but both raiders and traders penetrated it, possibly up to Darfur. Under the Middle Kingdom massive fortresses were built along a new frontier at the Second Cataract (c. 2000); eventually, around 1500, the Egyptians made the Fourth Cataract their frontier.

This land, with the Nuba Hills east of the Nile, they called Kush. Its attraction was that it was one of the richest gold-bearing areas of the ancient world and provided the finances for a policy of imperial expansion into the Levant. The Egyptian conquerors did not disturb the indigenous agriculturalists, but Egyptian traders, officials, clergy, and soldiers Egyptianized the population.

About 920 B.C. an independent Kushite dynasty began to rule at Napata. In 716 its ruler, Shabaka, conquered all of Egypt. His descendants lost it to the Assyrians in 667, but retired to Napata. From there, and then from Meroe, they ruled for a thousand years. No other African state can equal their record. Ruins of temples and numerous pyramids attest their prosperity. The land was not desiccated as it would later be; it supported huge herds of cattle, and corn cultivation and wine production flourished. In the fourth century B.C. the Kushites began to mine and exploit iron, an art which they may have learned from the Assyrians as the Assyrians had learned it from the Hittites, and the latter in turn from the people of Urartu in the mountains of Armenia. In this the Kushites had the advantage of Egypt, which had neither iron ore, nor wood with which to smelt it.

The wealth in wood proved to be Meroe's downfall. The woodlands were depleted by excessive smelting and were not renewed; thus the soil eroded, and the area could no longer support either human or animal populations of any size. It fell to Axum around A.D. 350. □

EGYPT AND NORTH AFRICA ACCORDING TO HERODOTUS

The Greek historian Herodotus (d. c. 429 B.C.) was the first writer to describe Egypt and Libya. Map 15 is a reconstruction of the North African areas covered in his History. Much of what he reported is mythical, but there are nuggets of valuable information. He states, for example, that asafoetida (a gum resin) was obtained near Cyrene, while near Barca date palms were cultivated and locusts caught, cooked, and made into a beverage. Near Syrtis rainwater was already being collected in cisterns. Herodotus contrasts the Garamantes, who shun all others and possess no warlike weapons, with the Macae, who coif their hair like crested helmets. The land of the Gindanes is inhabited by the Lotus-Eaters, a people who subsist on a fruit as sweet as the date. Among the Libyans are cattle herdsmen, hunters, and gatherers of salt. The Garamantes, the people of the Fezzan, use four-horse chariots and eat snakes and lizards. They have a language unlike that of any other people, and screech like bats. They are troglodytes (as some Libyans are even today). To the far west are the Atlantes, of whom it is said that "they eat no living thing, nor dream dreams." Beyond these regions salt mines were already being exploited. Among the Gyzantes monkeys are eaten (as indeed they are today in Zaïre). Some Gyzantes practice "silent trade" with the Carthaginians, "setting down gold in exchange for merchandise, and then retiring." □

14 NUBIA AND THE SUDAN IN THE TIME OF THE PHARAOHS

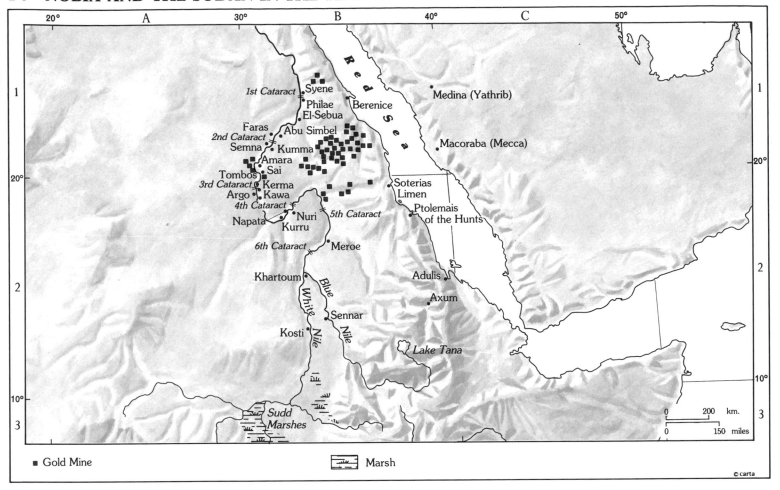

■ Gold Mine   ▨ Marsh

© carta

15 EGYPT AND NORTH AFRICA ACCORDING TO HERODOTUS

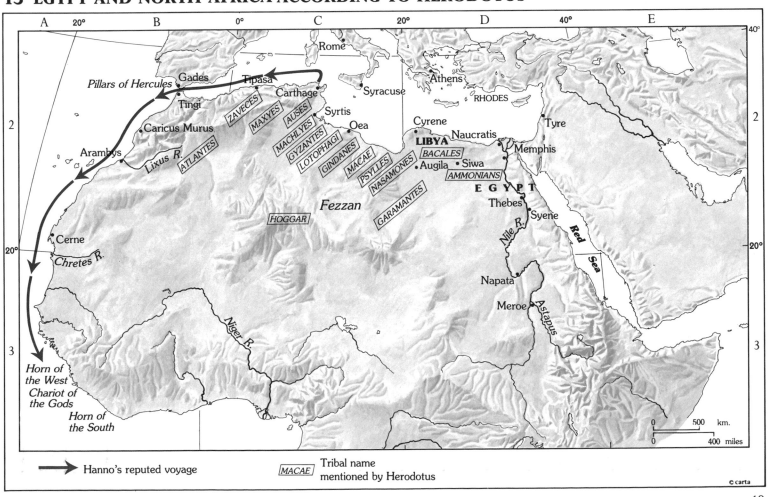

→ Hanno's reputed voyage   *MACAE*   Tribal name mentioned by Herodotus

© carta

CARTHAGINIAN AND ROMAN NORTH AFRICA

About 1110 B.C. Phoenicians from the Levant founded trading stations at Lixus (now Larache), in Morocco, and at Gades (present Cádiz), in Spain. Their objective was to obtain the produce of the gold and silver and tin mines of the Atlas Mountains and the Wadi Draa and from Huelva and the Sierra Morena respectively. According to tradition Utica was founded in 1105, as an entrepôt which would unite Phoenicia with the seaborne bronze and copper trade between the areas of present-day Tunisia and Sicily. These connections are attested by pottery and by funerary architecture dating back to the third millennium.

At first trade was conducted by what Herodotus called "silent trade," long after the foundation of Carthage, traditionally in 814, by Queen Dido, sister of Pygmalion, king of Tyre. The core of the legend attests a relationship between the prosperous Levant and the west as far as Morocco and Spain. Soon Carthage developed trading settlements throughout the western Mediterranean as well as with the oases (through the agency of the nomadic Berbers) and then with western Africa.

It was inevitable when Rome became mistress of all Italy in 272 B.C. that she should come into conflict with Carthage. The First (264–261 B.C.) and Second (209–206) Punic Wars swayed the issue in favor of Rome, which now acquired all the northern African seaboard as far as Morocco. A third Punic War (201–146) ensued against the Berbers under Masinissa, which ended with the destruction of Carthage. Resistance by local rulers still continued until in A.D. 25 the emperor Augustus organized a kingdom of Mauretania from Morocco to the Tunisian border, without, however, effecting any real easing of tribal resistance. □

ROMAN PROVINCES OF NORTH AFRICA UNTIL THE 3RD CENTURY A.D.

The years A.D. 40 to 238 were a golden age in the history of the Roman Empire. The Pax Romana extended from Britain to the Danube and the Black Sea, throughout the Mediterranean from the Atlantic to the Levant, and as far as the Euphrates.

In North Africa the area Rome occupied was not much greater than the coastal zone inland as far as the beginning of the desert and almost all of present-day Tunisia. From this area Rome drew the greatest part of its corn supply and the wild animals that were needed for the circus games (*panem et circenses*) that kept the Roman plebs content.

So as to exploit agricultural land to the utmost at the expense of pasture, land was seized and parceled out among large landowners or tax-farmers (*publicani*), who were responsible for collecting grain. The result was an impoverished peasantry that often had to till the lands it had previously owned. The peasants revolted again and again. Nevertheless, the sale of oil, wine, and marble, brought wealth to the landowners, and led too to the creation of splendid cities whose ruins are still a source of wonder to travelers and tourists. Theaters, baths, temples, markets, statuary, paved streets, public fountains fed by aqueducts — all were there for the pleasure of the townsfolk. The number of baths reflects the wealth of a leisured bourgeoisie cultivated enough to produce Latin writers, poets, grammarians, and rhetoricians, and even Christian theologians. Even here an undercurrent of resistance was demonstrated by the rapid spread of Christianity among the Berbers by way of reaction against the gods of Rome. The same undercurrent could also be sensed in the Berber tendency toward heterodoxy, exemplified by Tertullian and the Montanists in the second century and by that puritanical rigorism which erupted in the Donatist movement at the beginning of the fourth century. □

16 CARTHAGINIAN AND ROMAN NORTH AFRICA

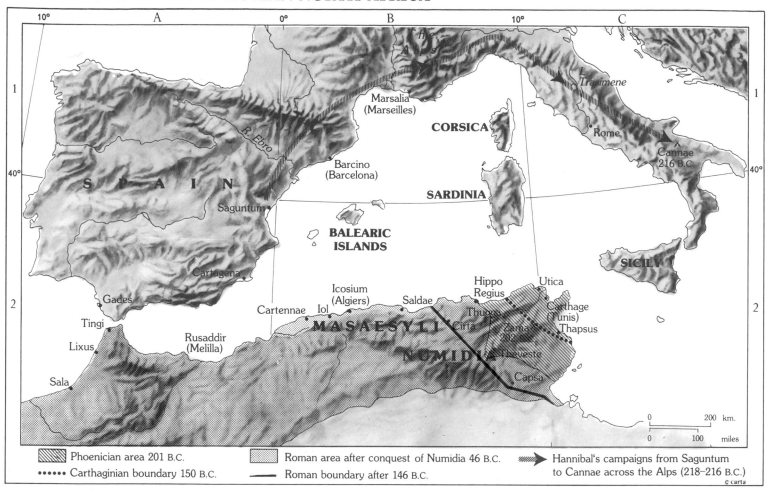

Marsalia (Marseilles)

CORSICA

Rome

SARDINIA

Cannae 216 B.C.

SPAIN

Barcino (Barcelona)

Saguntum

BALEARIC ISLANDS

SICILY

Cartagena

Gades

Icosium (Algiers)

Hippo Regius

Utica

Tingi

Cartennae

Iol

Saldae

Carthage (Tunis)

Lixus

Rusaddir (Melilla)

MASAESYLII

Thugga

Cirta

Zama 202

Thapsus

Sala

NUMIDIA

Theveste

Capsa

▨ Phoenician area 201 B.C.	▨ Roman area after conquest of Numidia 46 B.C.	➤ Hannibal's campaigns from Saguntum to Cannae across the Alps (218–216 B.C.)
•••• Carthaginian boundary 150 B.C.	— Roman boundary after 146 B.C.	

© carta

17 ROMAN PROVINCES OF NORTH AFRICA UNTIL THE 3RD CENTURY A.D.

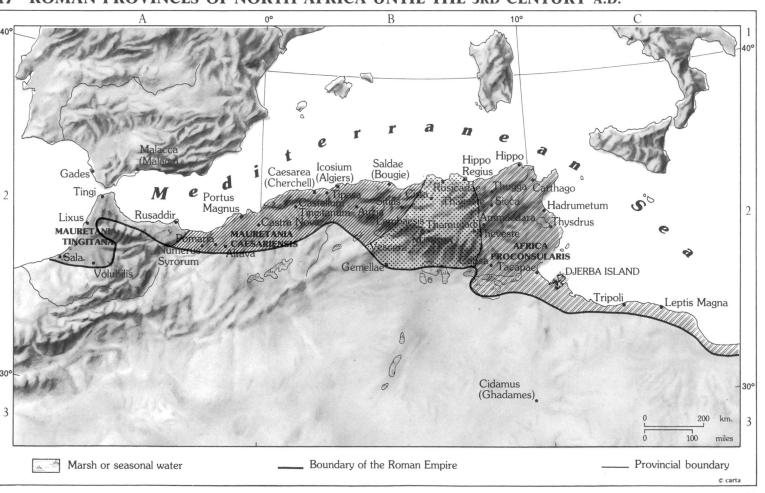

Mediterranean Sea

Malacca (Malaga)

Gades

Caesarea (Cherchell)

Icosium (Algiers)

Saldae (Bougie)

Hippo Regius

Hippo

Tingi

Portus Magnus

Rusicade

Thugga

Carthago

MAURETANIA TINGITANA

Rusaddir

Tipasa

Cirta

Thabraca

Sicca

Hadrumetum

Lixus

Castra Nova

Siga

Pomaria

Tingitanum

Lambaesis

Thamugadi

Ammaedara

Thysdrus

MAURETANIA CAESARIENSIS

Auzia

Theveste

Sala

Numerus Syrorum

Altava

Vescera

AFRICA PROCONSULARIS

Volubilis

Gemellae

Tacapae

DJERBA ISLAND

Tripoli

Leptis Magna

Cidamus (Ghadames)

▨ Marsh or seasonal water	— Boundary of the Roman Empire	— Provincial boundary

© carta

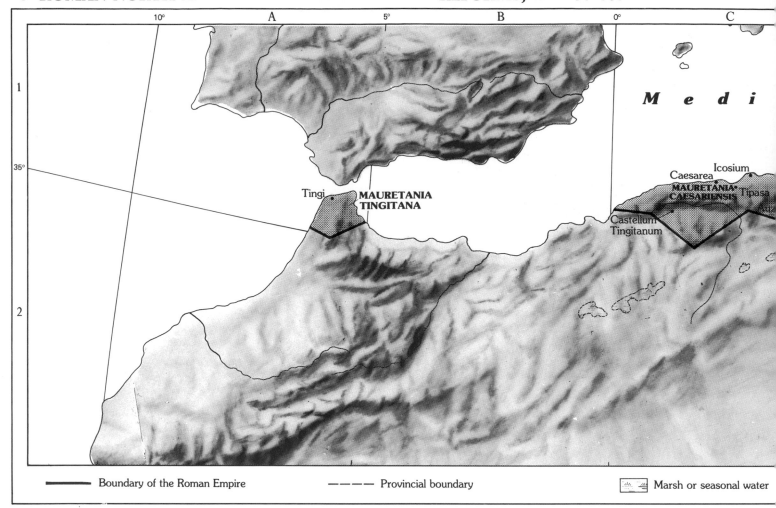

Boundary of the Roman Empire — — — — Provincial boundary

Marsh or seasonal water

ROMAN NORTH AFRICA AFTER DIOCLETIAN'S REFORMS, A.D. 284–305

The thirty years following the assassination in 235 of the emperor Alexander Severus were years of anarchy throughout the Roman Empire. In North Africa already in 238 the emperor Gordian I was forced to disband the famous Legio Augusta that formerly had kept the peace at the foot of the Aurès Mountains. Among the Berbers in the cities there was a recrudescence of national feeling that was to express itself in the Donatist movement (see map 22), while among the tribesmen there was open revolt.

About 246 a well-known public orator named Cyprian became Christian. Three years later he was acclaimed as bishop of Carthage. In 250 the order of the emperor Decius that all should sacrifice to the pagan gods provoked a crisis within the church. There were numerous apostates in the face of persecution. Were they to be read-

mitted to the sacraments, or indeed admitted at all? The correspondence of Cyprian with Pope Stephen I of Rome survives. Although he acknowledges, somewhat grudgingly, the Roman primacy, his thinking in terms of church government is distinctly democratic: bishops, priests, and deacons must be elected by the suffrages of the clergy and be acclaimed by people at large, as well as have the acceptance of the college of bishops. It was a view in full accordance with the Berber spirit. Cyprian himself died most courageously as a martyr in 258.

From 253 to 262 all Numidia and Mauretania was in rebellion. Insecurity persisted long after, and in 285 the emperor Diocletian determined to draw back the boundaries of the empire in North Africa (for previous boundaries, see map 17). The region of Tangiers was governed from Spain, while west of

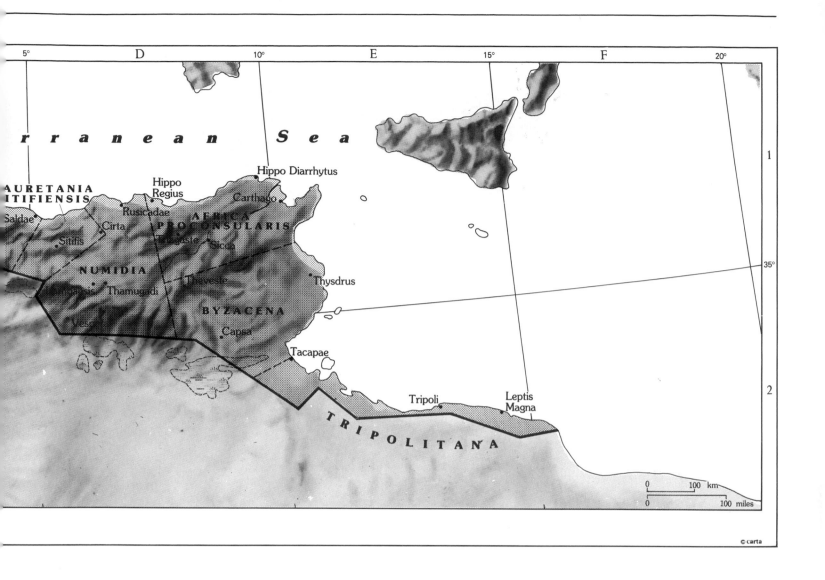

the line Batna-Mostaganem was unadministered. Nevertheless there was a further rebellion in 289, and order was restored only in 297. Even so, the army was largely locally recruited from Berbers, and could not be relied upon. Among them a form of pacifism was widespread, coupled with a refusal to sacrifice to the emperor (a ceremony of little more meaning than saluting a flag). Those who refused, soldiers or no, were regarded as confessors if they lived, martyrs only if they died. All this was the prelude to the Donatist movement, which was to condemn all those who took flight in the face of persecution — as indeed did many bishops, together with leading laymen and Roman officials. Diocletian's edict of persecution in 303 was yet another strand in a complex situation which only sharpened the different conflicts.

The history of the Donatist movement is outlined in map 22. It was only toward the end of the century that Augustine, the man who would be the greatest theological thinker of the early church, became bishop of the small town of Hippo (now Annaba). He was born at Thagaste in 354 and, after a brilliant academic career, became professor of rhetoric first at Carthage, then in Rome, and finally in Milan. A Berber by origin, he was attracted initially to Manichaeism, a system that regarded Satan, the personification of evil, as coequal with God. In 387 he was converted, largely by the influence of Ambrose, to orthodox Catholicism. He then returned to Thagaste and gave all his possessions to the poor. He was elected a priest in 391 and bishop of Hippo in 395. Here he reigned until 430, having formed what was the first cathedral monastery, in which study and church administration were combined. In *The City of God* and in his *Confessions* he rises above the nationalistic conceptions of Berber Donatism to a universality of doctrine for the entire church. This, together with the new direction that Augustine gave to monasticism, are the great contributions of a most troubled era to world history. □

TRADE CONNECTIONS OF AFRICA IN GRECO ROMAN TIMES

At the beginning of the Christian era three principal nomadic groups that are still found today in the Sahara already dwelt there: the black Tuba in the Tibesti region; the Tuareg in the central Sahara; and the Sanhaja, the ancestors of the people of southern Morocco and of Mauritania, on the Atlantic coast. About A.D. 1 the camel was introduced into Egypt and Cyrenaica, and then into Tripolitania and the Fezzan, from which point its breeding was spread rapidly by the Garamantes westward into Tunisia, and so on as far as the shores of the Atlantic. The Romans had only a limited interest in the Sahara. An expedition under Cornelius Gallus went to Ghadames and the Fezzan in 19 B.C. Ghadames (Cydamus) later became a legionary fort for the Third Legion Augusta. The expedition reached Ghat and perhaps Tassili 'n-Ajjer, following the ancient cattle route as far as the Niger bend. Tombs and funeral amphorae of Roman merchants have been found in the Fezzan; farther south, in the Hoggar, Roman arms, lamps and various objects in iron and copper have been recovered, together with coins of Constantine the Great. The Arabs and Berbers developed the trans-Saharan trade only after the eighth century A.D., as some of the genealogies of sub-Saharan African rulers suggest.

In the Indian Ocean the pharaohs had already sent expeditions to Punt (perhaps Somalia) in 2400 B.C., to bring back myrrh and frankincense. About 900 B.C. Solomon was taking advantage of the Phoenician fleet to bring back Indian Ocean products. Arabs, Indians, and Persians participated in this trade and somehow kept their knowledge from the Greek seamen, who went no further than Eudaemon Arabia, otherwise Aden, the entrepôt to which Arabs and Indians brought their cargoes and exchanged them.

In A.D. 6 Hippalos, an Alexandrine merchant, learned the secret of the monsoons, and now Roman trade with India grew steadily. The anonymous *Periplus* [Circumnavigation] *of the Erythraean Sea* describes this trade as it was around A.D. 50. The accuracy of its details is confirmed by finds of Roman coins and pottery in India as well as some in Somalia and, with less certainty, in Zanzibar. The *Periplus* was probably never published in ancient times: rather it is in the nature of a government trade report. In African waters the traders from Egypt stopped at various points along the Red Sea and down the eastern African coast, as far as the island of Menouthias (perhaps Pemba or Zanzibar?) and to Rhapta (perhaps somewhere near the mouth of the river Rufiji). On the Ethiopian shore they bought ivory, tortoiseshell, rhinoceros horn, some spices, and a little myrrh; from Somalia, myrrh, frankincense, spices, drugs, and some slaves; farther down, chiefly at Rhapta, ivory, tortoiseshell, and rhinoceros horn. Myrrh and frankincense fed the altars of countless temples in Egypt, Asia Minor and Greece, North Africa, Rome, and western Europe.

To Somalia and the Ethiopian coast were brought textiles, grain and iron and steel from India, and a few items only from the west: some wine ("to gain the good will of the natives"), olive oil, some tools, bronze vessels, and glass. From the Roman point of view the most lucrative trade was with India. On the African shore, important for its later history, the presence of Arab agents who had married locally and knew the local language is to be noted. Beyond India the author of the *Periplus* knew somewhat vaguely of Thina (China), where silent trade was conducted. It was the first seaborne contact with the silk route, whose secret was unveiled only in the reign of Justinian I (529–565).

□

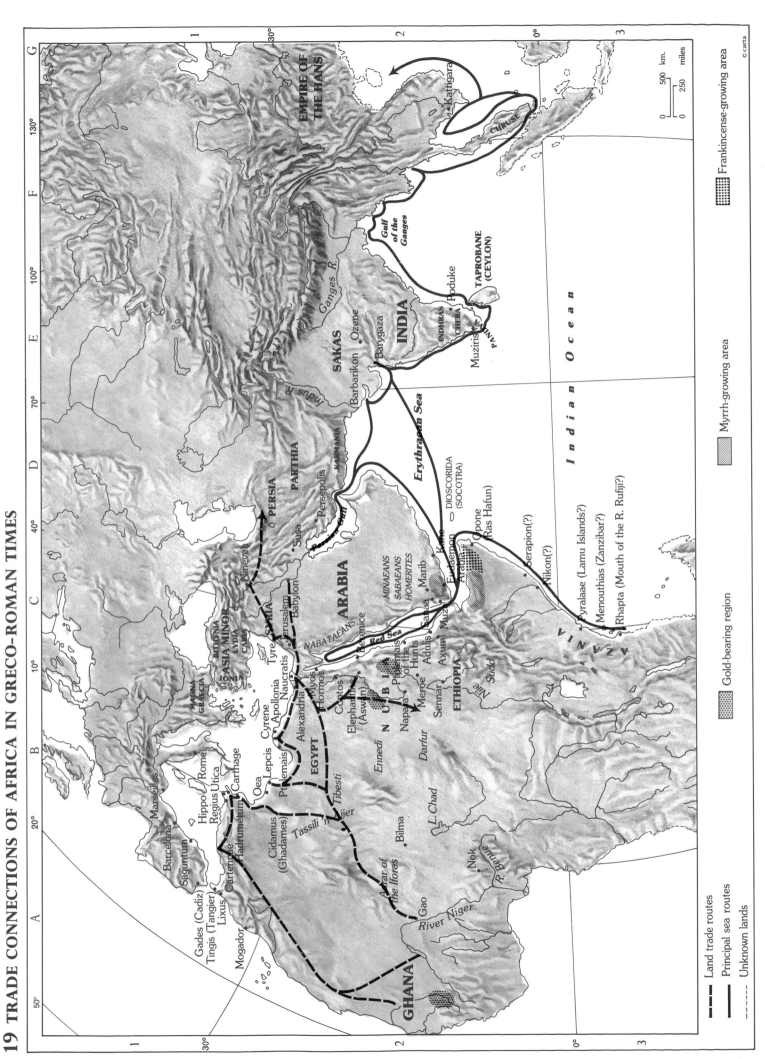

Land trade routes

Principal sea routes

Unknown lands

Frankincense-growing area

Myrrh-growing area

Gold-bearing region

© carta

THE SPREAD OF CHRISTIANITY UP TO c. 632

The northern seaboard of Africa, now chiefly Islamic, was once wholly Christian. It is extremely difficult to estimate the number of Christians in any given area during the first six centuries. The principal sources for any such determination include archaeological remains, tombstones with epitaphs, occasional dedicatory inscriptions, even graffiti, and a great number of ruined churches in Roman Africa, modern Tunisia, and ancient Numidia. There are also occasional lists of bishops of ancient sees, lists and acts of martyrs, and references in the fathers of the church. Not unexpectedly, many of these sources are not in former pagan areas, but in areas where the Jewish concept of monotheism and Greek philosophy met, intermingled, and coalesced. It is not always easy to isolate any particular reasons for successful missionary effort or for expansion in one area or another.

Although map 23 shows relatively small areas in Africa that converted to Christianity in the first two centuries, in early times these were among the most potent areas of theological development. Already before 155 a catechetical school had been founded in Alexandria by Pantaenus, which Clement of Alexandria (c. 155–220) made a center of advanced study. Irenaeus in Lyons, Hippolytus and Caius (Gaius) in Rome, and Tertullian at Carthage were his contemporaries. By fostering the imperial cult and the traditional protection of the Jews, Septimius Severus unleashed persecution in Africa and Egypt (c. 202–211), but the numbers martyred were not great. Their courage and blood was as seed to the church. In about c. 203 Origen, the most brilliant and original thinker the church had yet seen, became head of the catechetical school of Alexandria; around 225 he initiated in his *Hexepla* the systematic critical study of biblical texts. Contemporary with him at Carthage was Cyprian, the former Roman official who was named bishop in 248.

In the mid 3rd century Christianity developed in a fresh direction. Paul of Thebes, the first hermit, took to the eastern desert of Egypt around 250.

Antony the Hermit was born in the Fayyum around the same time. Later the "father of the monks", he gave order to the first monasteries. The origins and development of the monastic movement are studied in map 21. At first it was largely a peasant movement; then, after 296, when Menas died near Alexandria, a great cult city sprang up, with monasteries for both men and women. To this movement all Europe and much of the rest of the world was to owe its universities, schools and hospitals. Their foundation was accomplished wholly spontaneously, without any formal central organization.

Following attempts to destroy Christianity by persecution in the late third and early fourth centuries, under Constantine the Great (306–337) Christianity became the offical religion of the empire. Constantine's motives have been variously assessed: his concern for the unity of the empire was paralleled by concern for the unity of the church. About this time Arius, a Libyan priest, had questioned the incarnation of Christ as Son of God. In 323 he was expelled from Alexandria, but his doctrine spread like wildfire. The bishops appealed to the emperor. Thus the first general council of the church met at Nicaea in 325, attended by almost every bishop. Like subsequent councils, its decisions led to further controversy which persisted into the following century and beyond. If ecclesiastical unity was maintained by Rome in the west and Constantinople in the east, after the Council of Chalcedon the Copts of Egypt severed themselves, as did some sectarians in Syria. The Egyptians took with them the Ethiopians of the kingdom of Axum (see map 26). In North Africa the Donatist movement was just beginning (map 22), further dividing the Church. Egypt's great gift to Christianity, the institution of monasticism, grew nevertheless as a sturdy plant, while the isolation of its country of origin, along with the rise of Donatism and the lingering relics of Arianism, provided an effective preparation for Islam.

□

20 THE SPREAD OF CHRISTIANITY UP TO c.632

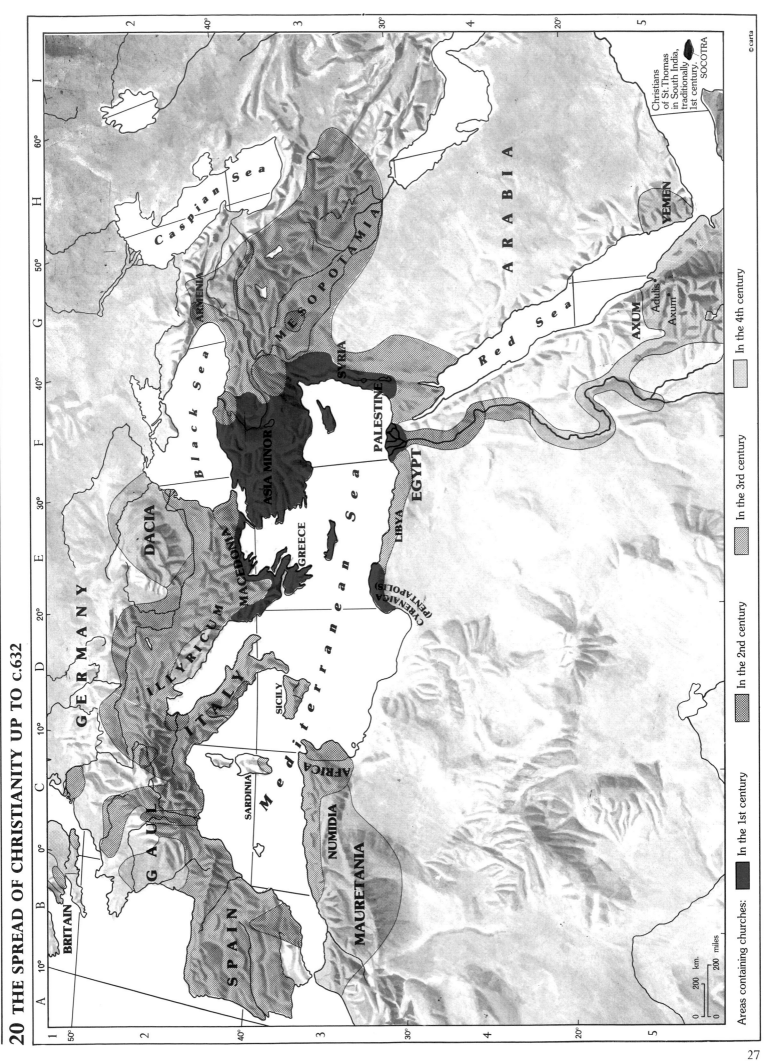

BRITAIN

GERMANY

GAUL

SPAIN

ITALY

SARDINIA

SICILY

MAURETANIA

NUMIDIA

AFRICA

Mediterranean Sea

ILLYRICUM

DACIA

MACEDONIA

GREECE

CYRENAICA (PENTAPOLIS)

LIBYA

EGYPT

Black Sea

ASIA MINOR

ARMENIA

SYRIA

PALESTINE

Caspian Sea

MESOPOTAMIA

Red Sea

A R A B I A

YEMEN

AXUM

Adulis
Axum

SOCOTRA

Christians
of St. Thomas
in South India,
traditionally
1st century.

© carta

Areas containing churches:

In the 1st century

In the 2nd century

In the 3rd century

In the 4th century

0   200 km.

0   200 miles

MONASTERIES IN EGYPT AND JUDAEA, 3RD TO 4TH CENTURIES

Ideas and ideals of asceticism are inherent in all religions, and the "sons of the prophets" (1 Kings 20:35) are cited in the Hebrew scriptures as if they were commonplace. The Jewish ascetics had various institutions, including a major center at Qumran. In Christianity monasticism as an institution became formalized only in the third century A.D., although individual ascetics and, for women, a *parthenon* (a community of virgins) are mentioned earlier.

In about 271 a certain Antony heard the Sunday gospel: "If thou wilt be perfect, go and sell all that thou hast and give to the poor, and come and follow me" (Matt. 19:21). After providing for his sister, he took himself to a desert place and finally to the Eastern Desert, to pray and to support himself by simple manual work. Shortly, others gathered near him; nearby was also Paul of Thebes, who had fled into the desert during the persecution of Decius (c. 250). The call to perfection and the spur of persecution were incentives added to the intolerable burden of imperial taxation and the *corvées* put upon the Egyptian peasantry.

Neither Antony nor Paul founded an institution. Around 310 a pagan boy, Pachomius, was converted and baptized; he had begun to practice asceticism even before his baptism. By about 320 the *schema*, the monastic habit had already evolved, and this he assumed. At Tabennisis Pachomius heard a voice: "Stay here, and make a monastery, for many will come to thee and become monks" (*Monachos*, "monk," referred both to solitaries or hermits and to those who lived in communities.) At much the same time the first settlements of monks were established by Amoun in Nitria, and then in Scetis, in the present Wadi el-Natrun, where still today four Coptic monasteries survive. In Palestine one Hilarion was sent to school as a boy in Alexandria, where at the age of fifteen,

he was drawn to Antony. After a period in which he lived in solitude, monasteries sprang up around Hilarion in the region of Gaza. It was the beginning of a mass movement that quickly penetrated the desert regions on the western bank of the Jordan.

The Pachomian monasteries were all built on cultivated land near the Nile. For a short while Pachomius had been a soldier, and his *coenobium* had a gatehouse and a guesthouse, a *sunaxis* (an assembly hall that later became a church), a kitchen, a bakehouse, stores, an infirmary, and houses that, barrack-like, held twenty to forty monks each. These buildings were of the simplest construction, and none of the early ones have survived. Each monk had a separate cell. There were no priests. For Mass, Pachomius called in a priest from one of the neighboring churches. He gave no encouragement for anyone to seek the priesthood lest he should think of "the love of command." Within a short while numerous monasteries had grown up, for women as well as men.

It might be thought that such an institution contradicted Christ's instruction to preach the gospel to every creature; yet its effect was to fulfill that call. In about 330 a Syrian merchant, Frumentius, was ordained bishop of Ethiopia by the patriarch of Alexandria and soon converted the Ethiopian court. In 340, when he was exiled from Alexandria to Rome, Athanasius took monks along with him: it was the first seed of monasticism in the West. In 357 the newly baptized Basil the Great made a monastic tour of Palestine and Egypt, the same year in which Athanasius wrote his classic life of Saint Antony. It remained for Benedict of Nursia (c. 480–547) to set out a rule of organized worship, study, and labor that was to transform the civilization of the West.

□

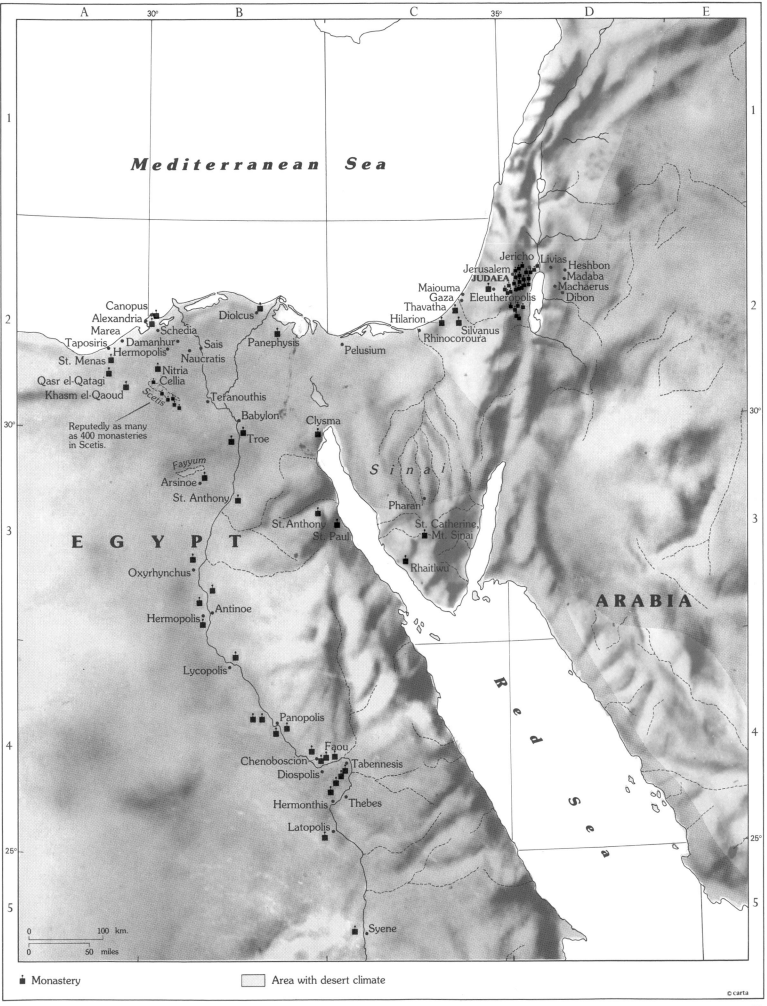

Mediterranean Sea

Canopus
Alexandria
Marea
Taposiris
Damanhur
Hermopolis
St. Menas
Qasr el-Qatagi
Khasm el-Qaoud
Scetis

Schedia
Sais
Naucratis
Nitria
Cellia
Terenouthis
Babylon
Troe

Reputedly as many
as 400 monasteries
in Scetis.

Diolcus
Panephysis
Pelusium

Clysma

Jericho · Livias
Jerusalem
JUDAEA
Maiouma
Gaza
Thavatha
Hilarion
Rhinocoroura
Silvanus

Heshbon
Madaba
Machaerus
Dibon

Eleutheropolis

Fayyum
Arsinoe
St. Anthony

E G Y P T

St. Anthony
St. Paul

Oxyrhynchus

Hermopolis
Antinoe

Lycopolis

S i n a i

Pharan

St. Catherine,
Mt. Sinai

Rhaitlwu

ARABIA

Panopolis
Chenoboscion
Diospolis
Faou
Tabennesis
Hermonthis
Thebes
Latopolis

R e d   S e a

Syene

0   100 km.
0   50 miles

■ Monastery   ▢ Area with desert climate

© carta

THE DONATIST MOVEMENT IN NORTH AFRICA, 4TH TO 5TH CENTURIES

In contrast to the See of Alexandria, which in the fourth century led the struggle against Arianism in favor of Catholic unity and orthodoxy, in Proconsular Africa, Byzacena, Numidia, and Mauretania Sitifiensis a schismatic body arose within the African church which threatened to cut it off from the main body. It was by no means an intellectual movement.

The initial cause of contention was the refusal of certain Christians to accept one Caecilian as bishop of Carthage in 311, because his consecrator, Bishop Felix of Aptunga had been a renegade during the persecution under the emperor Diocletian in 284. So in Numidia the bishops consecrated Majorinus as a rival to Caecilian; he was shortly succeeded by Donatus, who gave his name to the movement.

The bishops appealed to the pope, Miltiades, who investigated in 313 and decided in favor of Caecilian. Donatist appeals to the Council of Arles in 314 and to the emperor Constantine in 316 were likewise without success. The schism nevertheless throve, partly out of local patriotism, partly because the Catholics were supported by Rome. Numidia, too, was jealous of Proconsular Africa. Between 316 and 321 Constantine tried coercion without any success. It simply strengthened the schism.

Later, because of economic unrest and resentment of taxation, there arose violent bands of brigands and marauders known as Circumcellions. From 347 to 361 a further attempt at repression was made; it ceased only because of the emperor Julian's short-lived attempt to restore pagan cults. The Circumcellions were religious fanatics whose centers were the shrines of martyrs, where they collected food from pious donations, storing it in silos and barns. Central to their concept of religion was the idea of martyrdom to be attained on raids conducted against Catholics and pagans alike. They dressed in quasi-monastic habits; on their raids they carried relics of martyrs and clubs that they called "Israels". Their celebrations included dancing and ritual drunkenness, as had those dedicated to the god Bacchus in an earlier age. Martyrdom was an objective to be pursued at all costs, even that of instances of mass suicide are known from inscriptions. As Augustine described them, they lived as robbers, died as Circumcellions, and were honored as martyrs. Caecilian died in old age in 347. Shortly thereafter, although he had made overtures to reestablish unity, Donatus was exiled from Africa.

Apart from its extravagances, Donatist piety was of an extreme puritanical rigorism. It also opposed the fundamental Catholic doctrine of the unity of the church, maintaining that the Donatist "saints" alone formed the church, because they alone were one and holy.

Our knowledge of the Donatists comes from men who were Africans themselves (principally Augustine and Optatus). Many of the sect's ruined churches and funerary inscriptions have survived. It was the Donatists' violence rather than their doctrines that caused the state to intervene against them in 405. In 411 an imperial commissioner attended the Council of Carthage to pronounce against them. They were deaf to the persuasion of Augustine: it was the year before he completed the *City of God*. They continued to maintain that Felix of Aptunga was incapable of performing a valid consecration because of his personal unworthiness as a former *traditor*, or renegade. It was in vain that Augustine pleaded that the unworthiness of the minister does not affect the validity of the sacraments, because the true minister is Christ himself.

While the schism gradually diminished in numbers and order was restored, it greatly weakened the church in North Africa: it crumbled following the Arab invasion of the seventh century (see map 28) and the impact of militant Islam. Certain characteristics of Donatism still persist in the Islam of the area, especially in the puritanism of the Ibadhi and in the heterodox practices that surround the cults of the tombs of marabouts, or holy men. A syncretistic, unorthodox Christianity was replaced by a syncretistic, unorthodox Islam.

22 THE DONATIST MOVEMENT IN NORTH AFRICA, 4TH TO 5TH CENTURIES

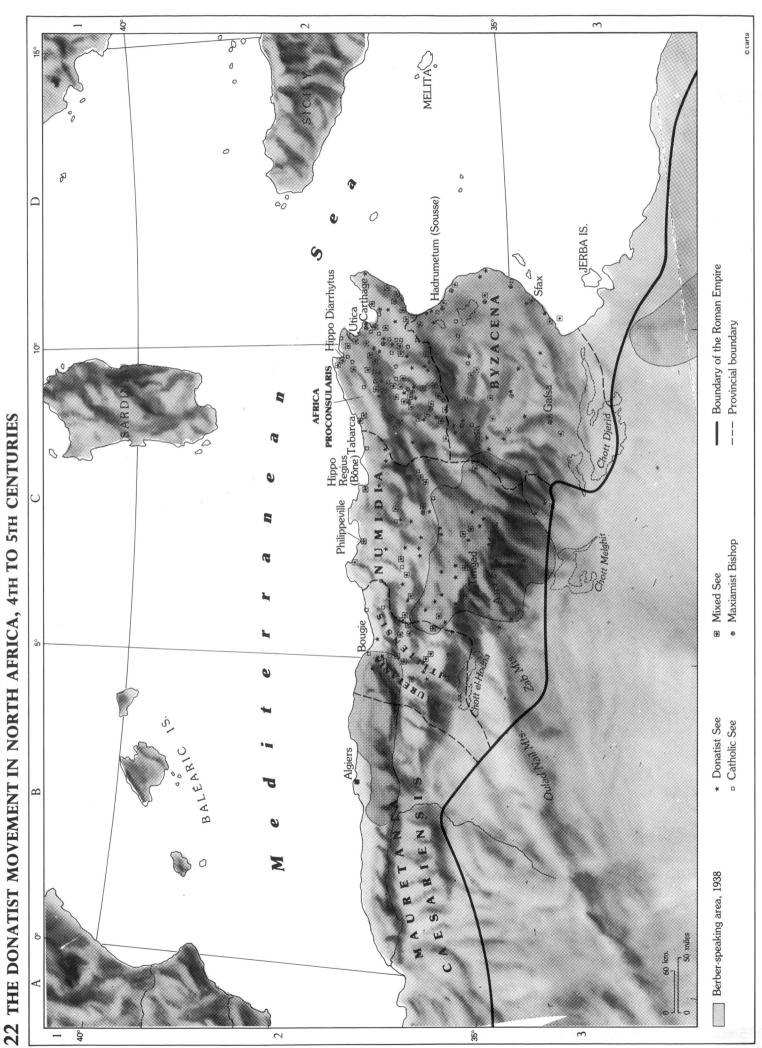

Boundary of the Roman Empire
Provincial boundary

★ Donatist See
□ Catholic See
⊞ Mixed See
⊕ Maxiamist Bishop

Berber-speaking area, 1938

SICILY

MELITA

Mediterranean Sea

SARDINIA

BALEARIC IS.

Hippo Diarrhytus
Utica
Carthage
Hadrumetum (Sousse)
Sfax
JERBA IS.

AFRICA PROCONSULARIS
BYZACENA

Tabarca
Gafsa

Hippo Regius (Bône)

Chott Djerid

Philippeville

NUMIDIA

Chott Melghir

Bougie

Timgad

URBANITANA MAURETANIA SITIFENSIS

Chott el-Hodna

Algiers

Oulad Naïl Mts.

Zab el Mts.

MAURETANIA CAESARIENSIS

60 km.
50 miles

©carta

THE VANDAL KINGDOM OF AFRICA, C. A.D.534

The Vandals, a tribe of Teutonic origins from near the river Oder, on the borders of modern Germany and Poland, migrated first to the Danube, where they made themselves a nuisance on the frontier, and then into Gaul, (c. 406). In 409 the whole tribe crossed the Pyrenees into Spain; in Galicia they were virtually exterminated in a series of wars, at the end of which the survivors moved south into Andalusia.

About 429 Boniface, count (Roman governor) of Africa, declared himself independent. He was short of military support, so he invited the Vandals over. They were led by Genseric, a man of spirit albeit lame, and crossed — men, women, and children — in vessels provided by Boniface. Genseric had taken all of Roman Africa except Carthage, Hippo, and Cirta when Boniface returned to his former loyalty in 430. Genseric besieged Hippo from May 430 until July 431, a period otherwise remembered for the last illness and death of Augustine.

At length the emperor Valentinian III reached a compromise with Genseric. He was to retain Carthage and Proconsular Africa, while the Vandals were given the rest. Genseric broke the treaty as soon as he found it convenient and took Carthage by assault on 19 October 439. From Carthage he plundered, pillaged, and organized a fleet which even took Rome in 455. He pillaged it for fourteen days, and carried off the sacred gold vessels that the emperor Titus had taken from the Jewish Temple in Jerusalem.

At home, an Arian like his followers, he took the side of the Donatists against the Catholics. The subsequent torture of Catholic priests and bishops and the destruction of their buildings earned the Vandals their name for destructiveness which has endured as a byword to this day. Genseric died in 476, but his successor, Huneric, took up the persecution with vigor. Huneric's successors, Gunthamund (484–496) and Thrasamund (496–523), were less aggressive in this respect. The latter was succeeded by Hilderic, a Catholic, who in 531 was usurped by his cousin Gelimer.

Recognizing the weakness of the Vandals at this point, the emperor Justinian sent Belisarius — one of the most distinguished generals in all history, ranking in genius with Alexander and Napoleon — with a small body of troops and a fleet. It was a combined operation. The troops landed in September 533. As they moved rapidly in a forced march, the fleet kept pace with them along the shore. Belisarius took Carthage on 14 September. It was a brilliant feat of arms by a small force trained in battle drill with every care.

The Vandal soldiers were taken as slaves, while the victors took the Vandal women. Among Belisarius's force was a Bulgar contingent speaking a language very similar to that of the Vandals. No vestige of Vandal buildings or institutions has survived in modern Tunisia, but one cannot fail to remark a high proportion of men and women of blond coloring, more than anywhere else in North Africa. These are the descendants of the Vandals, mixed over the centuries with the indigenous Berbers and with the different peoples that came into the region, first with the Phoenicians, then with the Romans, and then yet others. Attempts have been made by historians to whitewash the Vandals, but their century of power led to nothing and was largely destructive.

□

23 THE VANDAL KINGDOM OF AFRICA, c. A.D.534

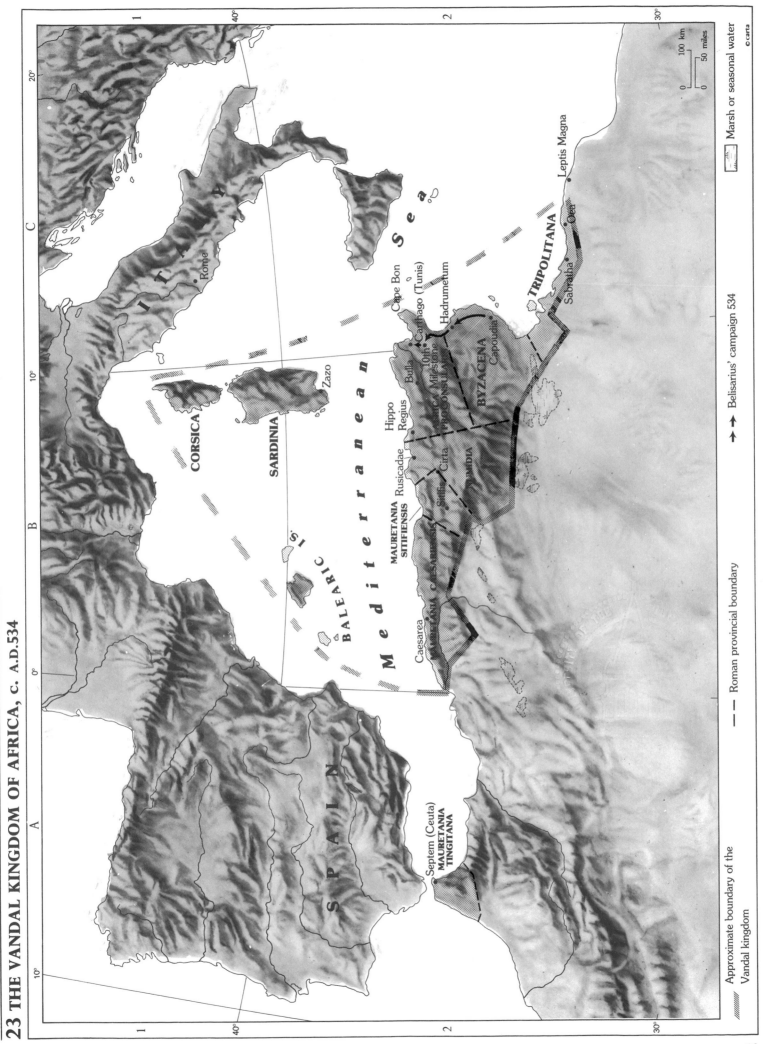

ITALY

Rome

CORSICA

SARDINIA

Zazo

BALEARIC

Mediterranean Sea

SPAIN

Septem (Ceuta)
MAURETANIA TINGITANA

Caesarea

MAURETANIA CAESARIENSIS

MAURETANIA
SITIFIENSIS

Rusicadae

Sitifis

Cirta

NUMIDIA

Hippo
Regius

Bulla

Carthago (Tunis)
Cape Bon

10th
Milestone
PROCONSULARIS

Hadrumetum

BYZACENA

Capoudia

TRIPOLITANA

Sabratha

Oea

Leptis Magna

100 km

50 miles

©carta

↑ Belisarius' campaign 534

— — Roman provincial boundary

Approximate boundary of the
Vandal kingdom

Marsh or seasonal water

33

PROVINCES OF EGYPT UNDER ROME AND BYZANTIUM

The years 31 to 30 B.C. marked a climacteric in the affairs of Egypt. Octavian (later emperor as Augustus) entered Egypt by the classic route of all previous armies via Pelusium. The fleet that the Ptolemies had created was burned by his Nabataean Arab allies, and Mark Antony and Cleopatra committed suicide. Egypt now became a Roman imperial province, while its treasury was carried off to Rome. Thus the process was begun by which, in A.D. 42, with Claudius as emperor, all North Africa was annexed. For the Romans the Mediterranean was indeed now Mare Nostrum, "our sea."

Two less dramatic events must be noted. About A.D. 1 the camel was introduced into the Sahara. The transport system thus inaugurated was soon to stretch westward to the Atlantic, and southward to the gold-bearing lands and the southern Sahara. Then, around A.D. 6, an Alexandrine merchant named Hippalos identified the periodicity of the monsoons in the Indian Ocean (see map 18). Soon, as documented in numerous papyri and in the *Periplus of the Erythraean Sea* (c. A.D. 50), the sea trade of Alexandria was reaching the eastern African coast, the seaboard of South Arabia and of western India, with a remote tentacle as far as China. Alexandria, principally a Greek city but with a Jewish population of one million, now became the greatest trading city in the world.

Still less dramatically, in Roman Palestine the Christian religion was born, to develop silently and to have its principal intellectual seat neither in Palestine nor in Rome, but among the Greco-Judaic intelligentsia of Alexandria. Already around A.D. 40 the Jewish philosopher Philo, writing in Greek, had set out to reconcile Greek philosophy with the teachings of the Septuagint. He was followed in the second century by celebrated Gnostic teachers such as Basilides, Carpocrates, and Valentinus, against whom a catechetical (or theological) school was set up by what came to be called "orthodox" Christians. Among these the most famous were Clement of Alexandria in the second century, Origen at the beginning of the third century, and Athanasius in the fourth century. It was the latter's skill, although he was still a deacon, that dominated the Council of Nicaea in 325, formulating orthodox belief in the divinity of Christ and in the Trinity.

By 391 the patriarch Theophilus closed all the pagan temples in Egypt. In Alexandria the pagans rebelled and took refuge in the temple of Serapis, where they were burned together with the famous library of the kings of Pergamum. At a lower level, Greek mobs attacked Jews, while from time to time Jews rebelled against Greek domination. Equally, Greeks under imperial orders had persecuted Christians; the most bitter of all the persecutions, waged under Diocletian in 284, is taken by Coptic (Egyptian) Christians as the first year of their calendar.

By this time the majority of the Egyptian peasantry under the Roman and then the Byzantine administration had a double effect, political and religious. Politically it generated a xenophobic nationalism; religiously, this distaste for Byzantium was given full effect in the Monophysite movement, the belief that Christ had one single nature in which the human nature was swallowed up by the divine nature, as against the orthodox doctrine that the two natures coexisted. As a result, the Coptic church broke away from orthodoxy after the Council of Chalcedon (451). Before this had taken place a monastic movement had arisen, again among the Egyptian peasantry, which was to have the most far-reaching results even throughout the Western world (see map 21).

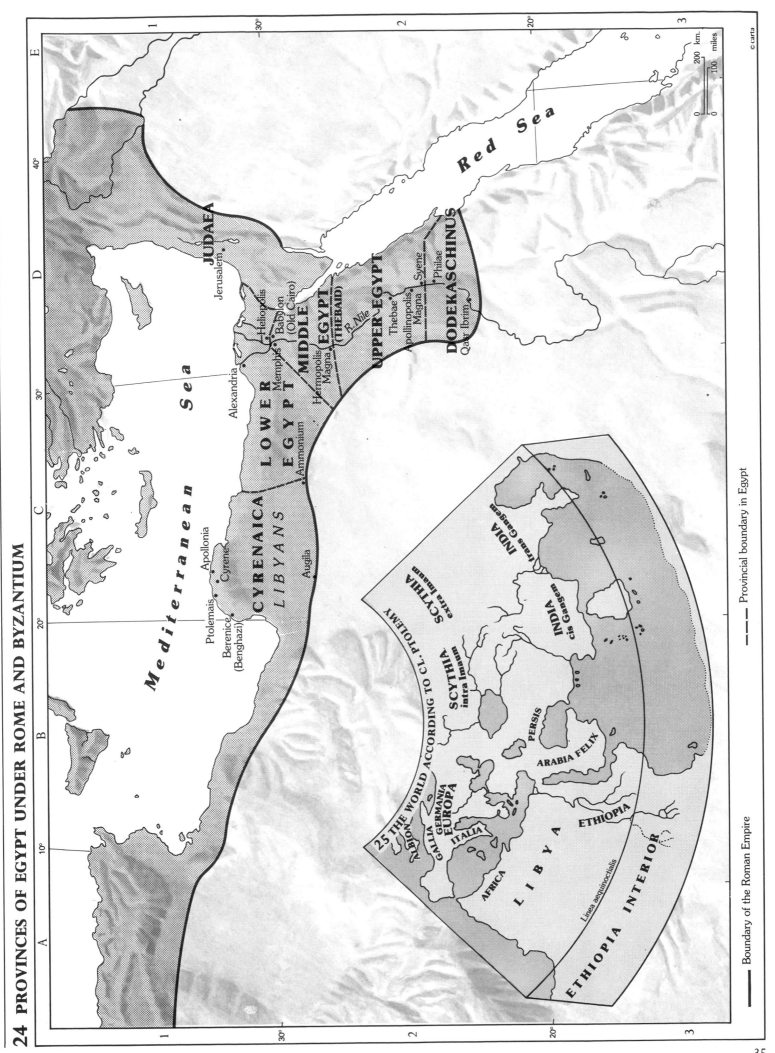

Red Sea

Mediterranean Sea

JUDAEA
Jerusalem

Heliopolis
Babylon
(Old Cairo)
Alexandria
Memphis
MIDDLE
EGYPT
LOWER
EGYPT
Hermopolis
Magna
R. Nile
Ammonium
(THEBAID)
UPPER EGYPT
Thebae
Apollinopolis
Magna
Syene
Philae
DODEKASCHINUS
Qaṣr Ibrim

CYRENAICA
LIBYANS
Augila
Apollonia
Cyrene
Ptolemais
Berenice
(Benghazi)

25 THE WORLD ACCORDING TO CL. PTOLEMY

ALBION
GALLIA
GERMANIA
EUROPA
ITALIA
AFRICA
LIBYA
ETHIOPIA
ARABIA FELIX
PERSIS
SCYTHIA
intra Imaum
SCYTHIA
extra Imaum
INDIA
cis Gangem
INDIA
trans Gangem
Linea aequinoctialis
ETHIOPIA INTERIOR

—— Boundary of the Roman Empire

--- Provincial boundary in Egypt

200 km.
100 miles
0

© carta

EGYPT, NUBIA, AND ETHIOPIA, C. 600

During the sixth century Byzantine strength declined. Soon, in a future of which there was no sign on the horizon, all the northern African provinces and the Levant would be shorn from Byzantium by the Arabs.

In Egypt in the mid-sixth century, in order to curb the power of the Augustalis, or viceroy, the emperor Justinian I had divided the country into five provinces (see map 24), subdividing them into eparchies, and these into small administrative districts, or pagarchies. The pagarch was both magistrate and tax collector, and apparently directly answerable to the emperor. There was a locally recruited army to maintain order, but as the century wore on it became slack and ineffectual. Some changes were made by the emperor Maurice; nevertheless, Egypt was on the verge of revolution.

In religion, after the Council of Chalcedon (451) the Egyptian church was in schism (see map 20). There now emerged a self-conscious Coptic nationalism, antipathetic alike to Byzantium and to the Melkite Orthodox Greeks of Alexandria. There were now two patriarchs, Coptic and Melkite, representing Monophysite and Orthodox Christianity. Efforts at conciliation and then, after 536, the persecution of the Monophysites, served only to harden the situation. While there was a certain revival during the reign of the patriarch Damian, in particular of monasticism, the intellectual leadership that once had been the mark of the Egyptian church was a thing of the past.

Below the First Cataract lay three Christian kingdoms, often confused with Ethiopia. Their history is extremely obscure. The northernmost was Nobatia or Nuba. Beyond the Third Cataract, Makuria or Makurra (later Dongola) was the heir of the ancient capital of Meroe (see map 14). From here perhaps came the eunuch treasurer of Queen Candace who is reported in Acts 8:27–40 to have been baptized by Philip after making a pilgrimage to Jerusalem. The effective conversion of Nobatia, however, did not take place until 543, when King Silko was converted to Monophysite Christianity by missionaries sent by the empress Theodora. Makuria was converted by Orthodox missionaries sent by Justinian around 550. The third kingdom, Alodia or Alwa, with its capital at present-day Soba, was converted to Monophysitism around 570. Christianity survived in Makuria until 1336, and in Soba until 1594. Even today women, nominally Muslim, may be seen crossing themselves as they draw water from the Nile, to protect themselves against crocodiles.

Recent excavations at Axum, with its splendid funerary stelae and other monuments, attest the prosperity and magnificence of the ancient kingdom which, alone in "black Africa," issued a gold coinage from about the mid-third century to the tenth. This coinage is the principal source for the history of Axum until the ruler and the court were converted to Christianity around 330. Thereafter some account is possible from the *History of the Patriarchs*. At this period the kingdom was not extensive. According to this source the Cathedral of Saint Mary at Axum was founded in 330. In 1564 it was deliberately wrecked by Ahmed Grañ. Somewhat earlier it was seen by Alvarez, a Jesuit whose plan shows a church with a broad nave and two aisles on either side. The site has never been excavated, but if Alvarez's plan is correct, its plan was modeled on other basilicas built by Constantine the Great in Jerusalem, Bethlehem, and Rome. Ever since the fourth century the Christian emperors of Ethiopia have been crowned at Axum, the last in 1931. The conversion was the work of a Syrian merchant, Frumentius, later the first patriarch as Abba Salama.

Four streams of influence may be discerned in Ethiopia, all reflecting its different directions of trade. The first is Arabian, for the ancient Ethiopic language, Geez, still the liturgical language, derives from the ancient Sabaean tongue of southern Arabia. The second of these is Jewish, for until recently the Falasha practised a form of Judaism which knew only the Torah and none of the later works in the Hebrew Bible. The third stream evident is Greek: of twenty-two rulers who minted in gold, only five used Geez, the rest Greek. From the same source too came numerous theological works which were translated. The fourth influence is Syrian. Not only did a Syrian merchant bring Christianity to Ethiopia; around 500 came the Nine Saints, Syrians who translated the Scriptures into Geez. In the mountain outpost Islam was never able effectively to overcome the Christian culture, in spite of many attempts to do so. Isolated, but always hospitable to outside influences, Ethiopia transmuted them and remained as a rock bastion.

□

26 EGYPT, NUBIA, AND ETHIOPIA, c. 600

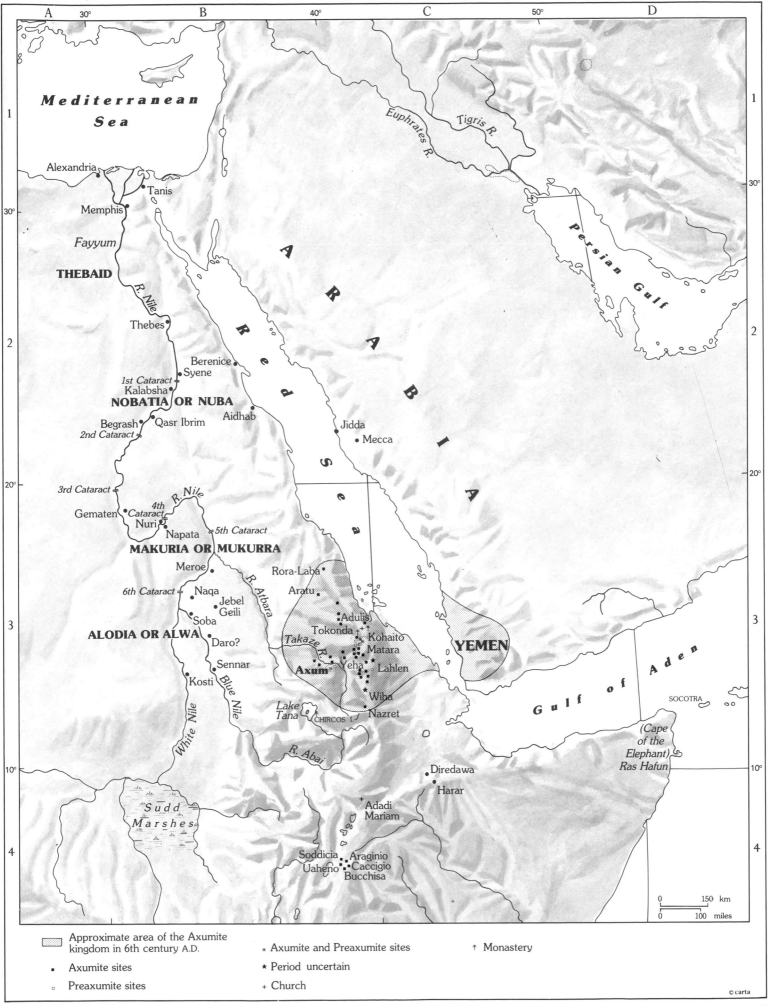

Mediterranean Sea

Alexandria
Tanis
Memphis
Fayyum
THEBAID
R. Nile
Thebes
Berenice
Syene
1st Cataract
Kalabsha
NOBATIA OR NUBA
Aidhab
Begrash
Qasr Ibrim
2nd Cataract
3rd Cataract
Gematen
4th Cataract
Nuri
Napata
5th Cataract
MAKURIA OR MUKURRA
Meroe
6th Cataract
Naqa
Jebel Geili
Soba
Daro?
Sennar
Kosti
ALODIA OR ALWA
R. Atbara
White Nile
Blue Nile
Sudd Marshes

A R A B I A

R e d   S e a

Euphrates R.
Tigris R.

Persian Gulf

Jidda
Mecca

Rora-Laba
Aratu
Adulis
Tokonda
Takaze R.
Kohaito
Matara
Axum
Yeha
Lahlen
Wiha
Nazret
Lake Tana
CHIRCOS I.
R. Abai

YEMEN

Gulf   of   Aden

SOCOTRA

(Cape of the Elephant)
Ras Hafun

Diredawa
Harar
Adadi Mariam

Soddicia
Uaheno
Araginio
Caccigio
Bucchisa

0 ——— 150 km
0 ——— 100 miles

▨ Approximate area of the Axumite kingdom in 6th century A.D.

▪ Axumite sites

◻ Preaxumite sites

▨ Axumite and Preaxumite sites

★ Period uncertain

† Monastery

✚ Church

© carta

THE ARAB CONQUEST OF EGYPT, 640–652

By 639 the Arabs, having come up from the desert, had taken Syria, Iraq, and, with somewhat inconclusive results, Persia. Egypt, still in Byzantine hands, lay dangerously on the exposed left flank of the Hijaz and Syria. For the Arabs its conquest was a military necessity. 'Amr ibn al-'As, the commander in Syria, took advantage of the caliph Umar's visit to Jerusalem to obtain permission. In January 640 he set out with four thousand cavalry and invested al-Farama. It gave way after a month. Other castles followed, and he immediately invested Babilyun (commonly Babylon, now Old Cairo). In July he attacked Ayn Shams (now Heliopolis) and routed the Byzantine forces. The patriarch Cyrus, who was governor, attempted to bribe 'Amr by offering three choices: Islam, the payment of tribute, or the sword. He refused them all. On 6 April the castle, which still stands today, was taken by assault. On 13 May Nikiu (Naqyus) fell with much slaughter; shortly thereafter 'Amr invested Alexandria with a force now increased to twenty thousand. The defenders had fifty thousand men and the Byzantine navy behind them. 'Amr had not a single ship.

Apparently hoping he could continue to administer Egypt as governor for the Arabs, Cyrus signed a treaty of capitulation on 8 November 641. It was ratified by the emperor. Thus through weakness the Byzantines lost their richest province. To the caliph 'Amr reported:

> I have captured a city from the description of which I shall refrain. Suffice it to say that I have seized therein four thousand villas with four thousand baths, forty thousand poll-tax paying Jews and four hundred places of entertainment for the royalty.

'Amr set up his capital at al-Fustat, just north of Babylon. His name survives as that of the mosque which was constructed on the site he selected, and which has been rebuilt again and again. Government offices now rose near the mosque, and the canal to the Red Sea that had been built by the Persians and cleaned under Trajan was reopened. Once again Egypt had direct access from the Mediterranean to Africa and the East.

Alexandria revolted in 645 but was retaken in 646, when the walls were demolished. 'Amr was now free for administration, and among his first acts was the creation of a fleet. This enabled Mu'awiyah, governor of Syria, to seize Cyprus in 649 and to defeat the Byzantine fleet in 652. The same fleet utterly destroyed the Byzantine fleet in 655 and enabled Sicily to be pillaged in 668 or 669.

To the south a treaty of peace on condition of payment of tribute was made with Nubia in 652, enabling it to survive as a Christian kingdom until the thirteenth century. □

THE ARAB CONQUEST OF NORTH AFRICA, 7TH TO 8TH CENTURIES

'Amr ibn al-'As had already made a cavalry raid into Cyrenaica in 642–643, occupying Barca, and then reached Tripoli and Carthage, taking tribute from them. No regular attempt to conquer Ifriqiya (as the Arabs called Proconsular Africa) until Qayrawan (now Kairouan) was founded by Uqba ibn Nafi in 670. He is said to have advanced until the waves of the Atlantic halted his horse.

It was not until the governorship of Hassan ibn al-Numan (c. 693–700) that any determination to end both Byzantine rule and Berber resistance was made. With the support of the fleet Hassan expelled the Byzantines from Carthage in 698, as well as from other towns on the coast nearby. These areas were principally in the hands of Romans and Byzantines, whereas the interior was held by Berbers, a Hamitic people believed to have originated from the same human stock as the Arab Semites.

Although at first Islam made slow progress among the Egyptian Coptic Christian and little or none among the Greeks and Jews of Alexandria, it made rapid progress among the Berbers even as their language was being Arabicized. While the Copts were largely agriculturalists, the Berbers were largely nomadic or seminomadic, which provided a common chord with the Arabs of the desert. They had also to some extent been prepared for Islam by the Donatist movement (see map 22).

From the alliance between Arab and Berber, and from their common inheritance of *ghazzu*, of raiding and violence, other movements of "Arab" expansion arose: the eighth century conquest of Spain, the sweep from Morocco to Cairo by the Fatimids (map 33), and the Almoravid and Almohad movements that took all of northern Africa and then Spain (maps 37, 38). □

27 THE ARAB CONQUEST OF EGYPT, 640–652

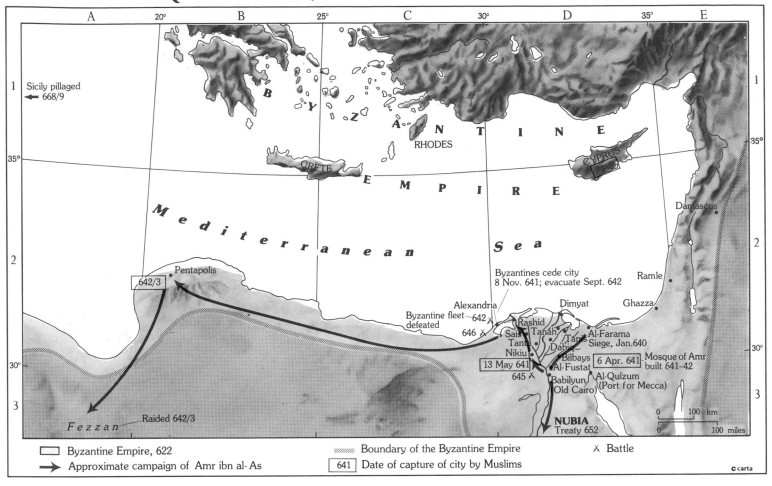

Sicily pillaged ← 668/9

B Y Z A N T I N E   E M P I R E

RHODES

CRETE

CYPRUS

Damascus

M e d i t e r r a n e a n   S e a

Pentapolis
642/3

Byzantines cede city 8 Nov. 641; evacuate Sept. 642

Alexandria
Byzantine fleet defeated — 642 X
646 X

Ramle

Ghazza

Dimyat

Rashid
Sais   Tanah
Tanta   Dabir
Nikiu   Tanis
Al-Farama Siege, Jan.640
13 May 641
Bilbays
Al-Fustat
6 Apr. 641   Mosque of Amr built 641–42
645 X
Babilyun
Old Cairo
Al-Qulzum (Port for Mecca)

NUBIA
Treaty 652

Fezzan   Raided 642/3

0   100 km
0   100 miles

☐ Byzantine Empire, 622
➤ Approximate campaign of Amr ibn al- As
▨ Boundary of the Byzantine Empire
☐ 641 Date of capture of city by Muslims
X Battle

© carta

28 THE ARAB CONQUEST OF NORTH AFRICA, 7TH TO 8TH CENTURIES

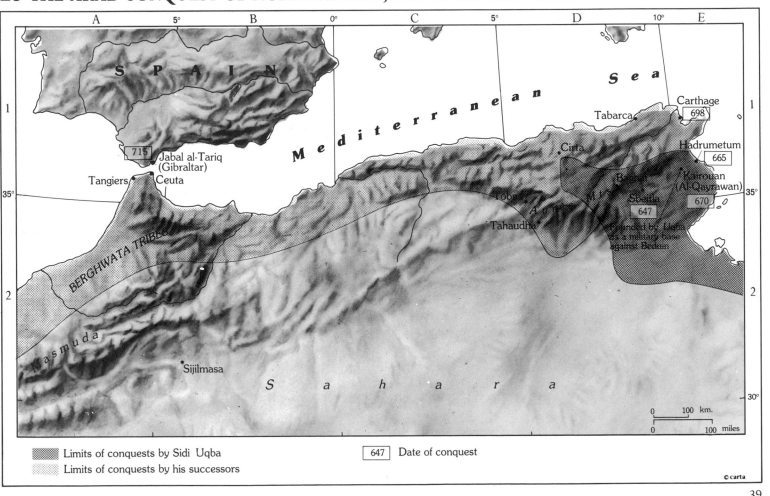

S P A I N

M e d i t e r r a n e a n   S e a

Carthage
698

Tabarca

715   Jabal al-Tariq (Gibraltar)

Hadrumetum
665

Tangiers   Ceuta

Cirta

BERGHWATA TRIBES

Babba
Sbeitla
647
Kairouan (Al-Qayrawan)
670
Founded by Uqba as a military base against Bedun

Tahaudha

Masmuda

Sijilmasa

S a h a r a

0   100 km.
0   100 miles

▨ Limits of conquests by Sidi Uqba
▧ Limits of conquests by his successors
☐ 647 Date of conquest

© carta

39

THE SPREAD OF ISLAM IN THE 7TH AND 8TH CENTURIES

While Muslim armies marched westward and into Spain, India and even Bukhara were raided. At first there was little conversion to Islam, in spite of military relations with the local population. The poet al-Mubarrad put the situation in a nutshell:

> Sons of slave women have become so common amongst us:
>
> Lead me, O God, to a land where there are no bastards.

Not until the early eighth century were Persia and India and the lands across the Hindu Kush effectively added to the Caliphate; the conquest was contemporaneous with the entry of Musa ibn Nusayr into Damascus with four hundred Visigothic princes captured by Arab-Berber forces in Spain, together with other prisoners, slaves, and booty in 715. The turning point of Islam's expansion was marked in 732, when Charles Martel defeated the Arab-Berber force between Tours and Poitiers, a move that was followed later by their ultimate expulsion from France.

The earliest mosques, which served also as administrative centers, were simple indeed. The mosque of 'Amr in Cairo and the first mosque of al-Aqsa in Jerusalem were no more than shelters, palm trunks supporting a roof of palm branches. The great stone mosque at Kairouan, with its Syrian echoes, was begun only in 670; the splendid Dome of the Rock in Jerusalem, with its echoes of the Holy Sepulcher, was constructed in 687–691. In 705 the cathedral of Damascus was reconstructed as a Friday mosque. It was the first of many such reconstructions; the Cathedral of Toledo (712) is another obvious example. Yet many years later a mosque might still be of the simplest materials, as was that of Shanga (map 42), a simple enclosure of reeds erected around 850.

The mosques were more than simply centers of worship and administration. They were teaching centers for study of the Koran and jurisprudence, including the *hadith*, or traditional sayings of the Prophet. Necessary concomitants were the study of grammar and lexicography, and in the face of Christian theology, the study of Greek philosophy (which was then reconciled with unitarian Islamic teachings). Such studies developed into a syllabus comparable with that of medieval universities in Europe.

A major shift took place in 706, when Arabic became the official language of administration in Egypt. Coptic, the descendant of the ancient language of the Pharaohs, was now relegated to second place, and ultimately declined to the status of a liturgical language, not comprehended by Coptic Christians. The shift strengthened the influence of an Islamic education upon opportunities for administrative employment. Other pressures toward Islamization were created by intolerant legislation under Harun al-Rashid (786–799) and al-Mutawakkil I (809–861), by cases of — wholly unlawful — individual and even collective forcible conversion, and by the tax imposed on *dhimmi*s, non-Muslims. Moreover, adherence to Islam conferred social prestige and security. There were, nevertheless, other currents. Between 724 and 743 John, bishop of Seville, translated the Bible into Arabic for Arabicized Christians and Moors. In about 744 the Koran itself was translated into Berber for a population which, albeit nominally Islamized, has obstinately retained its linguistic identity down to the present day.

Conversion to Islam was by no means evenly spread. Even today Lebanon has a Christian majority. In northern Iraq, Christianity lingers on in mountainous areas in appreciable numbers and with a recognized hierarchy. In Egypt Islam is in a majority in the Delta and in the Fayyum, and in Upper Egypt it is claimed that Christianity is the religion of perhaps as many as 60 percent or more of the population. In North Africa, where Donatism (map 22) had had a deep hold, Christianity lingered on for a century or two, during which Islam itself adopted its idiosyncratic cult of saints and martyrs, eventually reemerging in the puritanism of the Ibadhi and the Almoravids. ☐

29 THE SPREAD OF ISLAM IN THE 7TH AND 8TH CENTURIES

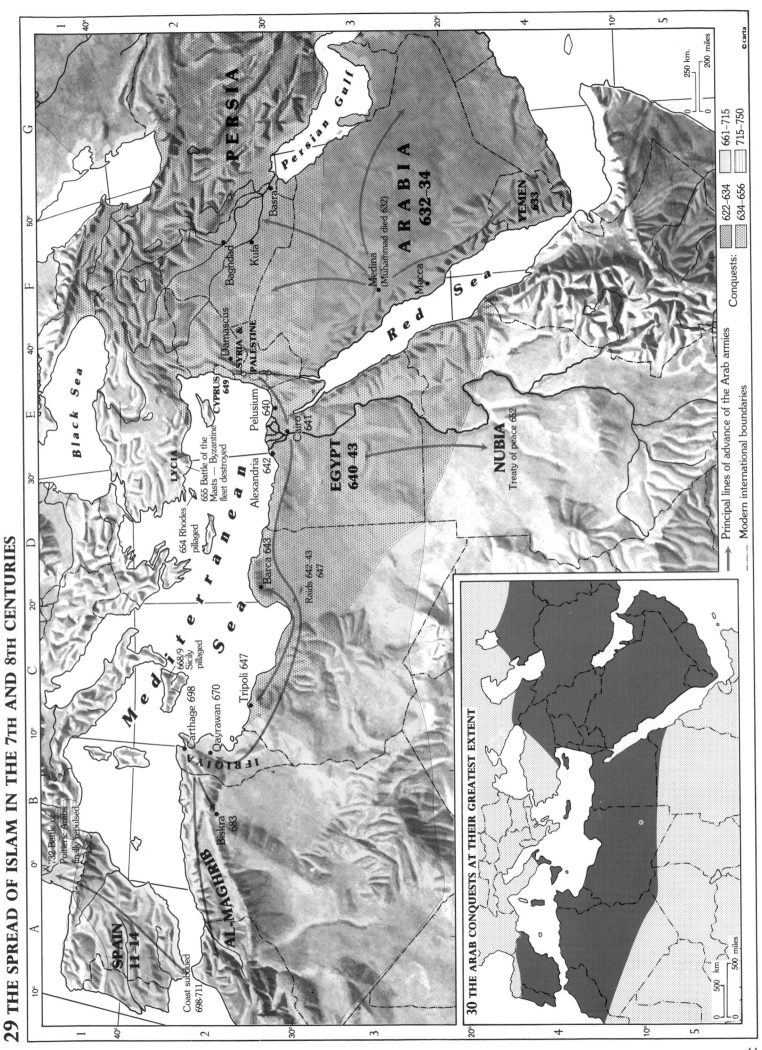

SPAIN
11-14

AL-MAGHRIB

IFRIQIYA

732 Battle of
Poitiers. Arabs
finally repulsed

Coast subdued
698-711

Carthage 698
Qayrawan 670

Tripoli 647

Biskra
683

Black Sea

Mediterranean Sea

668/9 Sicily
pillaged

654 Rhodes
pillaged

655 Battle of the
Masts — Byzantine
fleet destroyed

LYCIA

CYPRUS
649

Barca 643

Raids 642-43
647

Alexandria
642

Pelusium
640

Cairo
641

EGYPT
640-43

Red Sea

NUBIA
Treaty of peace 652

PERSIA

Persian Gulf

Basra

Baghdad
Kufa

Damascus
SYRIA &
PALESTINE

ARABIA
632-34

Medina
(Muhammad died 632)

Mecca

YEMEN
633

30 THE ARAB CONQUESTS AT THEIR GREATEST EXTENT

Conquests:
- 622-634
- 634-656
- 661-715
- 715-750

↑ Principal lines of advance of the Arab armies
--- Modern international boundaries

250 km.
200 miles

© carta

41

THE FURTHER SPREAD OF ISLAM IN AFRICA, 8TH TO 19TH CENTURIES

In the seventh and early eighth centuries the Arab armies had seized the entire world from Morocco to the Himalayas. In the eighth century the conquered peoples including Persians, Syrians, Copts, and Berbers, embraced Islam. Nationality disappeared; all spoke of themselves as Arabs.

Outside this area the progress of conversion seems to have been slow. In the tenth century the existence of a single Muslim ruler in East Africa is important enough to be noted by Arab authors. Islam does not seem to have reached the Tuaregs (Tawariq) south of Morocco until about 1040. South of Egypt the Nubian Church continued until the fourteenth or fifteenth century. In Somalia there is no evidence of Islam before the eleventh century.

Perhaps the most potent force in the spread of Islam in Africa is the mystical movement generally spoken of as Sufism. Sufi fraternities were established, the first in Baghdad, and spread to Algeria, Java and Guinea. The most important have been the Qadiriya, the Rifa'iya, and the Mawlawiya, of which last the Ottoman sultans of Turkey were members. Especially strong in Morocco was the Shadhiliya. In Egypt the Ahmadiya was the strongest. In the nineteenth century a new military-religious order originated in Algeria, which came to power in Libya as the Sanusiya in 1837. These fraternities, communities of devout persons bound together in religious purpose, occupied in Islam much the place of monasticism in Christianity. In contrast to Christian rules, however, membership in a Sufi order did not preclude marriage. Among the Berbers and in Egypt a popularized cult of Muslim saints arose, yet without any formal canonization. Its special ritual practice was *dhikr*, group recitation of the "beautiful names of God" and their private recitation on the *subhah* (or *tasbih*), or rosary. Although we have few details, it was from Sufi teachers that the courts of western African rulers learned Islam — Kanem in 1085–1097, Mali in the thirteenth century, Songhai after 1497, Wadai in the seventeenth century. Nubia, conquered from Egypt in the sixteenth century, forms an exception, as does the coast of eastern Africa. The most recent evidence of Islamic conversion in these areas is Islamic-type coinage locally minted before 750, and a mosque dating to about 850. Here there was no penetration inland.

Although Islam had reached Timbuktu in about 1100 and the Hausa by the fourteenth century, it was very thinly spread in western Africa. It was largely confined to the towns. In the eighteenth century the movement known as jihad, or holy war erupted, first in Futa Jallon (now in Guinea) around 1725, then in Futa Toro (now in Senegal) in the 1770s, and finally in Sokoto (now in Nigeria) in 1804. The author of this last movement was Usman dan Fodio, joined by his brother Abdullahi and his son Muhammad Bello. They entirely reorganized, both religiously and constitutionally, what is today Northern Nigeria as far as Bornu. In central and eastern Africa the progress of Islam was less dramatic, being carried along slave-trading and other trade routes by members of Sufi fraternities after 1823, when penetration began from Zanzibar, reversing the previous trend under which African traders brought their goods to the coast. In addition, with the increase of the settlement of Indian traders in Zanzibar after 1801, the Bohoras, Ismaili and Ithna'ashari Khojas, and other small sects built mosques on the coast and later inland. There are also some small Indian Muslim communities in South Africa. Arab traders succeeded in substantial conversions in the late nineteenth century in Uganda and eastern Zaïre. At the turn of the century Lamu became an intellectual center for this area, while the internment of Christian missionaries during World War I gave free rein to a successful campaign of conversion by Sufi missionaries in what is now southern Tanzania.

Spain, Sardinia, S. Italy and Sicily recovered by Christians

Beginning of large-scale conversion of area by preacher Abdallah b. Yasin c.1040

Rulers of Mali converted in 13th cent.

Songhai converted after 1497

Sultan Oume of Kanem (1085–97) initiates large-scale conversion of area to Islam

Nubia: Christian kingdoms 7th–13th cent. Islamized by conquest, late 16th cent.

Islam spread via Timbuktu (c.1100) and Gao, reaching the Hausa in 14th cent.

Wadai area converted from Dongola in 17th cent.

Islam brought by Egyptian slave traders in 19th cent.

Converted in 18th cent.

Darfur area converted from Lake Chad area

Ethiopia: Christian state from 4th cent. to present. Lowland areas Islamized from 8th to 16th cent.

Principal routes of Arab ivory and slave traders after 1823, bringing Islam into central Tanzania, Buganda and eastern Zaire

Extension of conversions to Islam after 1800 including "Jihad"

Expansion of Islamized Somali from 13th cent.

Arab and Egyptian traders on coastal route from 2nd cent. Mosque and coinage at Shanga, Manda Is., before 750. Muslim rulers by 10th cent.

Principal route of Arab ivory and slave traders after c.1830

Arab trading settlements from ?10th cent.

Indian immigration during 19th cent.

Extreme limit of Arab trade as shown by archaeology

32 PRESENT DISTRIBUTION OF ISLAM

Percentage of population:

- to 0.9%
- to 4.9%
- to 29.9%
- to 49.9%
- to 79.9%
- to 100%

Largely Indian and Malay

0   1000 km.
0   500 miles.

0   500 km.
0   250 miles

Rain forest   Arab possessions in A.D. 750   Arab coastal trade

Desert   Direction of spread of Islam

© carta

43

NORTH AFRICA AND EGYPT UNDER THE FATIMIDS

The Shi'ite Ismaili sect, which maintained against Sunni (orthodox) Islam that only the prophet's son-in-law Ali and his descendants could legitimately become caliphs, now produced a grave challenge to the Abbasid caliphate.

In North Africa in 909 Sa'id ibn al-Husayn usurped the Aghlabid dynasty, and proclaimed himself Imam Ubayd Allah al-Mahdi at Kairouan. Soon afterward he had control from Morocco to the Egyptian border. In 914 he seized Alexandria, and then ravaged the Delta. He had inherited a fleet from the Aghlabids, and with this he controlled Sicily, Malta, Corsica, Sardinia, and the Balearic Islands. In 920 he settled at a new capital, al-Mahdiya.

There was no further expansion until in 969 Jawhar al-Siqilli, a Sicilian, took al-Fustat (Old Cairo), and set about building a new capital of al-Qahira (Cairo: see map 39). Shortly thereafter the Fatimid caliph al-Mu'izz made his solemn entry, with the coffins of his ancestors carried in procession before him. The Fatimid empire now covered all of North Africa and the Mediterranean Islands to western Arabia and the holy cities of Mecca and Medina; very soon Syria was added. In 972 work began on the mosque of al-Azhar, destined to become the intellectual center of the Islamic world, as it is today.

The successor to al-Mu'izz was al-Aziz (975–996). His ambitions even reached Spain and Iraq. He built a palace in Cairo costing nearly two million dollars to house the Abbasid caliph, whom he had taken prisoner and brought there. Throughout Cairo there was intense building activity under his rule, including palaces, pavilions, mosques (including the huge mosque completed by his son al-Hakim), canals, bridges, and naval docks. Al-Aziz himself lived in the greatest luxury and was a connoisseur of precious stones. He had a Christian wife, and at her (quite irregular) wish her brothers were appointed orthodox patriarchs of Alexandria and Jerusalem. For the first fifteen years of his reign his wazir, Ibn Killis, a Jewish convert to Islam, managed the finances with commanding ability. Al-Aziz had a special predilection for Christians and Jews, and any Muslim opposition was promptly silenced. Power was maintained in the capital by a Berber bodyguard, and mixed troops of Sudanese and Turkish units, a sure recipe for future trouble. In this period the genius of Ibn Killis made Cairo the greatest power in the Mediterranean, with trade that stretched from the Atlantic and Europe to Arabia, East Africa and India (see map 34).

Al-Aziz fell dead in his bath in 996, and was succeeded by an eleven-year-old son, al-Hakim. During the regency Christians, Berbers, and Turks quarreled bitterly to the point of murder; at the same time al-Hakim grew more and more eccentric. His tutor called him "Lizard" for his slippery ways. He had a passion for darkness, summoning his council at night and making nocturnal journeys around Cairo on a gray ass. All business was ordered to take place after sunset, and women were forbidden to go out of doors. Soon he began to persecute Christians and Jews with impartial venom, and eventually his fellow Muslims as well. Al-Hakim aroused hatred on all sides. In 1005 he ordered the destruction of all the churches in Cairo. In 1009 he had the Holy Sepulcher in Jerusalem destroyed, and in 1014 he burned al-Fustat. Then he announced that he was the very incarnation of Allah, and rescinded the laws of fasting. Then, on 10 February 1021, he rode out to the Moqattam Hills and mysteriously disappeared. His bizarrre religion survives in Lebanon among adherents of the Druse sect propagated by Muhammad ibn Isma'il al-Darazi.

After 1033 the Fatimid empire declined steadily. Syria fell to the Seljuk Turks, and their capture of Jerusalem precipitated the Crusades. In Africa the western provinces threw up dynasties that acknowledged the Abbasid caliphate. In Tripolitania and Tunisia the Banu Hilal and Banu Sulaim tribes ravaged the country. In 1071 the Normans took Sicily. In 1058–1059 for forty days Baghdad acknowledged the Fatimid caliph, even issuing coinage in his name. □

33 NORTH AFRICA AND EGYPT UNDER THE FATIMIDS

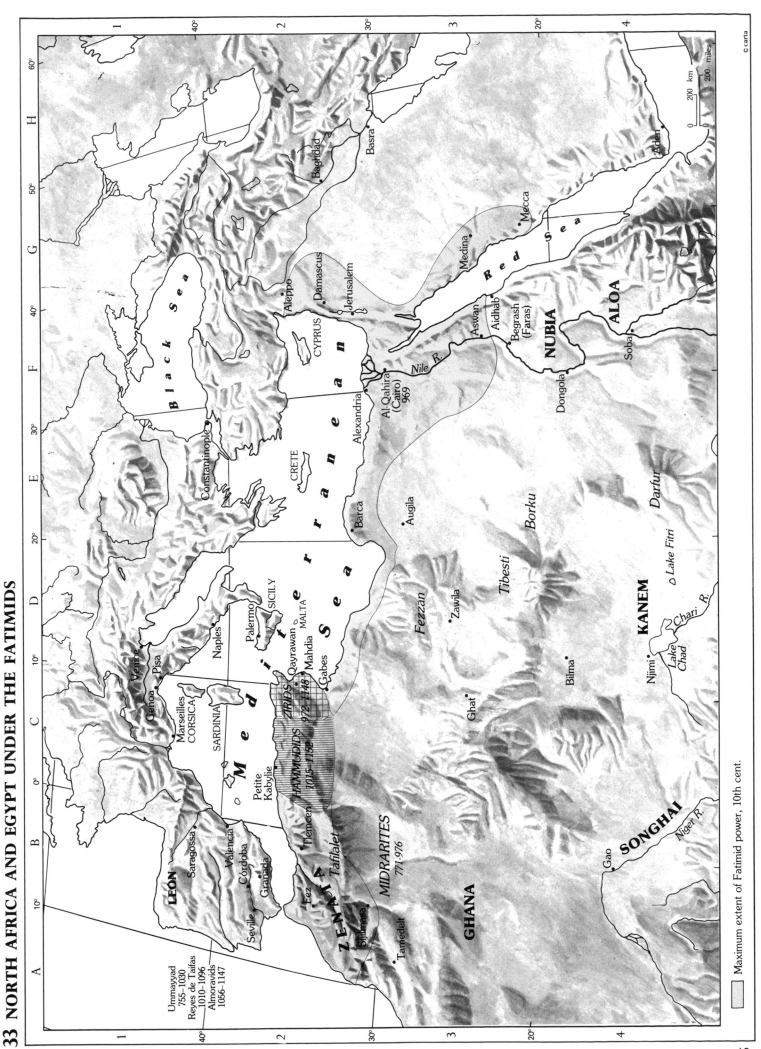

Ummayyad 755–1030
Reyes de Taifas 1010–1096
Almoravids 1056–1147

LEON

Saragossa
Valencia
Córdoba
Seville
Granada

Marseilles
CORSICA
SARDINIA

Genoa · Pisa
Venice
Naples

Petite Kabylie

Fez
Tlemcen
Sijilmasa
Tamedelt
Tafilalet

ZENATA

MIDRARITES
771–976

GHANA

Gao

SONGHAI

Niger R.

Njimi
Lake Chad

KANEM

Bilma

Ghat

Zawila

Fezzan

Borku

Tibesti

Chari R.
Lake Fitri

Darfur

SICILY
Palermo
MALTA
Qayrawan
ZIRIDS 972–1148
Mahdia
Gabes
HAMMUDIDS 1015–1152

Mediterranean Sea

CRETE

CYPRUS

Black Sea

Constantinople

Barca

Augila

Alexandria
Al-Qahira (Cairo) 969
Nile R.

Aleppo
Damascus
Jerusalem

Baghdad
Basra

Medina
Mecca

Red Sea

Aswan
Aidhab
Begrash (Faras)

NUBIA

Dongola

Soba

ALOA

Aden

©carta

Maximum extent of Fatimid power, 10th cent.

0   200 km
0   200 miles

45

CARAVAN AND SEA TRADE C. 1000

Originating as they did not far from the Sanhaja, the Fatimids and their supporters knew the desert routes as well as the sources of supply of gold and salt from Ghana and the western Sahara. How far the Fatimid conquest of western North Africa, of Tunisia and then Egypt, of the Mediterranean islands, and of the Hijaz and Syria was prompted by commercial considerations is an open question. The real conqueror of Egypt had been a Sicilian, while al-Aziz (975–996) had a wazir who was a convert from Judaism with also a Russian wife. Berbers, Turks, and Circassians thronged the court, and from around 1074 until the end of the dynasty in 1169 all of the wazirs were Armenians.

Al-Maqrizi's inventory of the treasures of the caliph al-Mustansir (1035–1094) gives some idea of the wealth accumulated in the palace and of its provenance. Included were jewels, crystal vases, gold plates, ebony and ivory, amber, musk, steel mirrors, parasols fitted with gold or silver sticks, chessmen in gold or silver, jeweled swords and daggers, and silks and other textiles for which Damascus and Dabiq were famous. The caliph reposed in the utmost luxury, listening to music, and drinking wine in a tent modeled on the Ka'aba. "This," said he, "is pleasanter than contemplating a Black Stone, listening to a droning muezzin, and drinking unclean water from Zemzem." The evidence that trade was being practiced with parts of Africa, with Syria, and with India is clear enough.

In architecture other affinities are discernible. the mosque of al-Hakim shows the influence of northern Iraq. Before Fatimid times building was chiefly in brick. Now, perhaps because of the employment of an Armenian architect, stone was preferred for mosques. The mosque of al-Aqmar is the first to display the corbeled "stalactite" niche that was to become commonplace under the Mamluks. The three surviving great gates of Cairo — the Bab al-Futuh, the Bab al-Nasr, and the Bab Zuwayla — were all constructed on Byzantine models and built by engineers from Edessa.

Marble, and occasionally mosaic, were now used for wall decoration in mosques. Some houses had exquisitely carved wooden paneling, with motifs which clearly have Sassanian Persian models. Olive-wood screens and doors were inlaid with carved ivory. Persia also inspired bronzes and textiles, as novelties replacing the older Coptic traditions. Sassanid traditions long prevailed in ceramic works, but al-Maqrizi notes the presence of Chinese wares. Only in bookbinding did Coptic art remain unchallenged.

As a Shi'ite region, hence separate from the main stream of Islamic tradition, Fatimid Egypt was to some extent an intellectual backwater. The great works of geography written by Arabs from the ninth century on were composed outside the Fatimid domains, with two exceptions. Except for India, Sijistan, and Spain, al-Maqdisi (so named for his birthplace, al-Quds [Jerusalem]) visited all the Muslim-held lands, as did his historian contemporary al-Mas'udi. The latter also reached India, and claimed to have reached China. He certainly visited Zanzibar. His *Meadows of Gold and Mines of Gems* is an encyclopedia of history and geography beyond the ordinary Islamic range, and includes even references to Indians, Jews, and Romans. Soon, however, their geography was to be surpassed by al-Idrisi, whose maps reflected his knowledge of trade routes (see maps 35, 36).

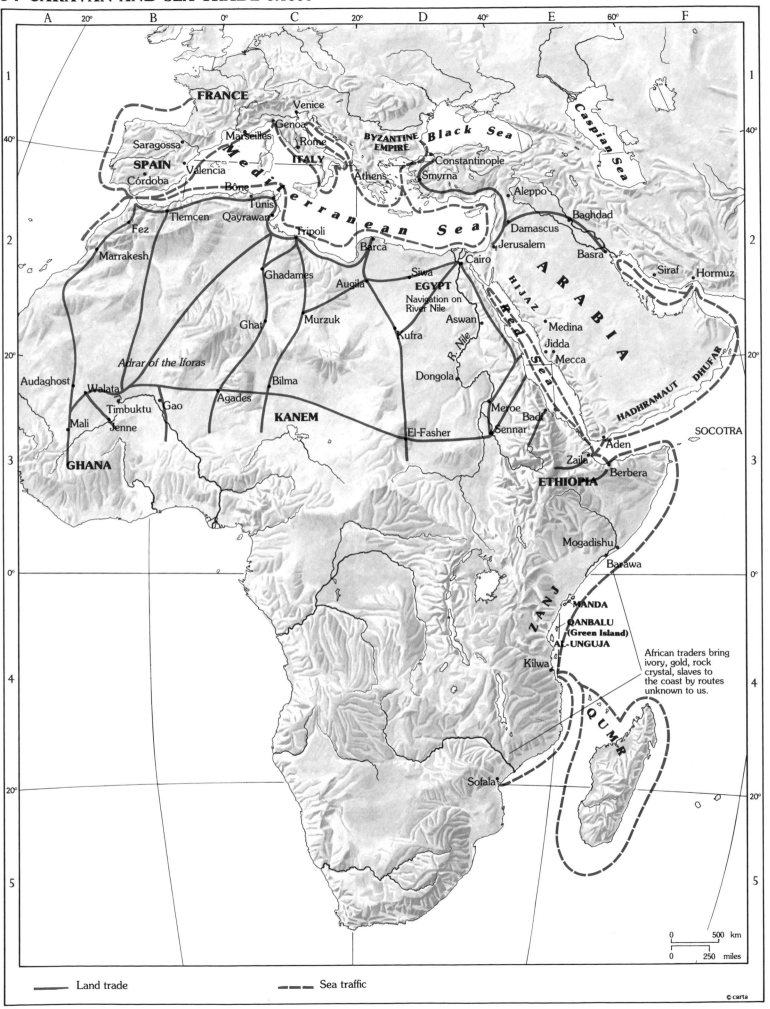

A map titled "Caravan and Sea Trade c.1000" showing Africa, southern Europe, and the Middle East with trade routes.

Labels on the map:

FRANCE
Venice
Genoa
Marseilles
Rome
Saragossa
SPAIN
Valencia
ITALY
BYZANTINE EMPIRE
Black Sea
Caspian Sea
Córdoba
Bône
Constantinople
Athens
Smyrna
Aleppo
Mediterranean Sea
Tunis
Tlemcen
Qayrawan
Tripoli
Damascus
Baghdad
Fez
Barca
Jerusalem
Basra
Marrakesh
Ghadames
Augila
Cairo
Siraf
Hormuz
Siwa
EGYPT
ARABIA
Navigation on River Nile
HIJAZ
Ghat
Murzuk
Aswan
Medina
Jidda
Kufra
Mecca
R. Nile
Red Sea
Adrar of the Iforas
Dongola
DHUFAR
HADHRAMAUT
Audaghost
Walata
Bilma
Agades
Timbuktu
Gao
SOCOTRA
Mali
Jenne
KANEM
Meroe
Badi
El-Fasher
Sennar
Aden
GHANA
Zaila
Berbera
ETHIOPIA
Mogadishu
Barawa
ZANJ
MANDA
QANBALU (Green Island)
AL-UNGUJA
Kilwa
African traders bring ivory, gold, rock crystal, slaves to the coast by routes unknown to us.
QUMR
Sofala

Legend:
—— Land trade
- - - Sea traffic

0   500 km
0   250 miles

© carta

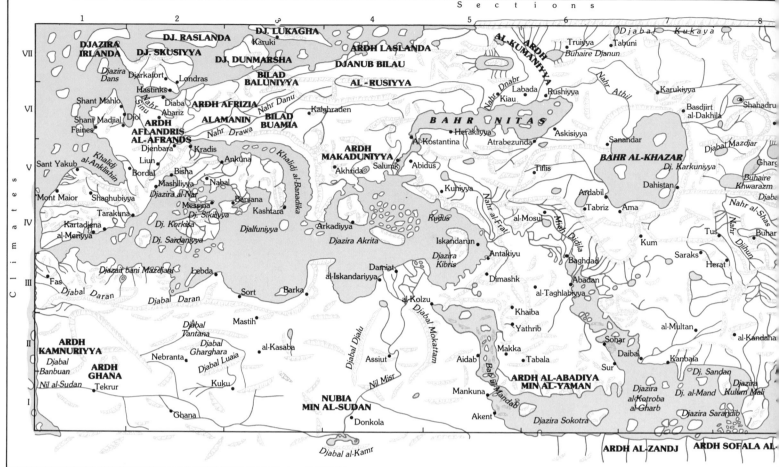

S e c t i o n s

1   2   3   4   5   6   7   8

VII   VI   V   IV   III   II   I

C l i m a t e s

DJ. RASLANDA   DJ. LUKAGHA   Djabal Kukaya

DJAZIRA IRLANDA   DJ. SKUSIYYA   Karuki   ARDH LASLANDA   AL-KUMANIYYA   ARDH   Truiyya   Tabuni

DJ. DUNMARSHA   DJANUB BILAU   Buhaire Djanun

Djazira Dans   Djarkafort   Londras   BILAD BALUNIYYA   Nahr Dnabr   Labada   Rushiyya   Karukiyya

Hastinks   AL-RUSIYYA   Kiau

Shant Mahlo   Diaba   ARDH AFRIZIA   Nahr Danu   Kalshraden   BAHR NITAS   Basdjirt al-Dakhila

Shant Madjial   Abariz   ALAMANIN   BILAD BUAMIA   Al-Kostantina   Atrabezunda   Askisiyya   Sanandar   Shahadru

Fajnes   Djol   ARDH AFLANDRIS AL-AFRANDS   Nahr Drawa   Heraklivya   Djabal Mazdjar

Khalidj al-Anklishin   Djenbara   Kradis   Tiflis   BAHR AL-KHAZAR   Gharg

Sant Yakub   Liun   Ankuna   ARDH MAKADUNIYYA   Salumik   Dj. Karkuniyya   Buhaire Khwarazm

Bordal   Bisha   Nabal   Akhrida   Abidus   Kuniyya   Dahistan   Djaba

Mashliiyya   Khalidj al-Banadika   Ardabil   Nahr al-Shas

Mont Maior   Shaghubiyya   Djazira al-Nar   Barsana   Ama   Tabriz

Tarakuna   Messina   Dj. Sikiliyya   Kashtara   Rudus   al-Mosul   Kum   Saraks   Buhar

Kartadjena   Dj. Korkisa   Djalfuniyya   Arkadiyya   Djazira Akrita   Iskandarun   Baghdad   Tus   Herat

al-Meriyya   Dj. Sardaniyya   Antakiyu   Abadan   Djijhun

Djazira Kibris   Dimashk   al-Taghlabiyya

Djazair bani Mazghani   Lebda   Damiat   al-Iskandariyya   al-Multan

Fas   Sort   Barka   al-Kolzu   Khaiba

Djabal Daran   Djabal Daran   Yathrib   al-Kandaha

Mastih   Djabal Djalu   Makka   Sohar

ARDH KAMNURIYYA   Djabal Tantana   Assiut   Tabala   Daibal   Kanbaia

Djabal Banbuan   Nebranta   Djabal Gharghara   al-Kasaba   Aidab   Sur   Dj. Sandan

ARDH GHANA   Djabal Luaia   ARDH AL-ABADIYA MIN AL-YAMAN   Djazira al-Kotroba al-Gharb   Dj. al-Mand   Djazira Kulum Mali

Nil al-Sudan   Tekrur   Kuku   Nil Mist   Mankuna   Djazira Sarandib

Ghana   Nahr Djihun   Akent   Bab al-Mandab   Djazira Sokotra

NUBIA MIN AL-SUDAN   Donkola

Djabal al-Kamr   ARDH AL-ZANDJ   ARDH SOFALA AL-

Nahr al-Frat   Nahr al-Athil   Mikl Didjla

AL-IDRISI'S MAP OF THE WORLD, C. 1154

Abu Abd Allah Muhammad ibn Muhammad ibn Abd Allah ibn Idrisi al-Hammudi al-Hasani al-Idrisi, to give him his full name, is commonly known as al-Idrisi. He was a sharif, a noble or descendant of the Prophet Muhammad by his grandson al-Hasan. He is believed to have been born at Ceuta, Morocco, around 1100. He studied in the Great Mosque of Córdoba, and traveled widely in Spain and North Africa.

In 1154, on the orders of Roger II, king of Sicily and a Norman, al-Idrisi produced the work of geography which brought him fame, *The Book for the Pleasure of Those Who Are Eager to Travel the Earth*. Its purpose was to illustrate a silver planisphere that he himself had constructed. How he came to be at the court of Roger II is not known, nor how or where he acquired the necessary skills

to assemble this monumental book (a complete edition of which was first produced in 1970). The court, however, gave the work its common name, the *Kitab Rujar* ("Roger's book"). Al-Idrisi is believed to have died in 1165. No other details are known of his life, possibly because medieval Arabian biographers considered him a renegade from Islam and deliberately refrained from mentioning him because he had resided at the court of a Christian ruler.

Comparison with other Arab geographers shows that al-Idrisi's work was to a great extent derived from his predecessors. According to the preface to his work, Roger II sent out in all directions to gather information for him. He ordered the construction of maps, and of these al-Idrisi produced no less than seventy, including some

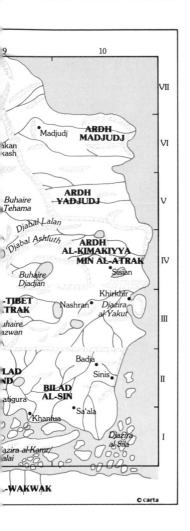

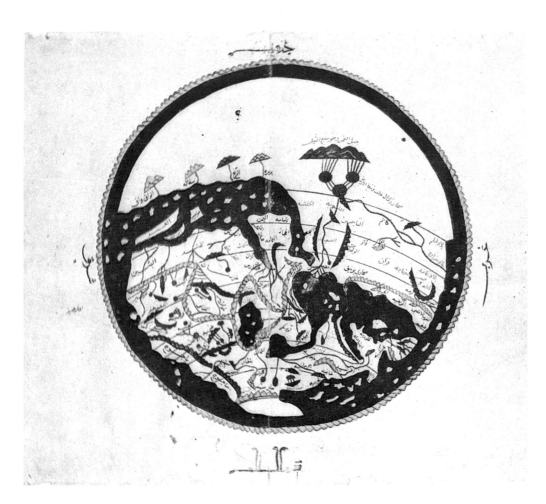

that survive in color. Put together, they would form an oblong quadrangle, much after the style of Claudius Ptolemy (see map 15), but his world map which precedes the other maps is round, in the traditional fashion. The map shown here is reproduced from the manuscript at Oxford in the Bodleian Library (map 36). Other manuscripts are in Paris, Cairo, Istanbul, Leningrad, and Tunis. This dispersion of manuscripts is not surprising, because at this period Sicily was a crossroads of trade between Africa, the East, and Europe.

Al-Idrisi's work is divided into ten sections and into seven geographical climes. To these is added an eighth as a kind of appendix, which shows the Mountain of the Moon (perhaps Kenya or Kilimanjaro?), two lakes in Ethiopia, and the eastern African coast from Ras Hafun as far as Sofala. His knowledge of place-names in Europe is extensive: his information stretches as far north as Britain, Iceland, and Norway, and as far east as China. He is much less informed about India than about the lands under Mongol control, and thus reflects

commercial knowledge so far as he knew it. In the same way his knowledge of West Africa as far as the Niger and Kanem reflects his knowledge of the gold and salt trades. His knowledge of Egypt tails off at the Cataracts, and becomes vague as far as Nubia and Ethiopia are concerned, although he seems to have a correct idea of the Nile sources that so puzzled later European geographers. He knows the eastern African coast as far as Malindi, but is unaware of the intervention of Mombasa or Kilwa before he reaches Sofala — another reflection, perhaps, of his knowledge of the gold trade. Because of his inherited lack of knowledge of the true shapes of Europe, Africa, and Asia, and because of the necessity as he understood it to compress the shape of the inhabited lands into a quadrangle, the picture presented is very distorted. This distortion extends to the islands off Africa, especially to the Comoro Islands, which are represented as huge in extent. It was nonetheless a noble attempt to comprehend so far-ranging a subject. □

THE ALMORAVIDS IN AFRICA AND SPAIN

Two African dynasties, the Almoravids and the Almohads, now successively invaded Spain, thus making a second and third conquest in Europe by African armies. These two were Berber dynasties, and both had religious movements as their origin.

The Almoravids (Arabic, *al-Murabitun*) take their name from their *ribat*, or fortified monastery, of soldier-monks in Senegal. They were chiefly Lamtuna tribesmen, nomads who wore face veils, as their Tuareg descendants do today. The Almoravids maintained the custom even when they had conquered all North Africa and much of Spain.

In 1055 the Almoravid army opened an era of expansion by taking the oasis town of Sijilmasa. Further successes followed, and in 1061 Yusuf ibn Tashfin was given command of an army to go northward. He was a quintessential soldier-monk, simple in dress, spare in diet, and of ascetic habits. He built a new capital at Marrakesh in 1062, and soon thereafter ruled all Morocco and western Algeria. Strict in orthodoxy, he acknowledged the Abbasid caliphs in Baghdad as suzerains.

Christian Spaniards retook Toledo in 1085. The Muslim rulers of Seville and other petty states were in confusion, and invited Yusuf ibn Tashfin to succor them. In 1086 he completely defeated Alfonso VI at Zallaqa and returned to Africa, as he had promised. Invited back to Spain, he took Granada in 1090, and Córdoba and Seville in 1091. Other towns followed, until his death in 1110. He had failed to capture the Christian capital, Toledo. "Victors," as Dryden says, "are by victory undone." It was a military regime without a civil policy; and constant pressure by the Christians and rebellions in 1144 and 1145 ended Almoravid rule in Spain. There followed a period of chaos and rule by petty kings, until a new Berber power arose in 1170.

One must not dismiss the Almoravids as mere barbarian soldiers. There was a two-way traffic, as the Arab-style coinage of Catholic Castile showed. The Great Mosque of Tlemcen was modeled on the Great Mosque of Córdoba. In Córdoba Arabic-speaking Jews maintained a Talmudic center where their culture flourished and underwent cross-fertilization with others.

□

THE ALMOHADS IN AFRICA AND SPAIN

The Almohads (Arabic, *al-Muwahhidun*) stemmed from Muhammad ibn Tumert, who claimed to be the Mahdi, the prophet sent by Allah to restore Islam to its original purity and orthodoxy before the Day of Doom. He preached *tawhid*, the unity and unicity of Allah and a spiritual conception of him, as opposed to the lax anthropomorphism then current in Islam. He lived as an ascetic, and eschewed wine, music, and other such indulgences.

In 1130 he was succeeded by Abd al-Mu'min ibn Ali, who shortly was to conquer Morocco. In 1146 he annihilated the Almoravids at Tlemcen, and then took Fez, Ceuta, Tangier, and Aghmat. Marrakesh fell after a siege in 1146–1147. In 1145 he sent an army into Spain, and within five years had all the Muslim possessions in the peninsula. Then he took Algeria in 1151, Tunisia in 1158, and Tripolitania in 1160. He died in 1163.

It was not until 1170 that his son Abu Yaqub Yusuf carried the Holy War again into Spain. He had little success. In 1184 his son Abu Yusuf succeeded, crossed to Andalusia, and secured a five-year truce with the Christian king of Castile and León. In 1195 he won a great victory over Alfonso VIII of Castile at Alarcos, but failed to exploit it. It was a stalemate until 1212 when an alliance of León, Castile, Navarre, and Aragon utterly defeated the Almohads at Las Navas de Tolosa. They were incontinently expelled from the peninsula. Thereafter they reigned in Marrakesh until the dynasty foundered in 1269, when the seminomadic Berber people Banu Marin took the city.

It was in architecture that Abu Yusuf's achievement was most splendid and lasting. The stupendous Giralda tower in Seville was built to mark his accession, as a minaret to the Friday mosque. The mosque was later built as a cathedral with the minaret serving as bell tower. The whole city known as Rabat (Arabic, *Rabat al-Fath*) was built by him, modeled on Alexandria. According to the writer al-Marrakushi the great hospital Abu Yusuf erected in Marrakesh had no equal in all the world.

□

37 THE ALMORAVIDS IN AFRICA AND SPAIN

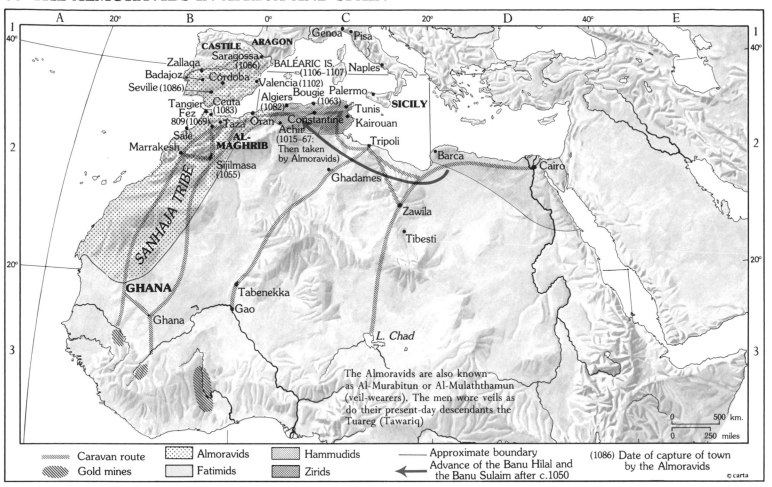

CASTILE
ARAGON
Genoa
Pisa
Zallaqa
Saragossa (1086)
BALÉARIC IS. (1106–1107)
Naples
Badajoz
Córdoba
Seville (1086)
Valencia (1102)
Tangier
Ceuta (1083)
Algiers (1082)
Bougie
Palermo
Fez 809 (1069)
Oran
Constantine
Tunis
SICILY
Taza
Kairouan
Salé
AL-MAGHRIB
Achir (1015–67: Then taken by Almoravids)
Tripoli
Marrakesh
Barca
Cairo
Sijilmasa (1055)
Ghadames
SANHAJA TRIBE
Zawila
Tibesti
GHANA
Tabenekka
Gao
Ghana
L. Chad

The Almoravids are also known as Al-Murabitun or Al-Mulaththamun (veil-wearers). The men wore veils as do their present-day descendants the Tuareg (Tawariq).

500 km.
250 miles

⫻ Caravan route	⬚ Almoravids	⫽ Hammudids	— Approximate boundary	(1086) Date of capture of town by the Almoravids
⫽ Gold mines	⫿ Fatimids	▨ Zirids	← Advance of the Banu Hilal and the Banu Sulaim after c.1050	

© carta

38 THE ALMOHADS IN AFRICA AND SPAIN

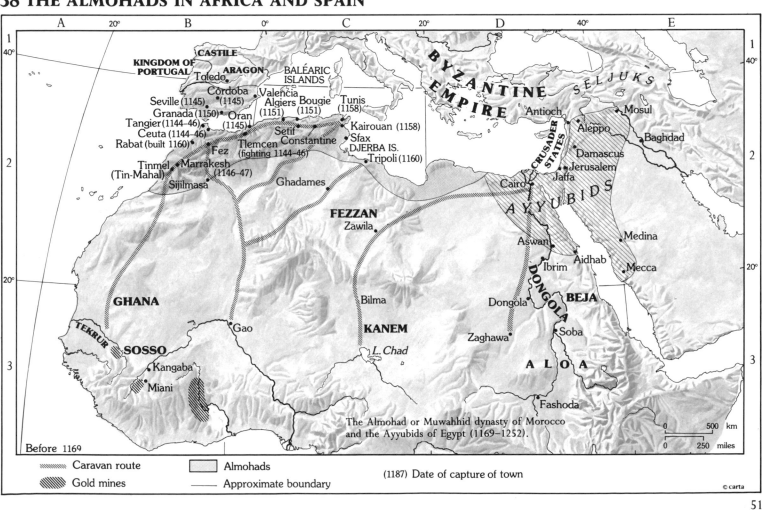

KINGDOM OF PORTUGAL
CASTILE
Toledo
ARAGON
BALÉARIC ISLANDS
BYZANTINE EMPIRE
SELJUKS
Seville (1145)
Córdoba (1145)
Valencia
Algiers (1151)
Bougie (1151)
Tunis (1158)
Antioch
Mosul
Granada (1150)
Oran (1145)
Aleppo
Tangier (1144–46)
Baghdad
Ceuta (1144–46)
Setif
Kairouan (1158)
CRUSADER STATES
Damascus
Rabat (built 1160)
Tlemcen (fighting 1144–46)
Constantine
Sfax
DJERBA IS.
Jerusalem
Fez
Tripoli (1160)
Cairo
Jaffa
Tinmel (Tin-Mahal)
Marrakesh (1146–47)
Sijilmasa
Ghadames
AYYUBIDS
FEZZAN
Zawila
Aswan
Ibrim
DONGOLA
Medina
GHANA
Bilma
Aidhab
Mecca
TEKRUR
Gao
KANEM
Dongola
BEJA
SOSSO
Zaghawa
Soba
Kangaba
L. Chad
ALOA
Miani
Fashoda

Before 1169

The Almohad or Muwahhid dynasty of Morocco and the Ayyubids of Egypt (1169–1252).

500 km
250 miles

⫻ Caravan route	⬚ Almohads	(1187) Date of capture of town
⫽ Gold mines	— Approximate boundary	

© carta

THE DEVELOPMENT OF CAIRO FROM 639 UP TO MAMLUK TIMES

Cairo is still the most glorious and populous city in Africa. Although it was given the name *al-Qahira* (the victorious) only in A.D. 969, it is largely on the site of the pharaonic Memphis, which reached as far as El-Giza and Saqqara. The pyramids and the Sphinx are its mute survivors. When the Romans acquired Egypt in 30 B.C., they stationed a legion at the apex of the Delta known as *Masr*, "the fortification," whence *Misr*, the ancient name for the country in Arabic. Close by was the Greco-Coptic town of Babilyun (Babylon), which had originated from a Persian fort of around 500 B.C. A Roman fortress which succeeded it in A.D. 27 and was rebuilt around 100 still survives. The adjacent town included a Jewish quarter. Here the Holy Family is believed to have taken shelter from the wrath of Herod, and here the apostle Peter and Mark the Evangelist are believed to have preached in A.D. 42. A synagogue and churches still survive from before 641.

In this year 'Amr ibn al-'As built his garrison town of al-Fustat (see map 27). A mosque still remains on his site, but all the remaining buildings, public and private, have long since disappeared. In 751 a new town, al-Askar ("the cantonment"), was built by the Abbasids. It also has disappeared.

In 868 the governor, Ibn Tulun, knowing the weakness of the caliphate, declared Egypt independent and seized all Syria as far as the Euphrates and Libya as far as Barca. He built a palace, offices, a racecourse, a polo ground, a hospital, a zoo, baths and markets, and a Great Mosque that would contain all the army. This alone survives.

In 969 the Fatimids (see map 38) conquered Egypt. Each preceding city had been built north of the last to catch the prevailing wind, and al-Qahira was no exception. On 5 August 969 the boundaries of the new palace city, surpassing all in magnificence, were demarcated with ropes on which bells had been hung. Astrologers stood by to determine the most propitious moment to turn the first sod. A raven anticipated them by alighting on the rope and setting the bells ringing. It was an unlucky moment: the planet Mars (Arabic, al-Qahira) was in the ascendant and gave the new city its name. By the eleventh century it had thirty thousand inhabitants, government offices, courts, stables, stores, halls and apartments, a hospital, and barracks. Near the palace a new mosque, al-Azhar, completed the city, making it a university to serve the Islamic world.

Fatimid rule finally collapsed in 1168. In 1169 Saladin (Salah al-Din Yusuf ibn Ayyub) was sent as governor by the Abbasid caliph. He made himself sultan in 1171. His great monument was the Citadel, a fortress built on the Syrian model. His commander-in-chief, Badr al-Jamali, of Armenian origin, began to ring the city with fortifications that have never been completed. He also built twenty *madrasa*s, colleges for teaching religion (i.e., that of Sunni orthodoxy in place of the Shi'ism of the Fatimids). There were also free hospitals and dervish monasteries. Only the Citadel survives.

Saladin's principal bequest to Cairo was the institution of Mamluks. *Mamluk* means "owned" or "slave," but for the Turks or Greeks whom he recruited and to whom he gave an Islamic education and training in all the arts of war and government, this classification was a passport to the highest offices of state. These early Mamluks, and the Circassian Mamluks who succeeded them, were the only dominating factor in Egypt until 1517.

On 8 August 1303 Cairo was devastated by an earthquake. Of some six hundred listed ancient buildings that survive today, only sixty-six were built before 1303. The older part of central Cairo thus belongs overwhelmingly to the Mamluk period, and to a lesser degree to the Ottoman Turks. The latter built little other than residences. To the Mamluks is owed the most splendid of the mosques, dervish monasteries, and hospitals, one of which is still in service as an eye hospital. These foundations, and the no less splendid mausoleums — all built on a grand scale — served as a form of publicity, testifying to the power and generosity of each ruler. A new palace and mosque were erected in the Citadel, but Mamluk architecture reached its apogee in the reign of Qayt Bay (1468–1495), whose elegantly decorated mosques remain unsurpassed in taste.

□

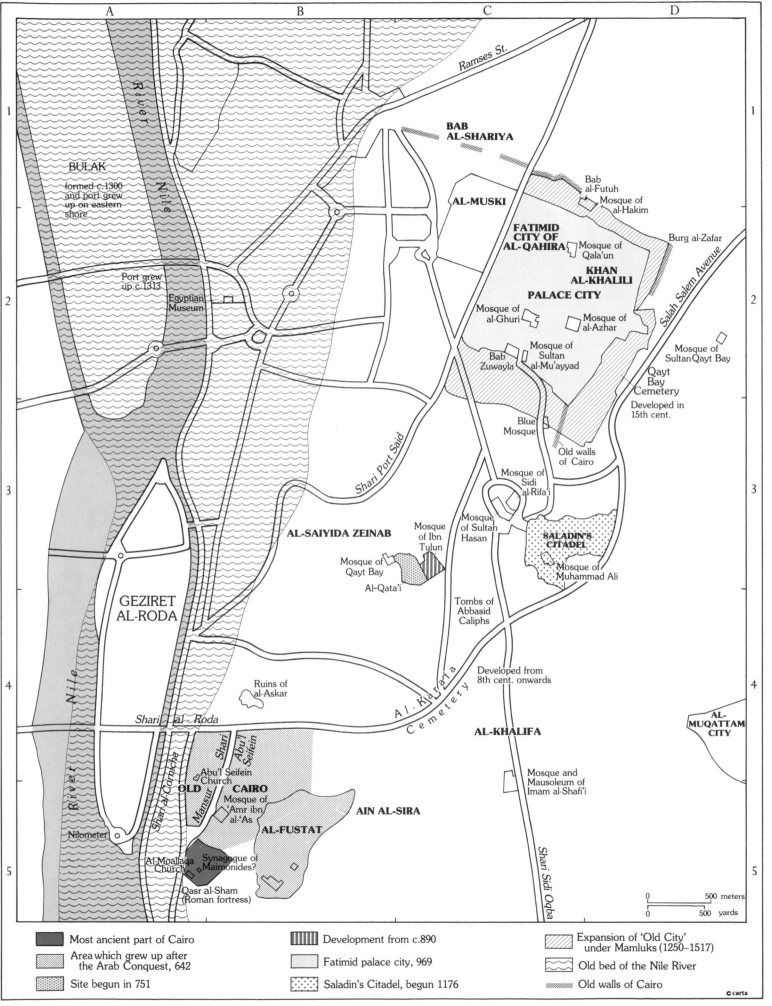

BULAK
formed c.1300
and port grew
up on eastern
shore

River Nile

Port grew
up c.1313

Egyptian
Museum

Ramses St.

**BAB
AL-SHARIYA**

AL-MUSKI

Bab
al-Futuh
Mosque of
al-Hakim

Burg al-Zafar

**FATIMID
CITY OF
AL-QAHIRA**
Mosque of
Qala'un

**KHAN
AL-KHALILI**

PALACE CITY

Mosque of
al-Ghuri

Mosque of
al-Azhar

Mosque of
Sultan Qayt Bay

Bab
Zuwayla
Mosque of
Sultan
al-Mu'ayyad

Qayt
Bay
Cemetery

Developed in
15th cent.

Blue
Mosque

Old walls
of Cairo

Shari Port Said

Mosque of
Sidi
al-Rifa'i

AL-SAIYIDA ZEINAB

Mosque
of Sultan
Hasan

**SALADIN'S
CITADEL**

Mosque of Ibn
Tulun

Mosque of
Qayt Bay

Al-Qata'i

Mosque of
Muhammad Ali

Tombs of
Abbasid
Caliphs

**GEZIRET
AL-RODA**

River Nile

Ruins of
al-Askar

Al-Karafa Cemetery

Developed from
8th cent. onwards

Shari al-Roda

AL-KHALIFA

**AL-
MUQATTAM
CITY**

Shari al-Corniche

Abu'l Seifein
Church
OLD CAIRO
Mansur
Shari Abu'l Seifein
Mosque of
'Amr ibn
al-'As

Mosque and
Mausoleum of
Imam al-Shafi'i

AIN AL-SIRA

AL-FUSTAT

Nilometer

Al-Moallaga
Church
Synagogue of
Maimonides?

Qasr al-Sham
(Roman fortress)

Shari Sidi Oqba

0   500 meters
0   500 yards

Legend:
- Most ancient part of Cairo
- Area which grew up after the Arab Conquest, 642
- Site begun in 751
- Development from c.890
- Fatimid palace city, 969
- Saladin's Citadel, begun 1176
- Expansion of 'Old City' under Mamluks (1250–1517)
- Old bed of the Nile River
- Old walls of Cairo

©carta

EGYPT AND SYRIA UNDER THE MAMLUKS, 1250 TO 1517

The Mamluks introduced by Saladin were Turks or Greeks, known as Bahri because their barracks was on Roda Island in the Nile (*Bahr al-Nil*). They ruled from 1250 to 1382. They were succeeded, with no real change of polity, by the Burgi (1382–1517), almost all Circassians from southern Russia, whose regiment was quartered in the Citadel (Arabic, *burg*). There are no other comparable dynasties. These were military oligarchies with no real law of succession, at least other than that enunciated by a sultan of Zanzibar in the nineteenth century, who said, as he touched his sword: The law of the sharpest.

Stranger yet, the actual initiator of the system was a woman, Shajar al-Durr ("tree of pearls"), widow of the Ayyubid al-Salih (d. 1249). For eighty days, she ruled using the male title sultan, striking coins in her name and being mentioned in the Friday prayers — all unprecedented in Islam. Then she married Sultan Aybak. When shortly thereafter he took a second wife, she had him put to death, only to be battered to death herself with the clogs of his first wife's servants.

The Mongols were now threatening western Asia and threatening to conquer Egypt. It was a moment of crisis. Their army was routed by Baybars I, who made himself sultan on 24 October 1260 and ruled for seven years. This remarkable soldier cleared Syria of the Mongols and destroyed the Assassins, while his generals were sent west to conquer the Berbers and south to take the Christian kingdom of Nubia. The army and navy were reorganized, fortresses built, canals dug, and a *barid* created, a relay postal service of swift horses that enabled the sultan to play polo in Damascus and Cairo within the same week. Numerous public works, mosques, *madrasa*s, and libraries were established. His diplomatic relations ranged from France, Sicily, Spain, and Constantinople to the river Volga and Persia. He brought the last Abbasid caliph to reside in Cairo, depriving him of all power except to legitimize him and his successors as sultans and to administer religious bequests.

Of the twenty-one Bahri successors to Baybars I, only two are of substantial significance. Qala'un (1279–1290) was distinguished as a soldier and a capable administrator. The remains of his teaching hospital in Cairo are of great elegance. Beside it is the plainer mosque of al-Nasir (1293–1294, 1298–1308, 1309–1340), who is especially celebrated as the restorer of Cairo after the earthquake of 1303 (see map 39). As a general he completely defeated the Mongol army in 1299, but stained his record with the devastation of Armenia in 1302. Lame and short, he was also *bon viveur* and a patron of the arts, and maintained diplomatic relations as far as India and China. In East Africa Ibn Battuta found his court ceremonies being imitated in Mogadishu.

Among the Burgi Mamluks, six reigned for 103 years out of a total of 134 years; the remaining seventeen reigned for less than two years each. The period is one of the darkest in Egyptian history, of intrigue, quarrels between Mamluks, degeneracy, and violence extending to every class, so that under Barsbay (1422–1438) women could not appear on the streets and the peasantry feared to bring meat to market lest it should be seized. Even the highest judge in the reign of al-Muayyad (1461–1462), the shaykh al-Islam, had bought his office. A Persian from Herat, he could speak no Arabic, and stole trust money. It was no wonder that in Alexandria the fishermen rose, shaved half the governor's beard, paraded him through the streets on a camel with a musical escort, and then killed him. In spite of all the chaos the religious institution went tranquilly on, and it was a time of the most outstanding achievements in Islamic architecture.

The most capable and distinguished of the sultans was Qayt Bay, who had worked his way up from the bottom. He was expert with the sword and javelin. A miser, he taxed without mercy. His long reign (1468–1495) was spent in travel throughout his dominions, Lebanon and Syria, the Euphrates, Upper and Lower Egypt, and in pilgrimages to Mecca and Jerusalem. In Jerusalem his *sabil* (drinking fountain) adorns the Haram al-Sharif. His mosques are matchless in beauty. In all this time he was watchful of the growth of Ottoman power, which had already usurped Constantiniople.

Some brief reigns followed. The Sultan al-Ashraf Qansawh al-Ghrawi was elected in 1501 at the age of sixty. He tried to restore order in the treasury and in the state. By now Vasco da Gama had rounded the Cape. The commercial links that Egypt held between Venice and other Italian cities and the East were outflanked and severed. In 1517 the Portuguese defeated an Egyptian fleet in the Indian Ocean, the same year in which the Ottomans seized Egypt. □

40 EGYPT AND SYRIA UNDER THE MAMLUKS, 1250 TO 1517

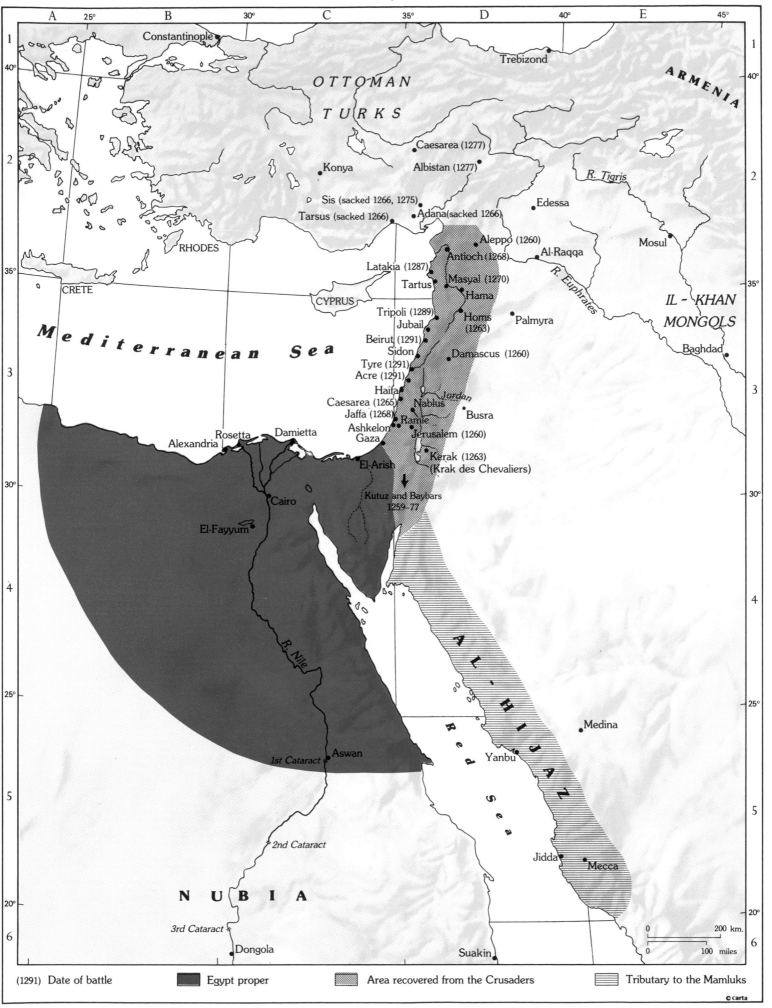

Constantinople

OTTOMAN
TURKS

Trebizond

ARMENIA

Caesarea (1277)

Konya

Albistan (1277)

R. Tigris

Sis (sacked 1266, 1275)

Edessa

Tarsus (sacked 1266)   Adana (sacked 1266)

Mosul

RHODES

Aleppo (1260)

Al-Raqqa

Antioch (1268)

Latakia (1287)

Masyaf (1270)

R. Euphrates

IL - KHAN
MONGOLS

CRETE

CYPRUS

Tartus

Hama

Tripoli (1289)

Homs
(1263)

Palmyra

Jubail

Baghdad

Mediterranean Sea

Beirut (1291)

Sidon

Damascus (1260)

Tyre (1291)

Acre (1291)

Haifa

Jordan

Caesarea (1265)

Nablus

Jaffa (1268)

Busra

Rosetta   Damietta

Ramle

Alexandria

Ashkelon

Jerusalem (1260)

Gaza

El-Arish

Kerak (1263)
(Krak des Chevaliers)

Cairo

Kutuz and Baybars
1259-77

El-Fayyum

R. Nile

AL - HIJAZ

Red Sea

Medina

1st Cataract   Aswan

Yanbu

2nd Cataract

Jidda   Mecca

N U B I A

3rd Cataract

0   200 km.

Dongola

Suakin

0   100 miles

(1291) Date of battle   ▓ Egypt proper   ▒ Area recovered from the Crusaders   ▤ Tributary to the Mamluks

© carta

ETHIOPIA AND EASTERN AFRICA, C. 1200 TO C. 1500

By the ninth century Axum was in decline; by the tenth century it had ceased to issue currency after nearly eight centuries. Tradition has it that the city was destroyed by a Queen Judith, but the details are very obscure. The dynasty said to be descended from King Solomon was now usurped by the Zagwe, which, under Lalibela, had hewn from virgin rock the famous churches of his capital, Lalibela, a "new Jerusalem," of which the chronology is unknown.

In 1270 the Solomonic line was restored by Yekuno Amlak (1270–1285), claiming descent from Menelik, son of Solomon and the Queen of Saba (Sheba). A succession of able and powerful rulers followed until 1527. Under Yagbea Sion (1285–1294) a successful campaign against Zaila pushed back the Muslim power of Ifat. Under Amda Sion the great (1314–1344) a series of campaigns more than doubled the empire. In 1328 Ifat and Fatagar were annexed. The expansion was accompanied by missionary effort in the conquered provinces, no less than by an increase of trade in the area, which brought prosperity even to the neighboring Somali sultanates. Of these there are substantial remains of some twenty cities. In Ethiopia itself some churches and monasteries of this period remain, evidence of surplus wealth to expend on building. Nevertheless, the growing strength of Islam in the plains of Somalia, isolating the Christian highland bastion, was a constant source of friction, an obstacle to its access to the sea. Holy War (jihad) is commemorated on many of the coins issued in the Mogadishu region, and would have been profitable as a source of slaves, who were exported chiefly to India in sufficient quantity to be known as "Habashi" (Ethiopians). They had varying fortunes: in Bengal they even ruled as the Slave Dynasty (1246–1290). At the same time in Ethiopia it was a period of great literary output, with translations from Coptic and Arabic. There were connections yet farther afield: in 1394 Venice sent masons, painters and artisans; an Ethiopian embassy visited Aragon in 1427, and another visited Lisbon in 1452, while Ethiopian monks were present at the Council of Florence in 1447.

Well to the south of Ethiopia in what is now Uganda, the states known collectively as Kitara arose between the tenth and twelfth centuries. These were ancestors of the Lacustrine kingdoms that became known to Europe in the nineteenth century, but whose genealogies and pottery appear to suggest a long history. At this time scarcely anything is known of them, and they appear to have been in isolation.

On the eastern coast of Africa inscriptions attest the stone mosques of Mogadishu of the thirteenth century. About 1300 both copper and billon (base silver) currency was issued. Ibn Battuta visited the city around 1330 and formed a favorable impression, after having greatly detested Zaila. Farther south lay a string of small Swahili city-states, of which the Lamu archipelago (map 42), Malindi, Mombasa, and Zanzibar (map 43) were the most important. One of the Lamu islands, Pate, had dynastic links with the Comorian sultanates in the far south.

Between the Rufiji and the Ruvuma rivers, but with possessions far to the south at Mozambique, Angoche, Quelimane, and Sofala, lay the Sultanate of Kilwa. From the Lamu area southward finds of Sassanian-Islamic pottery and coin finds demonstrate commercial activity in continuous sequence from the eighth century. Earlier evidence is at present lacking. Kilwa became prominent in the twelfth century, when it took possession of the gold trade with the Zambezi hinterland and controlled the series of small ports of the Mozambique coast. Its prosperity, evidenced by a large Friday mosque as well as by sumptuous houses and palaces, was built upon the carrying trade in gold and ivory. Here too, jihad was waged against the pagans of the mainland, with profit from slaves taken as prisoners of war. The luxury of the Kilwa sultans and merchants is described by Portuguese writers of the early sixteenth century.

In the gold-bearing areas of present-day Zimbabwe great stone fortified kraals were built, with foreign Swahili/Arab settlements at Sena and Tete. Thus wealth was to some extent shared. This was the very southern fringe of the medieval Islamic civilization from which the sons of the sultans of Kilwa were sent abroad to study.

□

41 ETHIOPIA AND EASTERN AFRICA, c.1200 TO c.1500

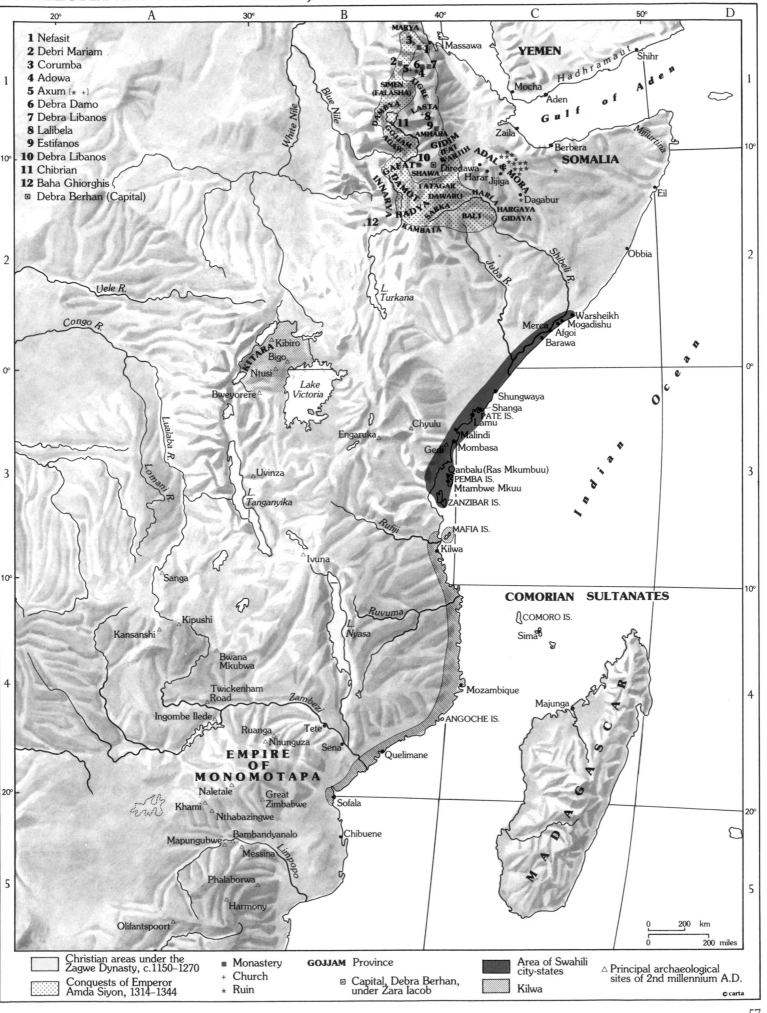

1 Nefasit
2 Debri Mariam
3 Corumba
4 Adowa
5 Axum [★ +]
6 Debra Damo
7 Debra Libanos
8 Lalibela
9 Estifanos
10 Debra Libanos
11 Chibrian
12 Baha Ghiorghis
▣ Debra Berhan (Capital)

MARYA
Massawa
YEMEN
Mocha
Aden
Gulf of Aden
Hadhramaut
Shihr

SIMEN
(FALASHA)
TIGRE
LASTA
DAMBIA
GOJJAM
AGAW
AMHARA
GIDIM
GAFAT
IFAT
WARJIH
ADAL & MORA
SHAWA
DAMOT
INNARYA
HADYA
DAWARO
FATAGAR
SABRA
HADYA
HARLA
BALI
HARGAYA
GIDAYA
KAMBATA

Zaila
Berbera
SOMALIA
Diredawa
Harar
Jijiga
Dagabur
Eil

Mijurtina
Obbia

White Nile
Blue Nile

L. Turkana

Juba R.
Shibeli R.

Uele R.
Congo R.

KITARA
Kibiro
Bigo
Ntusi
Bweyorere
Lake Victoria

Warsheikh
Mogadishu
Merca
Afgoi
Barawa

Shungwaya
Shanga
PATE IS.
Lamu
Malindi
Mombasa
Gedi
Chyulu
Engaruka

Lualaba R.
Lomani R.

Uvinza
L. Tanganyika

Qanbalu (Ras Mkumbuu)
PEMBA IS.
Mtambwe Mkuu
ZANZIBAR IS.
MAFIA IS.
Kilwa

Indian Ocean

Sanga
Kipushi
Kansanshi
Bwana Mkubwa
Twickenham Road
Ingombe Ilede
Ruanga
Nhunguza
Tete
Sena
Ivuna
L. Nyasa
Ruvuma

COMORIAN SULTANATES
COMORO IS.
Sima

Zambezi
EMPIRE OF MONOMOTAPA
Naletale
Khami
Great Zimbabwe
Nthabazingwe
Mapungubwe
Bambandyanalo
Messina
Limpopo
Phalaborwa
Harmony
Olifantspoort

Mozambique
Majunga
ANGOCHE IS.
Quelimane
Sofala
Chibuene

MADAGASCAR

Rufiji

0   200   km
0   200   miles

| | Christian areas under the Zagwe Dynasty, c.1150–1270 | ■ Monastery | **GOJJAM** Province | | Area of Swahili city-states |
| | Conquests of Emperor Amda Siyon, 1314–1344 | + Church | ▣ Capital, Debra Berhan, under Zara Iacob | | Kilwa |

△ Principal archaeological sites of 2nd millennium A.D.

© carta

57

THE LAMU ARCHIPELAGO AND ANCIENT SITES

There are no sheltered harbors on the eastern African coast until the islands that form the Lamu archipelago are reached. They are surrounded by a mangrove forest through which a natural channel passes. It is attested already by A.D. 50 in the *Periplus of the Erythraean Sea*. Flushed twice daily by the tides, this waterway, known as the Mkanda (Swahili) or Diorux (Greek), is the channel *par excellence* in English. Ivory was the principal export, exchanged for luxury goods, iron ware, and wine; the porters' tracks can still be seen.

From that point until about 750 history is silent. Then twenty-six sites, great and small, attest trade with the Persian Gulf, exchanging ivory and mangrove poles, still the staple trade. At Shanga the ruins of the fifteenth-century Friday mosque rest above the remains of no less than nine successive mosques, the earliest being a simple reed enclosure dating to around 750. This archaeological discovery accords with local traditions that claim trade connections with Damascus and Baghdad at this epoch.

The northernmost island, Pate, claims a dynasty of rulers from about 1200. Its trade connections, from the eighth century at least, later reached India and the Comoro Islands, where its princesses married. Lamu is least known in early history because most of the site was engulfed in sand dunes in the fourteenth century. Numerous mosques, chiefly of the eighteenth and nineteenth centuries, attest its prosperity after the Portuguese departure. Its old-fashioned, elegant Swahili houses are distinctive in design as is its antique furniture of camphor-wood and of ebony inlaid with ivory. It is famous for its Swahili poets and literary men, and is also known as a center of pilgrimage for the Muslims, who come to venerate a holy man of Arab and Swahili descent, and Comorian birth, in the Mosque College that he founded in 1901.

ZANZIBAR AND PEMBA

The history of the islands of Zanzibar and Pemba was not linked until the seventeenth century, when they fell under the suzerainty of Oman. They are part of the area known already by A.D. 6 as Azania, of which name *Zanzibar* is a mutation. Fishing from dugout canoes, fishing traps made of wicker baskets, and the exporting of tortoiseshell are attested by A.D. 50. Thereafter, although there are occasional references by eighth-century and later Arab writers, there is no solid archaeological evidence before the twelfth century. Stone mosques were built at Kizimkazi on Zanzibar and also on Tumbatu Island with Kufic inscriptions. Their calligraphy was inspired by sculptors at Siraf, in the Persian Gulf, but cut in local stone. Both islands have traditions of different sultans in different parts of the islands.

In the sixteenth century, when the islands became tributary to Portugal, they depended chiefly on agriculture and fishing, while some men took part in the coastal carrying trade in gold, ivory, and other commodities. In or about 1815 the first clove trees were planted, and soon, as a result of the commercial enterprise of Sayyid Said of Muscat and Zanzibar (1804–1856) it had captured the clove trade of the world. Further wealth accrued mid-century and after from slave caravans that reached Lake Malawi and far into the present Zaïre, but it was a commercial rather than a colonial empire. Only on the coast did the ruler exercise any real authority, with local governors and customs posts. A recent archaeological survey as a result of the initiative of the Zanzibar government has enabled an historical map to be drawn up. Not least interesting is the long series of coin finds. While those from imperial Rome and from Parthia are somewhat uncertain, local coinage would seem to have been current by the tenth century. There have also been finds of Chinese coins, perhaps connected with the visit of the Chinese admiral Cheng Ho in the fourteenth century. ☐

42 THE LAMU ARCHIPELAGO AND ANCIENT SITES

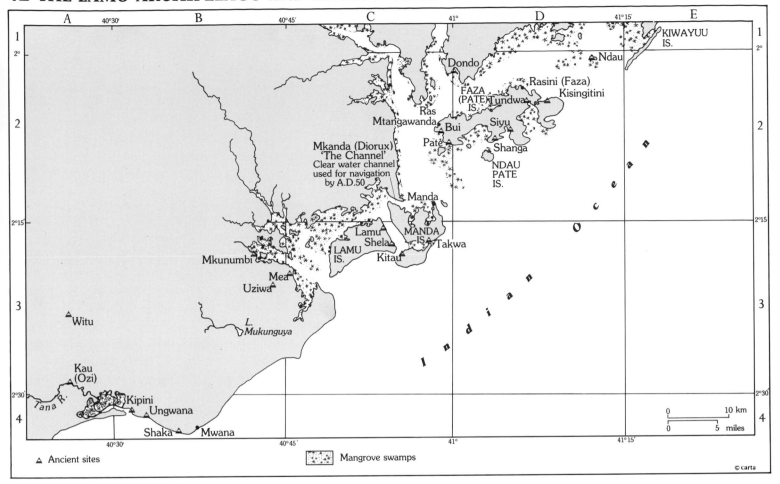

KIWAYUU IS.

Dondo

Ndau

FAZA (PATE) IS.

Rasini (Faza)

Kisingitini

Tundwa

Ras Mtangawanda

Siyu

Bui

Pate

Shanga

Mkanda (Diorux) 'The Channel' Clear water channel used for navigation by A.D.50

NDAU PATE IS.

Manda

MANDA IS.

Lamu

Shela

Takwa

LAMU IS.

Kitau

Mkunumbi

Mea

Uziwa

Witu

L. Mukunguya

Kau (Ozi)

Kipini

Ungwana

Tana R.

Shaka

Mwana

Indian Ocean

△ Ancient sites

Mangrove swamps

© carta

43 ZANZIBAR AND PEMBA

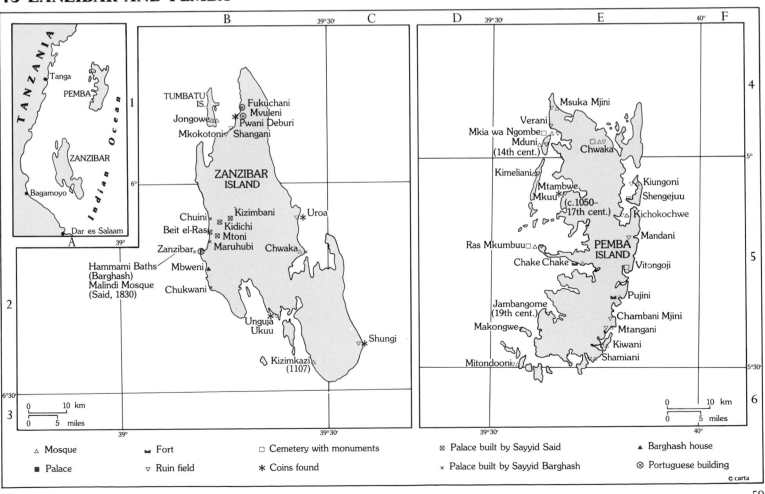

TANZANIA

Tanga

PEMBA

ZANZIBAR

Bagamoyo

Dar es Salaam

Indian Ocean

TUMBATU IS.

Fukuchani

Mvuleni

Jongowe

Pwani Deburi

Mkokotoni

Shangani

ZANZIBAR ISLAND

Chuini

Kizimbani

Uroa

Beit el-Ras

Kidichi

Zanzibar

Mtoni

Maruhubi

Chwaka

Hammami Baths (Barghash) Malindi Mosque (Said, 1830)

Mbweni

Chukwani

Unguja Ukuu

Shungi

Kizimkazi (1107)

Msuka Mjini

Verani

Mkia wa Ngombe

Mduni (14th cent.)

Chwaka

Kimeliani

Mtambwe Mkuu (c.1050–17th cent.)

Kiungoni

Shengejuu

Kichokochwe

Ras Mkumbuu

Mandani

PEMBA ISLAND

Chake Chake

Vitongoji

Jambangome (19th cent.)

Pujini

Chambani Mjini

Makongwe

Mtangani

Kiwani

Mitondooni

Shamiani

| △ Mosque | ◢ Fort | □ Cemetery with monuments | ⊠ Palace built by Sayyid Said | ▲ Barghash house |
| ■ Palace | ▽ Ruin field | * Coins found | × Palace built by Sayyid Barghash | ⊗ Portuguese building |

© carta

THE WESTERN SUDAN IN THE 11TH CENTURY

During the eighth century Berbers and Arabs penetrated the Sahara, by the coastal route from the Wadi Draa, and by northern and western routes from Tripoli and from the Nile, and mingled with the local people. The kingdom of Kanem is claimed to have been founded around 800; in 1085 the tenth ruler became a Muslim. The capital was at Njimi, west of Lake Chad.

Farther west, along the Niger bend, at some time during the seventh century, white nomads established the kingdom of Songhai in the region of Gao. They too intermingled with the local population, and became wholly identified with it. Unlike Kanem, with its Arab founders, these were Berbers of the Lamta and Howara tribes from Tripolitania. They had traveled down the ancient route known to the charioteers of Tassili 'n-Ajjer, the Hoggar and the Tilemsi valley. The capital was at Kukia, some ninety miles south of Gao; its kings, or dias, had authority over the river valley as far as it. Around 1010 Dia Kossoi became a Muslim, reflecting, as later in the century in Kanem, closer commercial links with Fatimid and North African prosperity.

A third kingdom was Ghana. Perhaps even in Carthaginian times it had exported its gold northward. Certainly the trade had begun by the beginning of the Christian era. The mines were in Bambuk, between the rivers Falémé and Senegal, and to the west of Niani. In 734 an Arab caravan brought back gold from the region; in 745 the Arabs established a series of wells along the caravan route as far as the mines, a sure indication of enhanced trade. According to tradition Ghana had forty-four white (Berber) rulers from the fourth century, but nothing is known of them or how their kingdom was organized. In the eighth century they were partly expelled by the Soninke, whose authority stretched over the greater part of the region by the tenth century. Gold was not the sole article of commerce: salt from Teggazza was no less important. In 977 the Arab geographer Ibn Hawqal speaks of the wealth of the trade. Another Arab, al-Bakri of Córdoba, writing in 1077, describes the wealth and gorgeous ceremonial of the court of Ghana, whose kings even had their horse harnesses decorated with gold.

□

THE WESTERN SUDAN IN THE 12TH TO 14TH CENTURIES

The empire of Ghana broke up at the end of the eleventh century into a number of kingdoms, in some of which the kings and their courts became Muslims. Among the masses the adoption of Islam meant no more than a new syncretism. Sosso took a large part of Ghana, and in 1224 took Walata, an oasis that now became a center of trade and Islamic teaching. Ghana itself became Muslim in the course of the century. In 1235 Sumanguru Kante of Sosso was overcome by Sundiata Keita, the son of a petty Mandingo ruler. He succeeded in establishing Mali as a larger empire than Ghana had ever been, controlling all the gold-bearing regions from Bundu to Mossi (1235–1255). Nominally Muslim, even today sacrifices are made to his name. The apogee of this empire was reached under the fabled kankan Mansa Musa (1312–1335). His brilliant reign and splendid pilgrimage to Mecca are recorded by Ibn Khaldun, the greatest of the Muslim historians. In Cairo, kankan Mansa Musa gave so much gold in alms as to depreciate the dinar. With a capital at Timbuktu, his empire stretched from the Atlantic to Gao on the Niger bend. It was visited by Ibn Battuta in 1352–1353 (see map 46). As the century wore on, the empire slowly dissolved, although the dynasty ended only in 1645.

To the east, among Hausa-speaking peoples, a number of states had developed in the tenth century. Unfortunately, most of their written records were destroyed in the nineteenth century, except in Kano. One at least paid tribute to Bornu, which as yet was not Islamized. To the south, unknown to the Arab historians, great kingdoms had evolved among the Nupe and the Yoruba in the present Nigeria. The cities of Benin and Ife, and Oyo on the fringe of their forest region, developed cultures of their own which were wholly unaffected by the outside world until the Portuguese made contact with them in the later fifteenth century. The peak of their prosperity was in the thirteenth to fourteenth century.

□

44 THE WESTERN SUDAN IN THE 11TH CENTURY

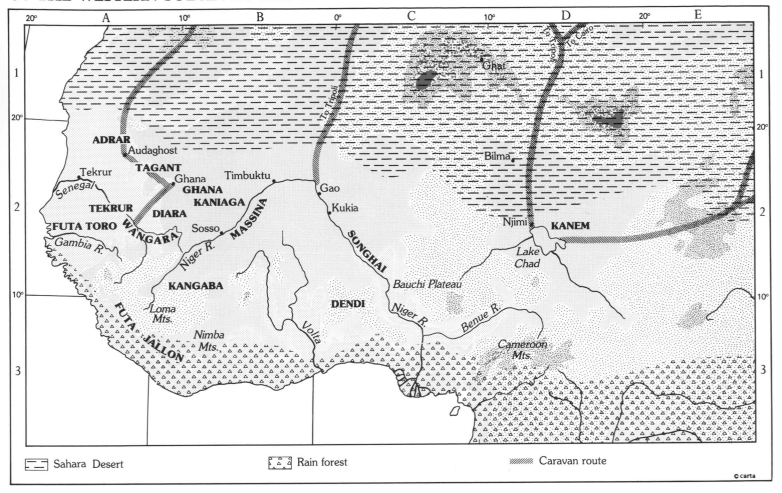

Sahara Desert   Rain forest   Caravan route

© carta

45 THE WESTERN SUDAN IN THE 12TH TO 14TH CENTURIES

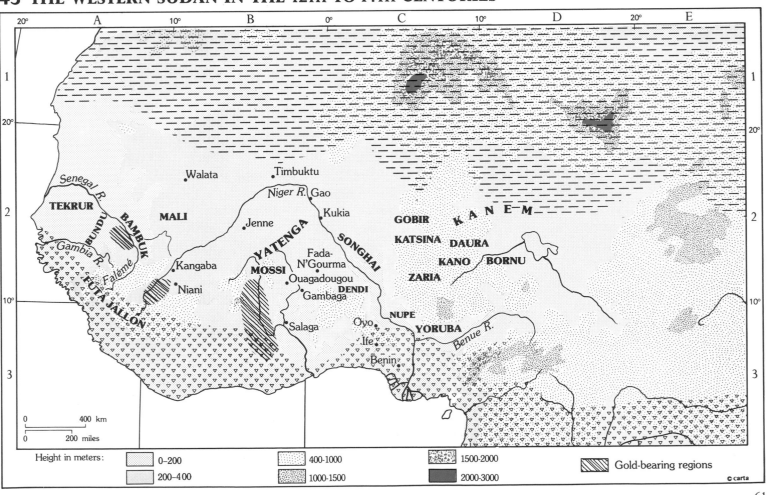

Height in meters: 0–200   400-1000   1500-2000   Gold-bearing regions
200–400   1000-1500   2000-3000

© carta

NORTHERN AFRICAN TRADE WITH THE WESTERN SUDAN, 13TH TO 14TH CENTURIES

By the mid-thirteenth century the Almohad empire (see map 38) had disintegrated. It had already ended in Spain in 1212. In 1235 the emir of Tlemcen created the independent Abdulwahid kingdom. In 1236 an independent Hafsid dynasty had been proclaimed. In 1248 the King of León and Castile had taken Seville, leaving only Grenada to the Muslims. In the same year the Marinids took much of Morocco, finally seizing Marrakesh in 1269 and killing the last of the Almohads.

The new kingdoms were soon in treaty relations with the leading Christian commercial centers — Venice, Pisa, Genoa, and Sicily — and with the new Mamluk sultanate in Egypt and its extension in Syria. Their existence was by no means untroubled, for they were harried in Tunisia and further west by the Banu Sulaim, nomads who had originated in Tripolitania. They attacked the oases that controlled the routes of the southern Sahara, and then Bougie, Bône, and Tunis itself. At Bougie they established the first organized pirate center which made Barbary a byword in later centuries. These cities were only recovered in 1370. At the end of the century the Hafsids held the coast from Tripoli to Biskra, and in 1410 they had extended their reach as far as Algiers. Piracy now spread from Bougie to Tunis and Bizerta.

In 1235 Tlemcen had freed itself from the Almohads. It was the entrepôt for the western Sudan as well as an important religious center. From Fez in the fourteenth century the Merinids pursued a career of conquest as far as Tunis, but were repulsed at Kairouan in 1347. The dynasty is especially notable for the glory of their public buildings in Meknès, Salé, Fez Jadi, Fez Bali, and Marrakesh. These owed much to Moorish refugees from Spain. Of particular importance were the *medersa*s (classical, *madrasa*s), institutes of advanced religious learning, from which the Qadiriya *tariqa*, or Sufi confraternity, propagated their ideas and devotional practices along the trade routes to south of the Sahara. The conversion to Islam of large tracts of western Africa was to a great extent the work of the Qadiriya. At the same time their toleration of the cult of saints and holy places made possible the absorption and syncretism of earlier religious thought and practice.

Ibn Battuta's journey to Mali and back in 1352–1353 was the last of his adventures which had taken him from Tangier to Cairo and Mecca, the Yemen, East Africa, India, and the Maldives. Salt, slaves, and gold were the main stock-in-trade that flowed northward, a trade that was long established. Mali had already sent an embassy to Fez when he was in East Africa in 1331. Mali, moreover, looked in another direction, and in 1310 had sent a fleet of canoes into the Atlantic to ascertain whether there might be land westward. It was a total disaster, for only one vessel returned. Kankan Mansa Musa's journey to Mecca with an immense retinue shows how well organized for water supplies were the desert mercantile routes. Gold was the primary source of prosperity, as was commemorated in England by the coin known as the guinea. Of importance, too, were the copper mines of Takedda; copper was exported also to the south. There, on the Bauchi plateau of modern Nigeria, local tin was used as an alloy to make funeral masks by the *cire-perdue* (lost-wax) method. Away to the east, bordering on Lake Chad, the kingdom of Kanem-Bornu had its own routes to Tripoli and to Cairo. Other routes connected it with the Fezzan and with Wadai. Theoretically a Muslim land, it remained obstinately pagan, venerating the king as a god whose face was to be veiled from the eyes of the crowd. □

46 NORTHERN AFRICAN TRADE WITH THE WESTERN SUDAN, 13TH TO 14TH CENTURIES

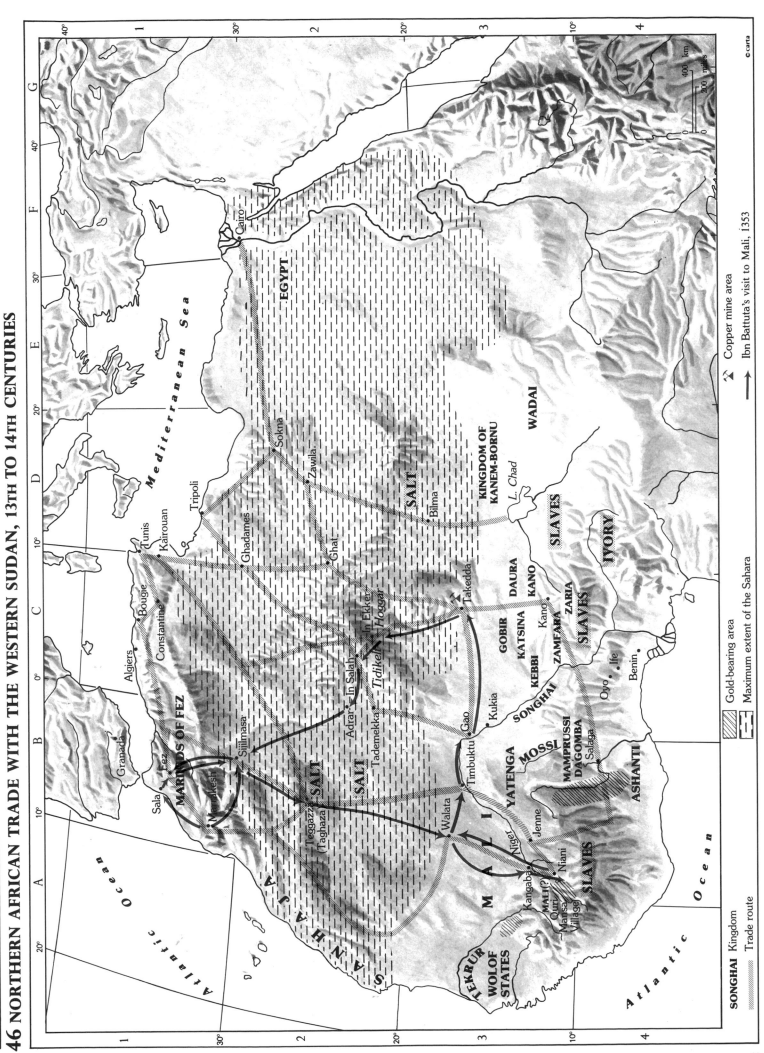

Mediterranean Sea

Atlantic Ocean

Atlantic Ocean

EGYPT

Cairo

Tripoli
Tunis
Kairouan
Ghadames
Sokna
Zawila
Ghat

Bougie
Constantine
Algiers
Granada
Sala
Fez
MARINIDS OF FEZ
Marrakesh

Sijilmasa

SALT
Teggazza
(Taghaza)

Adrar
In Salah
In Ekker
Hoggar
Tidikelt
Tademekka

SALT
SALT

Walata
Timbuktu
Gao
Kukia

Takedda
Bilma
SALT
KINGDOM OF KANEM-BORNU
L. Chad
WADAI

GOBIR
DAURA
KATSINA
KANO
Kano
ZARIA
ZAMFARA
KEBBI
SONGHAI
SLAVES
SLAVES

Jenne
Niger
M   A   L   I
YATENGA
MOSSI
MAMPRUSSI
DAGOMBA
Salaga
ASHANTI

Kangaba
MALI(?)
Mansa
Quri
Niani
village
SLAVES

TEKRUR
WOLOF
STATES

SANHAJA

Oyo
Ife
Benin
IVORY
SLAVES

200 miles
400 km

SONGHAI Kingdom

⚔ Copper mine area

→ Ibn Battuta's visit to Mali, 1353

▨ Gold-bearing area

- - - Maximum extent of the Sahara

⟋⟋⟋ Trade route

c carta

63

NORTHERN AFRICA, 15TH TO 16TH CENTURIES

As the fifteenth century drew to a close, Egypt lost a ruler of exceptional brilliance, the Mamluk sultan Qayt Bay (see maps 39, 40). Egyptian commerce reached the Atlantic and western Africa and eastward as far as India and China. Its prosperity was reflected in the public buildings of Egypt, Syria, and the Hijaz. In the university mosque of al-Azhar free provision was made for scholars from Mali to as far afield as Java, with a special institute (which still exists) for the blind. It dominated the intellectual world of Islam.

Politically and commercially it was an Indian summer. The Portuguese had reached India and captured the spice trade. Alexandria and Venice were ruined. Then the Ottoman Turks took Syria, Palestine, and, in 1517, Egypt. They hanged the last Mamluk sultan in the al-Mu'ayyad mosque by the Bab Zuwayla, one of Cairo's city gates. Their acquisition of North Africa was more leisurely, but just as deadly. Once proud and independent states were at the mercy of corrupt Ottoman officials and tax gatherers.

Aruj took Algiers in 1516. After he was killed in 1518, his brother Khair al-Din I (Barbarossa) succeeded him and ceded the conquest to the Ottoman sultan, whom he confirmed as *beylerbey*.

Khair al-Din slowly extended the Ottoman possessions. A new port was built in Algiers. In 1534 Tunis was taken, to be ruled by deys until 1705. Khair al-Din was recalled to Istanbul in 1536 to become admiral of the Ottoman fleet. The Hafsids still survived in southern Tunisia, and revived temporarily in 1573–1574. The Ottomans took Tripoli (in Libya) in 1551, the same year in which English merchants took up residence in Morocco, supplying the ruler with arms. From Algiers systematic piracy was organized; Philip II of Spain's fleet of Germans, Italians, and Spaniards sent against them in 1559 was utterly destroyed. In 1564 France posted a consul to Algiers, followed by England in 1569: these were tokens of new directions of trade.

Westward the Ottoman tide flowed no farther than Tlemcen. A line of *sharifs*, claiming descent from the Prophet, slowly extended their power from the south, and took Fez in 1549. The sensitive political ability of the first few rulers and the prestige of their descent enabled them to maintain an army and resist the Ottomans. Their artillery came from England. Their power soon extended throughout Morocco, until their line failed in 1659.

□

THE MOROCCAN CONQUEST OF SONGHAI, 1591–1753

Songhai is remarkable among African states for the continuity of its history and relative stability from about 800 until the Moroccan conquest in 1591. It was founded at Gao by a dynasty who converted to Islam around 1100. The next three hundred years were years of prosperity and expansion. About 1375 Songhai fell under the empire of Mali, and its fortunes were bound up with those of Timbuktu.

This prosperity was based principally on Songhai's control of the gold export of the Akan states in Guinea, and its control of the caravan routes. Along these routes in the Teghazza region not less important were the salt mines, whose product was used not only for consumption but in certain places as currency. Further, the frequent wars in which the Songhai rulers engaged made it a primary source for slaves. (Statistics are difficult to obtain, but it seems that Morocco had 150,000 slaves in the eighteenth century.) These commercial activities were confined to a relatively small merchant class, the mass of the people being agriculturalists.

All these branches of commerce supplied principally Songhai's neighbor Morocco, which had long cast envious eyes on the salt mines and resented the customs dues. During the reign of the *askia* Dawud (1549–1582) Morocco conducted raids on the salt deposits. These continued under his successors, and, finally, under Ishaq II, Sharif Ahmad al-Mansur of Morocco sent Judar Pasha across the desert with four thousand men. Judar himself was a renegade Spaniard, and his army included riffraff from England, France, Italy and Spain. Only fifteen hundred were true Moroccans. Altogether only some one thousand men completed the journey, but their possession of firearms, which Songhai did not have, made conquest inevitable. Talleyrand was later to remark that war is far too important a matter to be left to military men. Here, having conquered and occupied the capital, Judar's troops proved themselves incapable of ruling in peace. Soon the position of pasha was filled by popular acclaim. There followed 150 pashas in the course of 162 years, a period of instability that ruined a hitherto prosperous economy.

□

47 NORTHERN AFRICA, 15TH TO 16TH CENTURIES

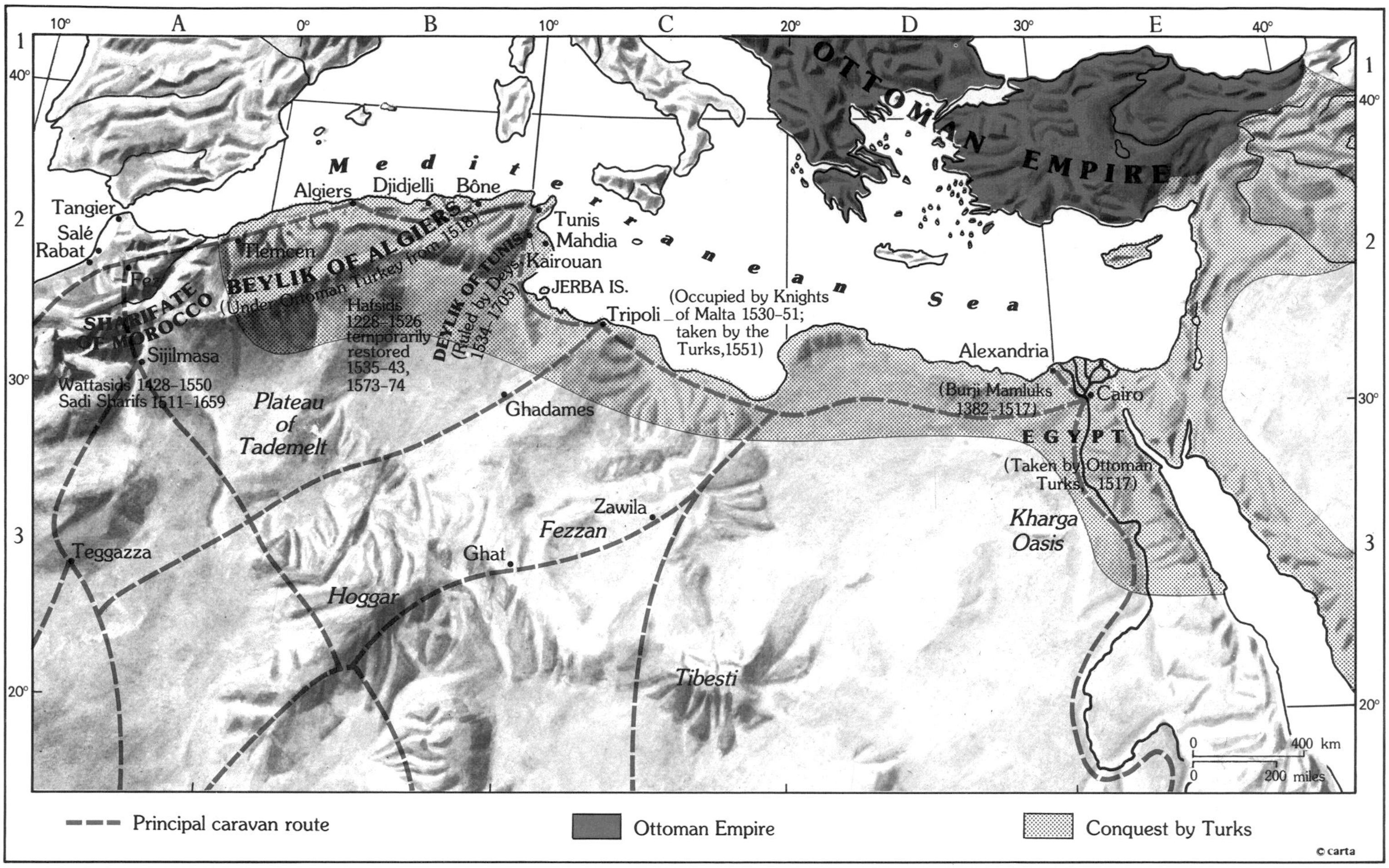
OTTOMAN EMPIRE
Mediterranean Sea
Algiers
Djidjelli
Bône
Tangier
Salé
Rabat
Fez
Tlemcen
Tunis
Mahdia
Kairouan
JERBA IS.
BEYLIK OF ALGIERS
(Under Ottoman Turkey from 1518)
BEYLIK OF TUNIS
(Ruled by Deys 1534–1705)
SHARIFATE OF MOROCCO
Hafsids 1228–1526 temporarily restored 1535–43, 1573–74
Sijilmasa
Wattasids 1428–1550
Sadi Sharifs 1511–1659
Plateau of Tademelt
Tripoli
(Occupied by Knights of Malta 1530–51; taken by the Turks,1551)
Ghadames
Alexandria
(Burji Mamluks 1382–1517)
Cairo
EGYPT
(Taken by Ottoman Turks, 1517)
Kharga Oasis
Zawila
Fezzan
Ghat
Teggazza
Hoggar
Tibesti
0 400 km
0 200 miles
Principal caravan route
Ottoman Empire
Conquest by Turks
© carta

48 THE MOROCCAN CONQUEST OF SONGHAI, 1591–1753

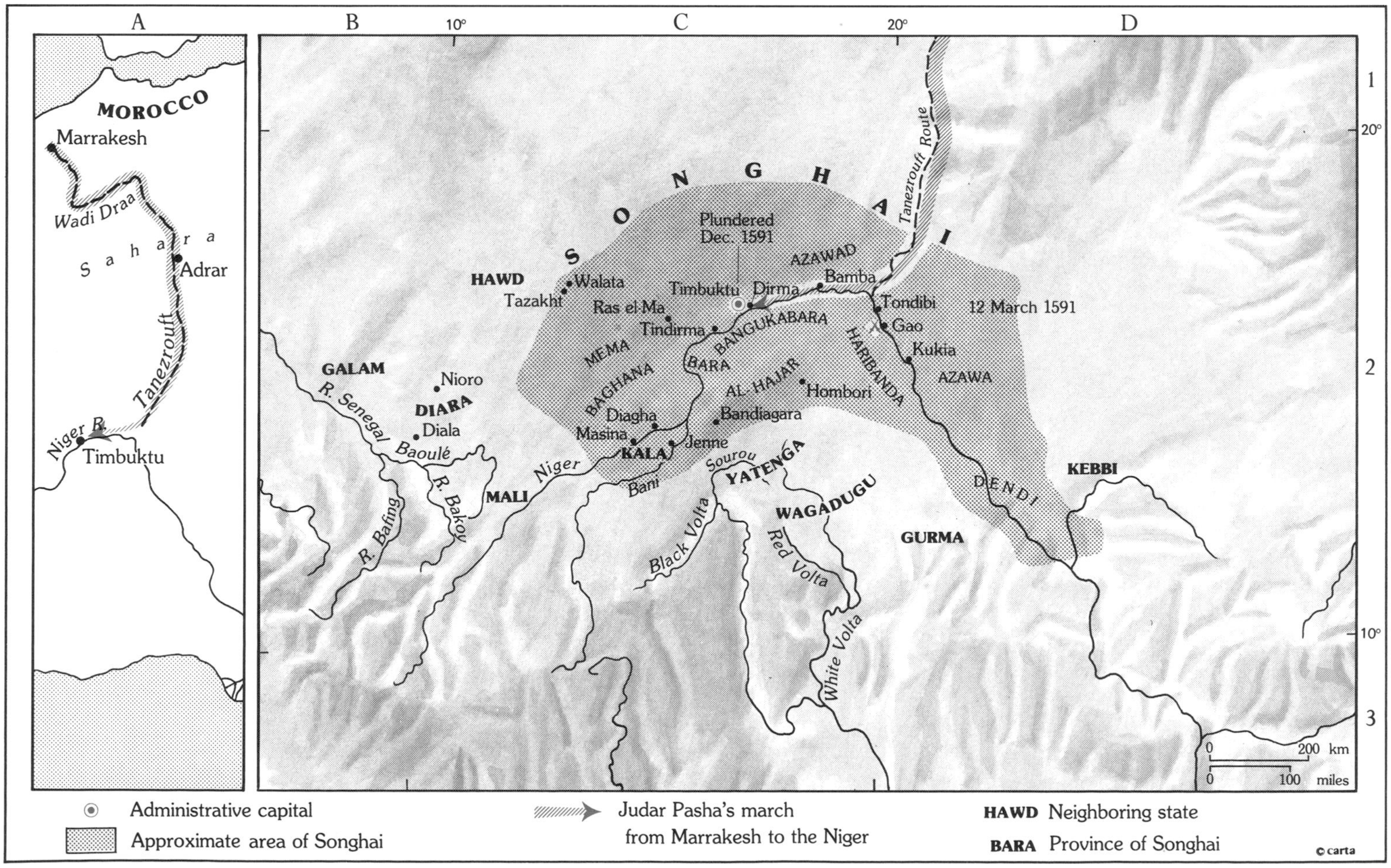
MOROCCO
Marrakesh
Wadi Draa
Sahara
Adrar
Tanezrouft
Niger R.
Timbuktu
SONGHAI
Plundered Dec. 1591
Tanezrouft Route
AZAWAD
HAWD
Walata
Tazakht
Bamba
Timbuktu
Dirma
Ras el-Ma
Tondibi
12 March 1591
Gao
Tindirma
BANGUKABARA
MEMA
BARA
HARIBANDA
Kukia
AZAWA
GALAM
Nioro
BAGHANA
AL-HAJAR
Hombori
DIARA
Diala
Diagha
Bandiagara
Masina
KALA
Jenne
R. Senegal
Baoulé
R. Bakoy
R. Bafing
MALI
Niger
Bani
Sourou
YATENGA
WAGADUGU
Black Volta
Red Volta
White Volta
GURMA
DENDI
KEBBI
0 200 km
0 100 miles
Administrative capital
Approximate area of Songhai
Judar Pasha's march from Marrakesh to the Niger
HAWD Neighboring state
BARA Province of Songhai
© carta

PORTUGUESE SETTLEMENTS IN AFRICA, 15TH TO 16TH CENTURIES

Five reasons are said to have prompted the *infante* Henry, commonly called Henry the Navigator (although he never went to sea), to promote African discovery: he desired first, to extend geographical knowledge; second, to extend Portuguese trade; third, to discover the real strength of the Moors; fourth, to see whether he might find any Christian prince who could become an ally against them; and finally, "to make increase in the faith of Our Lord Jesus Christ and to bring to him all the souls that should be saved."

His school of cartography, navigation, science, and shipbuilding was established at Sagres in 1415. By the time he died in 1460, Sierra Leone had been reached and a small trade begun. Contact with the Slave Coast of the Bight of Benin belongs to the period 1469–1474, and almost a decade after that the kingdom of Kongo was reached. It was here that the first real attempts at colonial control were made, by conversion to Christianity and the establishment of the kingdom as a vassal of the Portuguese crown. In the Portuguese *feitorias* (factories or trade agencies) commerce began, and, despite papal prohibitions, slaves became the prime object of trade to provide labor for the colony of Brazil.

A second phase, following Bartolemeu Dias's unsuccessful voyage of 1487–1488, was opened by Vasco da Gama's voyage of 1497–1499. After the discovery of the route to India and the establishment of a Portuguese base at Goa, refreshment stations combined with trading posts were established on the eastern African coast. These were never truly profitable, and often barely paid their way. The *infinito ouro* ("infinite gold") that Gama had reported was not there in such quantity or else vanished under the nimble fingers of Swahili and Arab traders. Likewise the Portuguese failed to control the ivory trade so important to India, except when they could ally with one local ruler against a rival, as they did in Pate. Attempts to introduce Christianity were null save in Angola and Mozambique, and successful there largely because Portuguese immigrants intermarried and carved out estates. In East Africa missionary effort, begun only in 1596, was ended when the Portuguese Fort Jesus of Mombasa was captured by the rising power of Oman in 1698. The fort still stands, a grim sentinel over Mombasa harbor. The Portuguese were now driven back to Mozambique.

This retreat perhaps meant no great imperial loss, for from Ormuz on the Persian Gulf, bases at Goa and Calicut in India, and at Colombo in Sri Lanka, trade was maintained that stretched through Malacca to Java, the Celebes, the Moluccas, and as far as Macao. Spices, not gold, were the main source of wealth in the Portuguese eastern empire, and the only serious attempt at conquest or colonization was confined to Brazil. In this the Portuguese were in sharp contrast with the Spanish.

During the seventeenth century the rising star of the Netherlands steadily encroached upon Portuguese interests. By the nineteenth century Cape Verde and Guiné remained, with Angola and Mozambique, in Portugal's sphere of influence. It was only in the 1890s, however, when in the "scramble for Africa" other European powers were seizing African territories, that Portugal began to think in terms of developing their own colonies. They were to become "overseas territories of Portugal," and from them, with the discovery of diamonds in Angola, new wealth began to flow to Lisbon. □

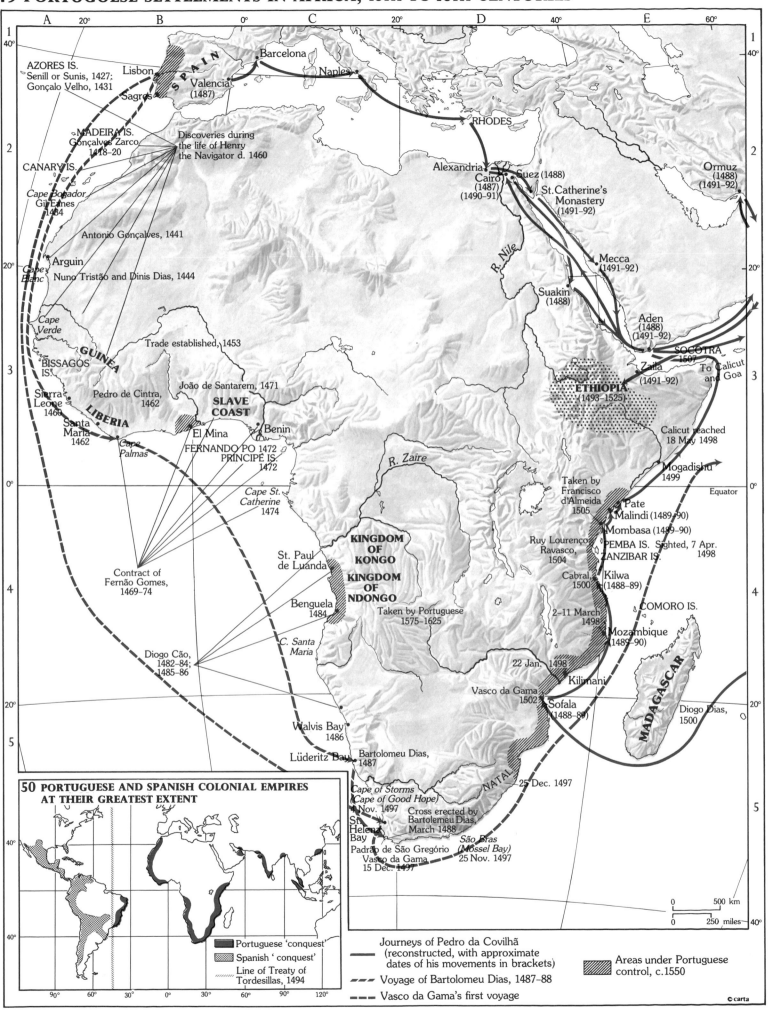

AZORES IS.
Senill or Sunis, 1427;
Gonçalo Velho, 1431

MADEIRA IS.
Gonçalves Zarco
1418–20

CANARY IS.

Cape Bojador
Gil Eanes
1434

Antonio Gonçalves, 1441

Lisbon

Sagres

SPAIN

Barcelona

Valencia
(1487)

Naples

RHODES

Discoveries during
the life of Henry
the Navigator d. 1460

Alexandria
Cairo
(1487)
(1490–91)

Suez (1488)

St. Catherine's
Monastery
(1491–92)

Ormuz
(1488)
(1491–92)

R. Nile

Mecca
(1491–92)

Suakin
(1488)

Aden
(1488)
(1491–92)

SOCOTRA
1507

Zaila
(1491–92)

To Calicut
and Goa

Cape
Blanc
Arguin

Nuno Tristão and Dinis Dias, 1444

Cape
Verde

BISSAGOS
IS.

GUINEA

Sierra
Leone
1460

Santa
Maria
1462

LIBERIA

Cape
Palmas

Trade established, 1453

João de Santarem, 1471

Pedro de Cintra,
1462

SLAVE
COAST

El Mina

Benin

FERNANDO PO 1472
PRINCIPE IS.
1472

Cape St.
Catherine
1474

R. Zaire

ETHIOPIA
(1493–1525)

Calicut reached
18 May 1498

Mogadishu
1499

Equator

Taken by
Francisco
d'Almeida
1505

Pate
Malindi (1489–90)

Mombasa (1489–90)

PEMBA IS. Sighted, 7 Apr.
1498

ZANZIBAR IS.

COMORO IS.

Contract of
Fernão Gomes,
1469–74

St. Paul
de Luanda

KINGDOM
OF
KONGO

KINGDOM
OF
NDONGO

Ruy Lourenço
Ravasco,
1504

Cabral,
1500

Kilwa
(1488–89)

2–11 March
1498

Benguela
1484

Taken by Portuguese
1575–1625

Mozambique
(1489–90)

MADAGASCAR

Diogo Cão,
1482–84;
1485–86

C. Santa
Maria

22 Jan.
1498

Kilimani

Vasco da Gama
1502

Sofala
(1488–89)

Diogo Dias,
1500

Walvis Bay
1486

Lüderitz Bay

Bartolomeu Dias,
1487

NATAL

25 Dec. 1497

Cape of Storms
(Cape of Good Hope)
4 Nov. 1497

St.
Helena
Bay

Cross erected by
Bartolemeu Dias,
March 1488

São Bras
(Mossel Bay)
25 Nov. 1497

Padrão de São Gregório
Vasco da Gama
15 Dec. 1497

50 PORTUGUESE AND SPANISH COLONIAL EMPIRES
AT THEIR GREATEST EXTENT

Portuguese 'conquest'

Spanish 'conquest'

Line of Treaty of
Tordesillas, 1494

Journeys of Pedro da Covilhã
(reconstructed, with approximate
dates of his movements in brackets)

Voyage of Bartolomeu Dias, 1487–88

Vasco da Gama's first voyage

Areas under Portuguese
control, c.1550

500 km

250 miles

© carta

EUROPEAN TRADING FORTS IN WESTERN AFRICA, 15TH TO 19TH CENTURIES

Between 1482 and the beginnings of colonial times Europeans and Africans lived, worked, and often died, in more than forty trading forts. The map shows that the majority were on the coast of present-day Ghana. They belonged to nine different European countries. The first one was founded by the Portuguese at Elmina in 1482; the last was built by the Danes at Keta in 1784.

Although they vary greatly in size and style, these forts all derive their ground plans from Elmina, itself modeled on the Castello de São Jorge, the first royal residence in Lisbon. All the Portuguese forts belonged to the Crown, but most of the others were operated by chartered companies. (The key to the map shows the nationality of the founders.) The primary object of all the forts was trade, not colonial domination; but the fact that they were the only suppliers of arms and ammunition to the local people and had a vested interest in keeping trade routes open and at peace led imperceptibly to European domination. Few of the forts were ever used for warlike purposes. Occasionally they changed hands, sometimes as a result of wars in Europe.

Until Vasco da Gama reached India in 1498, pepper was an important export. Elmina ("the mine") was so called because the Portuguese had high expectations of quantities of gold, but their purchases came largely from stocks that had built up over a long period. For gold and ivory, the Portuguese brought copper ware, cloth, hatchets, knives, and wine. Export of slaves did not begin until the mid-sixteenth century, as a result of the demand for labor in Brazil and the Caribbean. Of greatest importance to the European traders was the function of the forts as supply depots or ships' stores that held fruits and vegetables, above all citrus fruit (whose juice was necessary on long voyages to combat scurvy). In this way many American, Asian, and European fruit trees, plants, and vegetables were introduced: Asiatic yams, avocado, pears, bananas, cabbages, cassava (manioc), cauliflowers, coconuts, peanuts, guavas, lemons, lettuce, maize, mangoes, melons, oranges, pawpaws, pineapples, sugarcane, tamarind, and tomatoes, as well as aloes, sisal, and tobacco.

Each fort had its garrison of soldiers, under a governor who was served by a clerical and merchant staff as well as workmen with the knowledge of all skills necessary for the operation of the fort. Apart from officers, there were one or more chaplains, an apothecary, a barber who could bleed the sick, a chief cook, a blacksmith, a cooper, carpenters, masons, tailors, and armorers. The number varies with the size of the fort. In addition, each fort had its own slaves, whose rights of residence and food were recognized long after the abolition of slavery. None of the Europeans was accompanied by wives, but many married or had liaisons locally, so that even today along the coast many Ghanaians are encountered with European names.

Life in the forts was regulated with the same discipline as on board a ship. A fixed timetable was followed, its changes announced by a bell. Sentries patrolled to prevent theft or uprisings among the slaves. There were few amusements, and heavy drinking among the Europeans led to brawls. Deaths from malaria and other fevers were common, and the low expectation of life attracted only the roughest sort of persons to "the Bight of Benin, where few come out though many come in." Nevertheless, because life in the forts was kept somewhat apart, there was little friction with the local populations so long as trade was advantageous to both parties. □

51 EUROPEAN TRADING FORTS IN WESTERN AFRICA, 15TH TO 19TH CENTURIES

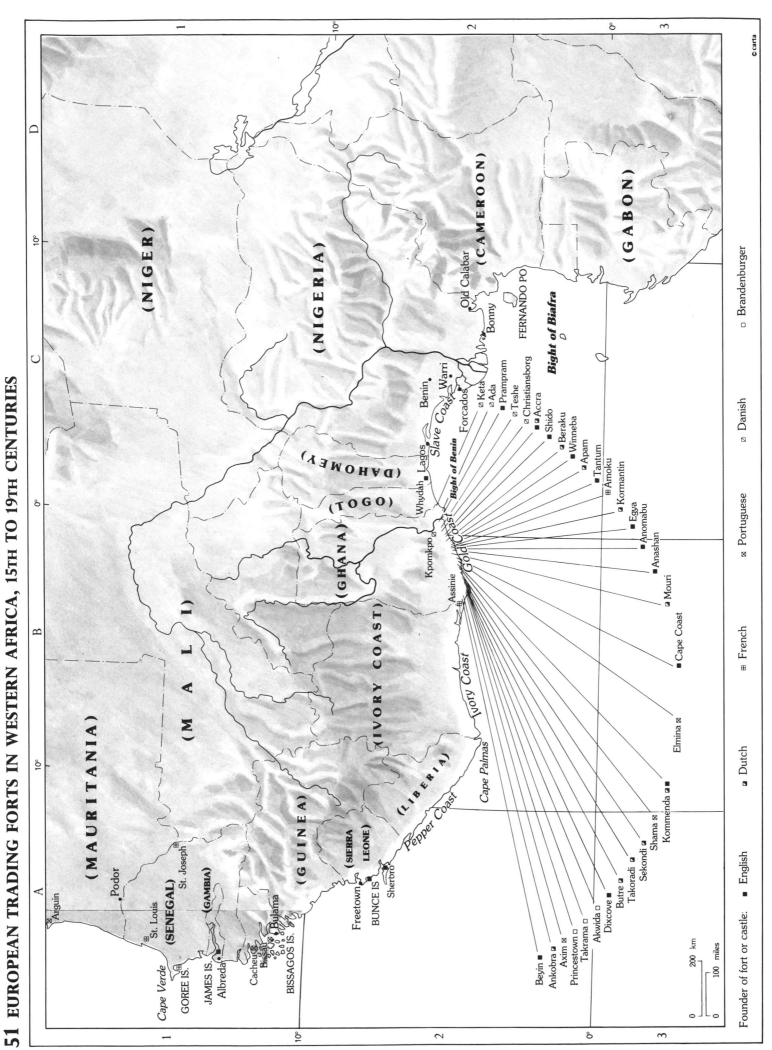

(MAURITANIA)

(NIGER)

(MALI)

(NIGERIA)

(SENEGAL)

(GAMBIA)

(GUINEA)

(SIERRA LEONE)

(IVORY COAST)

(GHANA)

(TOGO)

(DAHOMEY)

(LIBERIA)

(CAMEROON)

(GABON)

Cape Verde
Arguin
Podor
St. Louis
St. Joseph
GOREE IS.
JAMES IS.
Albreda
Cacheu
Bissau
Bulama
BISSAGOS IS.
Freetown
BUNCE IS.
Sherbro
Pepper Coast
Cape Palmas
Ivory Coast
Gold Coast
Beyin
Ankobra
Axim
Princestown
Takrama
Akwida
Dixcove
Butre
Takoradi
Sekondi
Shama
Kommenda
Elmina
Cape Coast
Mouri
Anashan
Anomabu
Egya
Kormantin
Amoku
Tantum
Apam
Winneba
Beraku
Shido
Accra
Christiansborg
Teshe
Prampram
Ada
Keta
Forcados
Kpomkpo
Assinie
Whydah
Lagos
Benin
Warri
Slave Coast
Bight of Benin
Bight of Biafra
Old Calabar
Bonny
FERNANDO PO

Founder of fort or castle:

■ English ⊞ French ◪ Dutch ⊠ Portuguese ◪ Danish □ Brandenburger

CENTRAL AFRICAN KINGDOMS, 15TH TO 19TH CENTURIES

In the center of the African continent, south of the Sudanic belt and stretching from the Atlantic toward the Great Lakes, is the huge forest belt (cf. map 6). Much of this forest is still intact. Below this area, and extending southward as far as the Kalahari Desert (cf. map 2) and crossing eastward to both north and south of Lake Malawi, a group of Bantu-speaking peoples installed themselves between the fifteenth and nineteenth centuries. The earlier of the various dates is simply when we first learn of them from Portuguese writers.

An exception is the realm of the Monomotapa, where mining for gold had been conducted since the fifth century, in the west of present-day Zimbabwe. Here, by the twelfth century those who were builders of the first stage of the Zimbabwe complex and others like it would have arrived. Early in the fifteenth century people called the Karanga arrived. Ruled by the Rozvi clan, they set up a kingdom under Mutota. His son Mutapa (1450–1480) made this an empire which embraced all southern Zimbabwe and much of Mozambique. About 1490 in Butwa one of his provincial governors, Changamire, broke away and founded a separate kingdom. This was the situation when the Portuguese arrived in 1505.

On the western side of Africa an Empire of Kongo ruled from Teke as far as Ndongo and the river Cuanza. Highly organized for trade, the commercial system stretched from west to east. Arab and Swahili traders coming from the east coast do not seem to have penetrated beyond Tete, nor have any imported objects of pottery, porcelain, or metal been found west of this area.

The Portuguese reached the Congo estuary in 1482. In 1489 the ruler, the Manikongo, requested missionaries and artisans to build a capital. In 1491 he became a Christian. His son and successor, Afonso (1507–1543), was an ardent Christian and modeled his court on Lisbon. Now dukes, marquesses, and counts strutted in European dress, and São Salvador, the capital, had as many churches as Lisbon. In 1555 the Jesuits moved into Ndongo, where the ruler, the Ngola (whence the name Angola), readily welcomed them. Yet Franciscans, Capuchins, Carmelites, and Jesuits were too few in number to penetrate beyond the coast, while from the early sixteenth century the hinterland was treated more as a hunting ground for slaves for the plantations of Brazil. In this way the Portuguese defeated the missionary impulse. In East Africa the Portuguese were more interested in gold and ivory than missions, and to a lesser degree in slaves. It is estimated that between 1560 and 1880 three million persons were sold into slavery from Angola, or nearly half the present population.

In 1629 Monomotapa Mavura was baptized and swore fealty as a vassal of Portugal. In Butwa Changamire was building in stone in the gold-bearing area, at Dhlo-Dhlo, Khami, Naletale and elsewhere. In 1725 Zimbabwe was taken by Changamire, who enlarged the famous stone buildings. The dynasty was to last until 1830, when the Nguni from South Africa overran his kingdom.

Farther north, to the west of Lake Tanganyika the Luba and Lunda peoples were populating the area. We know of them chiefly from oral traditions, mainly of genealogies, but it may be surmised that they functioned as commercial intermediaries and providers of ivory to the Portuguese. Man as a whole is migratory, and the Bantu are no exception. We need not consider that at any time there was a mass migration. Rather one may conceive a slow trickle, as families grew by natural increase, as a demand for fresh land grew, and as there grew too the natural desire for the benefits brought by trade. These objectives differed wholly from those sought by the Portuguese, whose principal interest at this period lay in Goa, the Far East, and Brazil. The African possessions were less productive and less profitable, of value only as sources of metals and of men. In this way, before the advent of any "scramble for Africa," Africans went forth to populate vast areas in the New World. ☐

52 CENTRAL AFRICAN KINGDOMS, 15TH TO 19TH CENTURIES

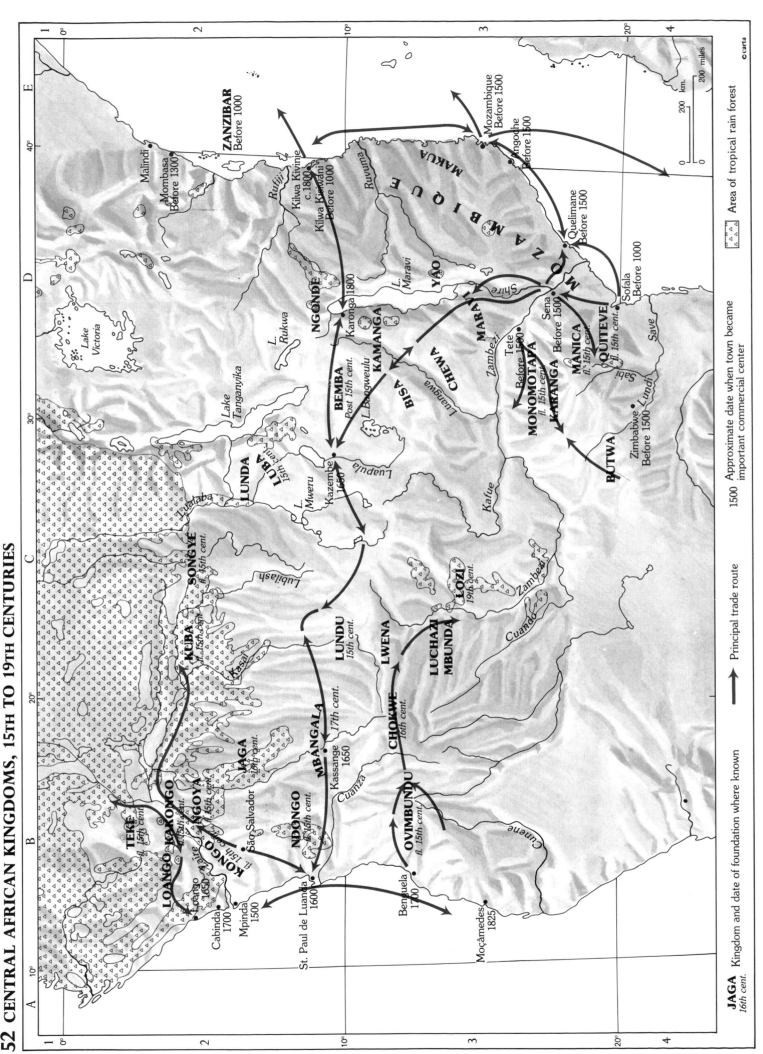

JAGA Kingdom and date of foundation where known
16th cent.

1500 Approximate date when town became important commercial center

→ Principal trade route

⬚ Area of tropical rain forest

© carta

THE MERINA KINGDOM, 16TH TO 18TH CENTURIES

By the eighth century Arabs were certainly reaching the Comoro Islands; possibly they had done so long before. It would be strange if they had not reached Madagascar. The great island is shown on al-Idrisi's map (see maps 35, 36), but with no details. There is thus no firm historical information before 1509, when Diogo Dias, driven by a storm, put in to shelter in the belief that he was in Mozambique. Madagascar first appears on a Portuguese map of 1502. Until the seventeenth century the Portuguese took little interest in it, but commercial relations were maintained with the northwest part of the island and Mozambique. The Dutch established themselves in Mauritius in 1638, and used Madagascar as a refreshment station and to obtain slaves. English attempts to found bases in 1636 and 1644 came to nothing. A more determined French attempt in midcentury was likewise fruitless, and from 1684 to 1724 the island was a haunt of pirates, American, English, and French alike.

The history of the people of the island, so far as it can be recovered, is one of many small kingdoms and chiefdoms whose boundaries — insofar as they recognized any such thing — are not fully known. During the seventeenth century the Sakalava became prominent under Andriandahifotsi (c. 1610–1685), the founder of a kingdom whose rulers were sacred persons and who organized his conquests in quasi-feudal fiefs. Under his son Andrianmanetriarivo (c. 1685–1718) commerce with Europeans was greatly encouraged. Other Sakalava kingdoms were instituted in the northwest, but the extreme north was a virtual desert. On the eastern coast small tribes and clans were highly mobile. By the early eighteenth century the Sakalava held about one-third of a thinly populated island in which the active populations were mainly on the coasts.

☐

MADAGASCAR c. 1750: THE MERINA EXPANSION

During the sixteenth century, the Merina people, who dwelt in the forests in the center of the island, evolved a small kingdom some six miles long and four miles wide, hardly more than a large village. During the seventeenth and eighteenth centuries it increased gradually as a sacred monarchy with an elaborate ceremonial, backed with guns. A series of wars provided prisoners for sale as slaves. As the population increased, so did its markets and local industries (iron work, pottery, and textiles). Forests were cleared to provide pasture and swamps drained to grow rice. By 1790 the kingdom had twenty thousand men capable of bearing arms. The neighbors of the Merinas on the west and south, albeit independent, acknowledged kinship with them. The south was important for its iron mines, its textile industries, and its paddy fields. Its commerce enabled it to purchase arms and so to resist the raids of the Sakalava.

Under Andrianampoinimerina (1787–1810), commonly known as Nampoina, the Merina peoples united under a single monarchy, which after two failed attempts seized the state and capital of Tananarive. There followed a period of expansion until Nampoina's death in 1810. With a firm base in his army and with the wealth he had captured as booty, he could now organize his kingdom. The king was the only master, god made visible, distinguished by his scarlet umbrella, with the sole right to grant fiefs and to impose taxation. Chiefs dispensed justice in defined districts, but lost the independence they had hitherto enjoyed. The king was assisted by a privy council and by a great *kabary*, an assembly where his speeches explained his policies on every conceivable subject, from war to law and even private morals. It was the seed of a yet greater kingdom to come (see map 77).

☐

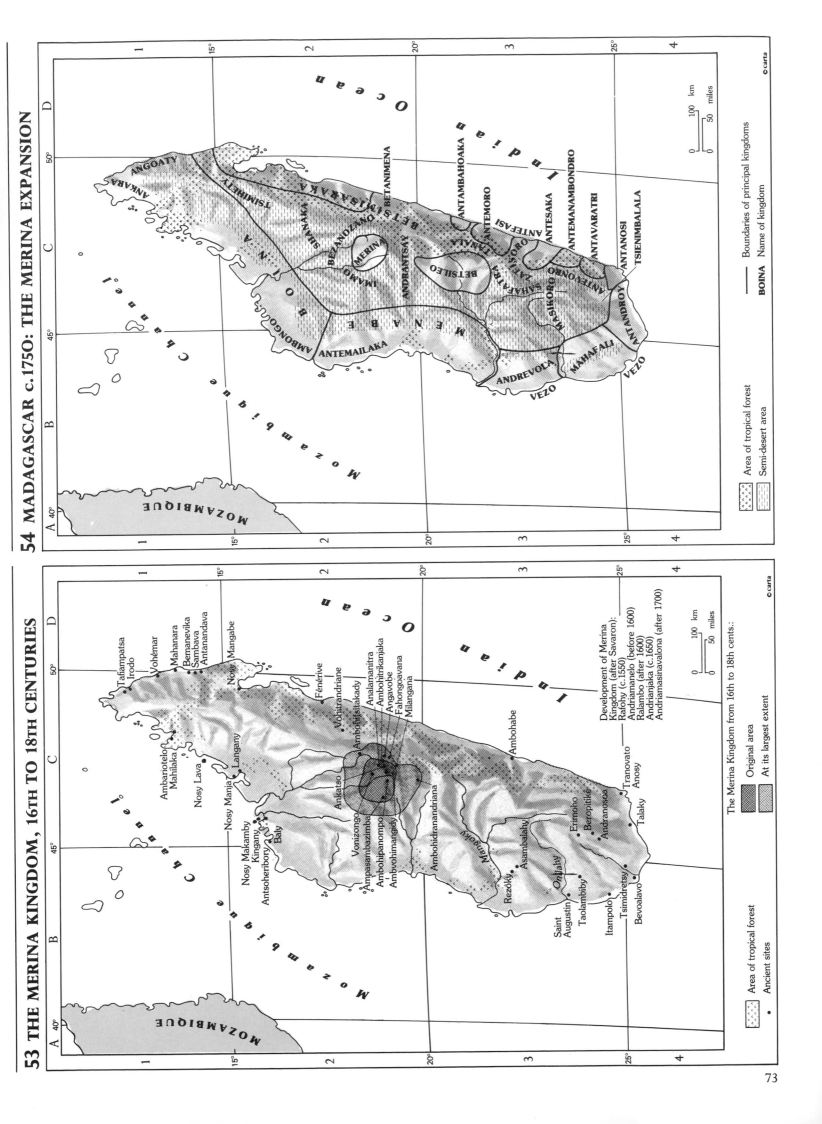

53 THE MERINA KINGDOM, 16TH TO 18TH CENTURIES

Tafiampatsa
Irodo
Vohémar
Mahanara
Bemanevika
Sambava
Antanandava
Nosy Mangabe
Fénérive
Vohitrandriane
Amboh ... fiakady
Analamanitra
Ambohitrikanjaka
Angavobe
Fahongoavana
Milangana

Ambariotelo
Mahilaka
Nosy Lava
Langany

Ambohabe

Ankatso
Vonizongo
Ampasambazimba
Ambohipanompo
Ambovohimanged

Ambohidranandriana

Tranovato
Anosy
Erimoho
Beropitiké
Andranosoa
Talaky

Nosy Makamby
Kingany
Antsoheribory
Balu

Rezoky
Asambalahy

Saint
Augustin
Taolambiby
Itampolo
Tsimidretsy
Bevoalavo

Onilahy

Indian Ocean

Mozambique Channel

MOZAMBIQUE

The Merina Kingdom from 16th to 18th cents.:

■ Original area
▨ At its largest extent

Development of Merina
Kingdom (after Savaron):
Rafohy (c.1550)
— Andriamanelo (before 1600)
Ralambo (after 1600)
Andrianjaka (c.1650)
Andriamasinavalona (after 1700)

▨ Area of tropical forest
• Ancient sites

© carta

54 MADAGASCAR c.1750: THE MERINA EXPANSION

ANGOATY
ANKARA
TSIMIHETY
ANTANKARANA
SIHANAKA
BEZANOZANO
IMAMO
MERINA
BETSIMISARAKA
BETANIMENA
ANTAMBAHOAKA
ANTEMORO
ANTEFASI
ANTESAKA
ANTEMANAMBONDRO
ANTAVARATRI
TSIENIMBALALA
ANTANOSI
ANTANDROY
VEZO
MAHAFALI
ANDREVOLA
MASIKORO
ANTONNO
SAHAFATRA
ZAFISORO
TANALA
BETSILEO
ANDRANTSAY
MENABE
ANTEMAILAKA
AMBONGO
BOINA

Indian Ocean

Mozambique Channel

MOZAMBIQUE

—— Boundaries of principal kingdoms
BOINA Name of kingdom

▨ Area of tropical forest
▨ Semi-desert area

© carta

73

EASTERN AFRICAN TRADE IN THE INDIAN OCEAN, c. 1500

We learn of eastern African trade from three vantage points. Ahmad ibn Majid's journals name the ports and give astronomical bearings. From two Portuguese, Tomé Pires, in Malacca from 1512 to 1515 (before becoming Portuguese ambassador to China), and from Duarte Barbosa, in Cananor on the Malabar coast, around 1517–1518, we learn of the participants and details of their commerce.

Aden was the entrepôt to which merchants from Cairo brought merchandise — chiefly luxury goods — from Italy, Greece, and Syria. From Zaila and Berbera Aden obtained horses as well as Ethiopian slaves who were captured in battle and sent to Asia: none came from farther south. From the Somali ports came local products; gold and ivory came from farther south. The greatest volume of trade from the west and from eastern Africa was directed toward Cambay, India, which in turn was the entrepôt for all the products of Malacca, principally spices. Cambay was a true entrepôt, for the trade with Malacca was conducted by Gujaratis, who brought foreign merchants to Cambay with them, whereupon the latter tended to settle there. These included Cairenes and Ethiopians; men from Kilwa, Malindi, and Mogadishu in East Africa; Persians from various provinces; Greeks from Asia Minor; and Turkomans and Armenians.

The African ports were to some extent specialized. Cambay sent large vessels to Malindi, Mombasa, and Kilwa, selling their goods for gold and then proceeding south as far as Sofala in Mozambique, where trade was carried on with the kingdom of the Monomotapa. Here were collected gold, ivory, and some ambergris, with trade connections reaching out to the far south as far as the Cape. (This much is attested by finds of Chinese porcelain as far south as Port St. John.) Mozambique itself had several smaller ports, which previously had been vassals of the ruler of Kilwa, the chief town of the area. Mombasa too had direct connections with Sofala and Cambay, and it, like its northern neighbor, Malindi, had a rich agriculture. Only Malindi is mentioned as a port having relations with Madagascar, whose many kings, both Moors and heathen, engaged solely in fishing and agriculture and traded with no one. The chief articles taken south were rice, wheat, soap, indigo, butter, lard (ghee?), oils, carnelians, coarse pottery "like that of Seville," and all kinds of cloth. It is perhaps indicative of the wealth of these African cities that they imported food, rice, millet, and some wheat, apart from the obvious imports of luxury textiles.

Excavations in eastern Africa since 1948 have provided a few further details. The quantities of broken Chinese porcelain that litter the beaches and ancient settlements along the eastern African coast are mute evidence of a preference for Chinese porcelain wares. These were not merely used commonly as tableware, but were set into or hung on the walls of houses as decoration and were placed in the more important tombs. Even more prolific are beads, to which it is difficult to assign a provenance; some are certainly from Cambay and Malacca. Finally, an export too commonplace to earn itself mention in literature — the mangrove pole — is nevertheless attested throughout the treeless areas of southern Arabia and in the Persian Gulf by its presence in ancient buildings. The two principal areas from which mangrove poles were harvested were (and still are) the Lamu archipelago and the steamy swamps of the Rufiji delta. Other, smaller areas provided them also. □

55 EASTERN AFRICAN TRADE IN THE INDIAN OCEAN, c.1500

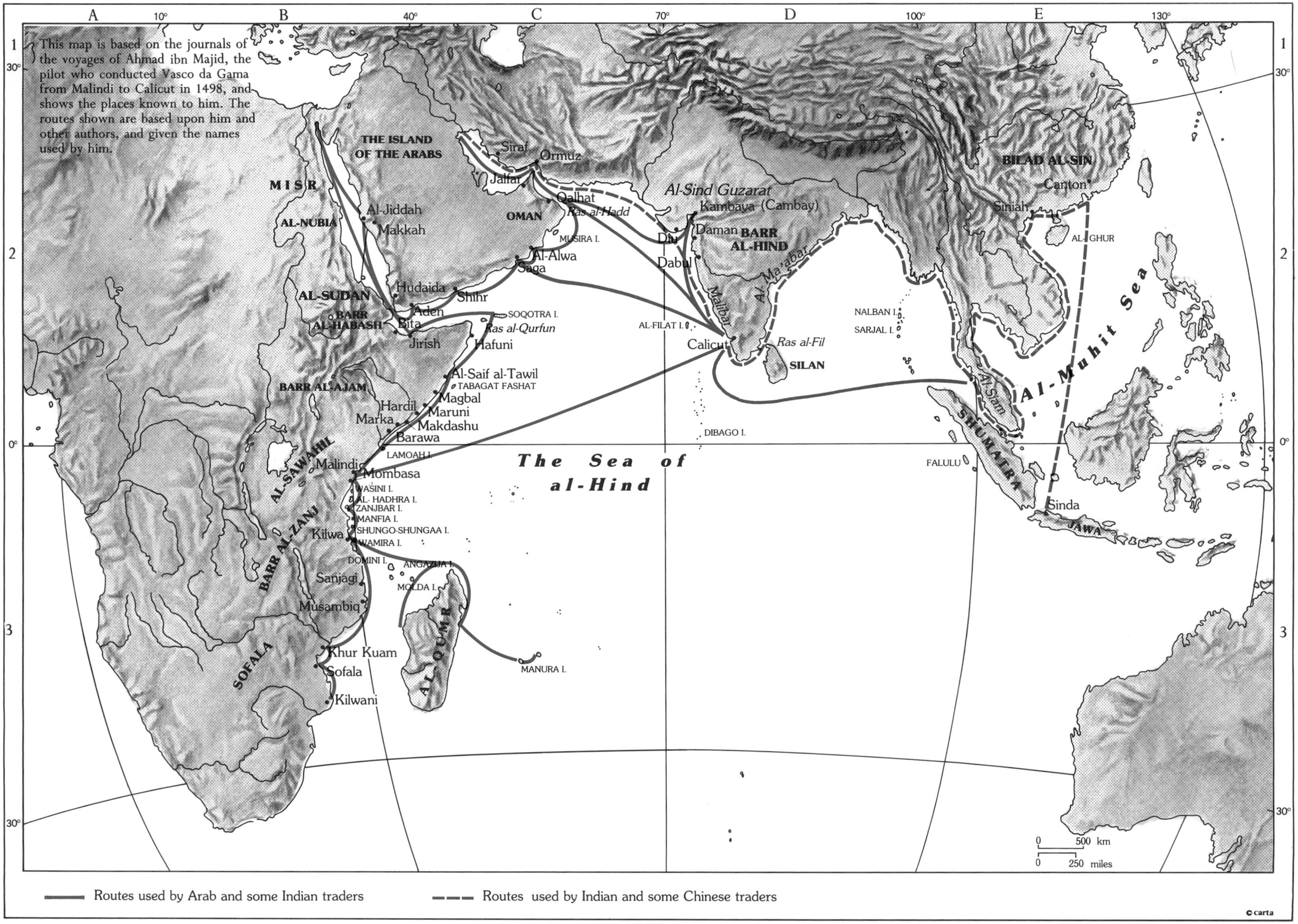

This map is based on the journals of Ahmad ibn Majid, the pilot who conducted Vasco da Gama from Malindi to Calicut in 1498, and shows the places known to him. The routes shown are based upon him and other authors, and given the names used by him.

Al-Muhit Sea

BILAD AL-SIN

Canton

AL-GHUR

Sinah

Al-Siam

SHUMATRA

JAWA

Sinda

FALULU

NALBAN I.

SARJAL I.

Al-Sind   Guzarat
Kanbaya (Cambay)

Daman BARR AL-HIND

Malibar

Ras al-Fil

SILAN

Dabul

Calicut

AL-FILAT I.

DIBAGO I.

The Sea of al-Hind

Siraf Ormuz

Jaffar

Qalhat Ras al-Hadd

OMAN

MUSIRA I.

Al-Alwa

Saga

THE ISLAND OF THE ARABS

Al-Jiddah

Makkah

MISR

AL-NUBIA

AL-SUDAN

BARR AL-HABASH

Hudaida

Aden

Zila

Shihr

SOQOTRA I.

Ras al-Qurfun

Hafuni

Jirish

Al-Saif al-Tawil

TABAGAT FASHAT

Maqbal

Maruni

Hardii

Marka

Makdashu

Barawa

LAMOAH

Malindi

YASINI I.

Mombasa

AL-HADHRA I.

ZANJBAR I.

MANFIA I.

SHUNGO-SHUNGAA I.

HAMIRA I.

BARR AL-ZANJ

AL-SAWAHIL

DOMINI I.

ANGOJAH

MOLDA I.

AL-QUMR

MANURA I.

Kilwa

Sanjagi

Musambiq

Khur Kuam

Sofala

Kilwani

SOFALA

500 km
250 miles

© carta

─────── Routes used by Arab and some Indian traders

─────── Routes used by Indian and some Chinese traders

- - - - - Routes used by Indian and some Chinese traders

THE WESTERN SUDAN IN THE 16TH AND 17TH CENTURIES

By the sixteenth century, European slave traders, led by the Portuguese, increasingly dominated the coast from the river Senegal as far as Angola. Soon the Bight of Benin would be thick with their forts (see map 51), as they traded in textiles, liquor, and arms, provoking slave-catching wars and expeditions. Up to 1600 Spain and Portugal were the chief participants in the transatlantic slave trade, aided by the African chiefs of the hinterland. The Portuguese concentrated especially on Angola, a source of silver as well as slaves.

Farther north, Songhai had been seized by a Moroccan army in 1590 (see map 48), which held it nominally until 1753. After the first honeymoon of conquest its progressive weakness was evident from the instability of its governance. Nevertheless it served Morocco as a recruiting ground in which to catch slaves. For the rest it was a time of disorder, during which the white Tuareg nomads had every opportunity to rob the sedentary black agriculturalists to the south as far as the Niger.

In the east the rulers of Kanem had moved their capital from the northeast of Lake Chad to Bornu, southwest of the lake. Here Mai Idris Alooma (c. 1571 or 1580 to 1603 or 1617) made Bornu a great power in the region. He had trade relations with the Ottomans of Tripoli and Tunis, who provided him with arms. These were employed in well-organized raids to provide quantities of slaves. The ever-aggressive Tuareg later undermined Bornu and brought it to ruin. Farther east three states emerged and gradually grew in importance: Baguirmi, Wadai, and Darfur. They likewise raided and forwarded slaves to the Ottomans. North of the river Benue the city states of what is now northern Nigeria had little stability and fought among themselves as well as against the Tuareg and other nomads. They did not find unity until the nineteenth century.

□

THE WESTERN SUDAN IN THE 18TH AND 19TH CENTURIES

In the seventeenth century the Dutch had come to dominate the slave trade, with smaller competitors in Brandenburg, Denmark, and England. During the eighteenth century the English overtook the Dutch and became the dominant force in the area into the nineteenth century and up to the colonial period. This was the peak of the Atlantic slave trade, but now with an ever-increasing number of slaves going to North-American plantations. The trade was fed by the African kingdoms that served the European traders on the coast in what became a symbiotic relationship between African and European to the point of frequent interbreeding. The names of many of the English, Irish, and Portuguese traders are perpetuated in present-day Ghana and elsewhere. In Benin (then named Dahomey or Abomey) the rulers became a byword for the export and ritual sacrifice of slaves.

The most important development took place in Northern Nigeria, where in the Hausa states Usman dan Fodio established a new Islamic empire with Sokoto as capital. On a military basis it united the whole area as far as Bornu and Adamawa. It was an intellectual and religious movement as well as a military one, and its founder spent the last years of his life solely in religious exercises and pious study.

In Segu in 1818 a similar movement, led by Shehu Ahmadu Lobo, conquered Jenne and Timbuktu. A puritan and mystic, Shehu Ahmadu rigorously enforced Islamic law. Farther west an adherent of the Tijaniya dervish confraternity, Omar Sedu Tal, conquered first Bambuk and Kaarta, and then Segu and Macina. He had previously made long stays in Mecca and Cairo, and then spent thirteen years preaching in Futa Jallon. He died in mysterious circumstances in 1864.

In the eastern part of the region near Lake Chad trade was maintained with the north and with Egypt and the Nile Valley.

□

56 THE WESTERN SUDAN IN THE 16TH AND 17TH CENTURIES

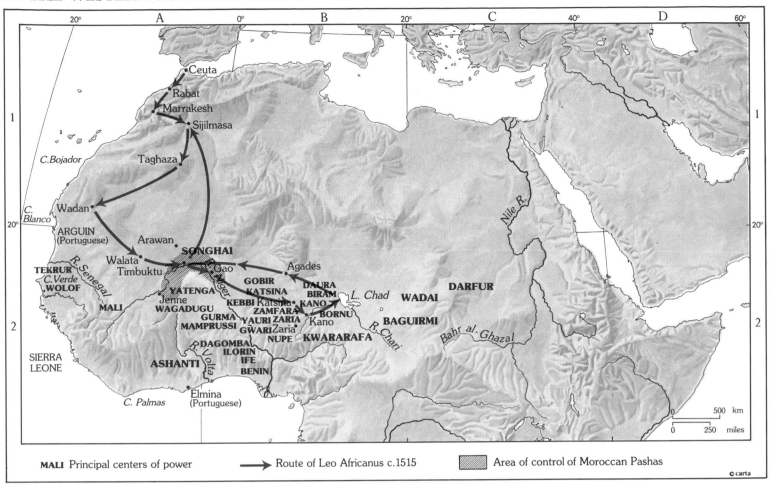

20° A 0° B 20° C 40° D 60°

Ceuta
Rabat
Marrakesh
Sijilmasa
1
Taghaza
C.Bojador
C.Blanco
Wadan
ARGUIN
(Portuguese)
20° Arawan
SONGHAI
Walata Gao Agades
Timbuktu
TEKRUR *R. Senegal* **GOBIR** **DARFUR**
C.Verde **KATSINA** **DAURA**
WOLOF **YATENGA** **BIRAM** *L. Chad* **WADAI**
Jenne **KEBBI** Katsina **KANO**
MALI **WAGADUGU** **ZAMFARA** **BORNU** **BAGUIRMI**
GURMA **YAURI ZARIA** Kano *R. Chari*
2 **MAMPRUSSI** **GWARI**Zaria **KWARARAFA** *Bahr al-Ghazal*
DAGOMBAI **NUPE**
SIERRA **ILORIN**
LEONE **ASHANTI** **IFE**
BENIN
Elmina
(Portuguese)
C. Palmas

500 km
250 miles

MALI Principal centers of power   → Route of Leo Africanus c.1515   ▨ Area of control of Moroccan Pashas
© carta

57 THE WESTERN SUDAN IN THE 18TH AND 19TH CENTURIES

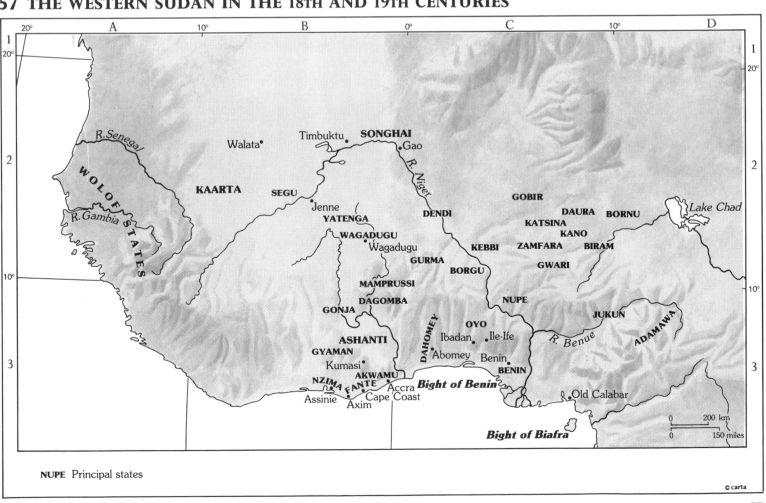

20° A 10° B 0° C 10° D

20°
R. Senegal
Walata Timbuktu **SONGHAI**
2 Gao
W *R. Niger*
O
L **KAARTA** **GOBIR**
O SEGU **DAURA** **BORNU**
F Jenne **DENDI** **KATSINA**
R. Gambia **YATENGA** **KANO**
S **WAGADUGU** **KEBBI** **ZAMFARA** **BIRAM**
T Wagadugu **GURMA** **GWARI**
A **BORGU**
T
10° **E** **MAMPRUSSI** **NUPE**
S **DAGOMBA** *Lake Chad*
GONJA **JUKUN**
D **OYO** **ADAMAWA**
ASHANTI **A** Ibadan Ile-Ife *R. Benue*
GYAMAN **H** Abomey Benin
Kumasi **O** **BENIN**
NZIMA **AKWAMU** **M**
Assinie **FANTE** Accra **E** *Bight of Benin* Old Calabar
Axim Cape Coast **Y**
3

Bight of Biafra

200 km
150 miles

NUPE Principal states
© carta

77

TRADE IN CENTRAL AND SOUTHERN AFRICA FROM THE VIEWPOINT OF AFRICAN TRADERS IN KONGO

Eduardo Lopez's account of trade in Africa south of the Equator, derived from African traders in the kingdom of Kongo, is notoriously deficient. It is interesting, however, as much for its omissions as for what it asserts, and it is this information perhaps which is of real value.

The two great river systems of the Zaïre and the Zambezi, and the smaller one of the Limpopo, account for the greatest number of names on Lopez's map. In western Africa his omissions and inaccuracies are the most obvious. It is perhaps pardonable that he only mentions the kingdom of Congo (Kongo) and assumes that we can fill in for ourselves the names of its vassals and satellites. Nevertheless, the Portuguese were firmly established by this time in Ndongo (Angola) and would build St. Paul de Loanda (now the city of Luanda) in 1600: the Jesuits had set up a mission at Loanda by 1575. Trade then may be assumed to be principally a riverine interest for Lopez's informants, extending far up the Zaïre and reaching up its tributaries.

There is a substantial gap between the sources of the Zaïre and those of the Zambezi in which Lopez places no names at all. Yet it was on the east coast at the end of the sixteenth century that the Portuguese Dominican missionary father João dos Santos was casually offered a blanket which had traveled across the continent all the way from Ndongo. Probably some link was provided by a route which crossed Lake Tanganyika or passed by land to the south of it.

At the eastern end of the route Lopez is at his most vague. There was certainly no recorded empire west of Lake Tanganyika that could be called "Imperio de Moen-Hemuge." *Moen* presumably represents something like the Swahili *mwinyi*, ("lord, master," a title of respect); *Hemuge* is not identifiable. Farther east the river Rufiji is named in its correct position but denominated "Quiloa" in its lower reaches. *Quiloa* is simply the Portuguese spelling of *Kilwa*, the name of the ancient capital of the sultanate which lies about one hundred miles to the south (see map 41). "Songo" presumably represents Songo Songo Island: it lies somewhat south of the sultanate which lies somewhat south of the Rufiji estuary near Kilwa. The Mafia Islands stand some fifteen miles out to sea. Lopez's "C. del Grido" is clearly Capo Delgado, south of the river Ruvuma off Mozambique. His "Mongulo" appears often on other contemporary maps as Mongalo or Mongallo, and is present-day Mingoyo, a village that lies up a creek on a small river, all of which bear the same name.

North of these place Membaca (Mombasa) and Melinde (Malindi) are historic coastal city-states, but with no possessions much more than a mile or so inland, where *nyika* (dry bush) takes over from the well-watered coastal zone. Strange, nevertheless, is Lopez's entry "Azania" in inland territory in present-day Tanzania then occupied by the Sukuma people, a tribal conglomeration bound together by a common language but fragmented under different chiefs. It was never united until colonial times. Both Strabo and Pliny record the name *Azania*; in Arab and Swahili literature it occurs in the words *Zanj* and *Zanzibar*, and always refers to the coastland.

The entry "Embeoe" plausibly represents the Bemba people. Most interesting is the entry "Mozimba" at the foot of Lake Malawi (Lake Nyasa). The Mozimba first appear in recorded history near modern-day Sena, and were long known for the practice of eating prisoners of war and slaves who could no longer work. Suddenly in 1587 they moved northward and at Kilwa ate three thousand persons out of a population of four thousand. Eventually they reached Mombasa, but were driven off. At Malindi they were met by the Segeju tribe, who took them in the rear as they laid siege to the city. The Segeju killed all but one hundred men, and so the Mozimba disappeared from history but not from the stock-in-trade of Lopez's informants. □

58 TRADE IN CENTRAL AND SOUTHERN AFRICA FROM THE VIEWPOINT OF AFRICAN TRADERS IN KONGO

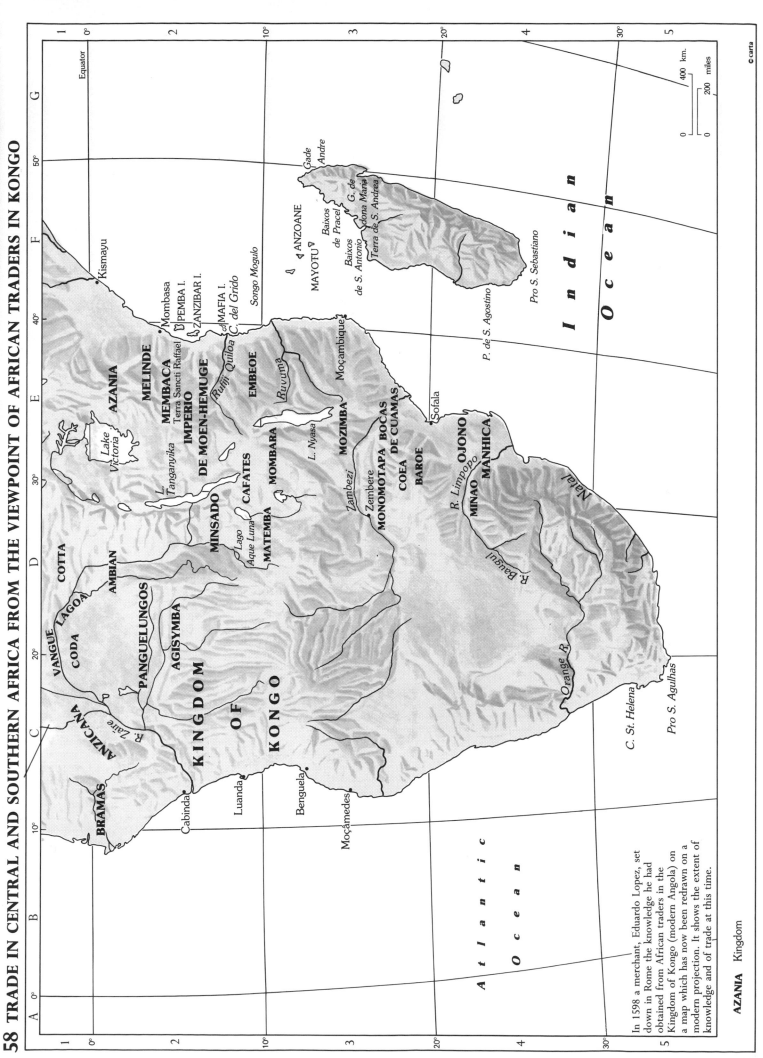

In 1598 a merchant, Eduardo Lopez, set down in Rome the knowledge he had obtained from African traders in the Kingdom of Kongo (modern Angola) on a modern projection. It shows the extent of knowledge and of trade at this time.

AZANIA Kingdom

79

ETHIOPIA AND EASTERN AFRICA, 16TH TO 19TH CENTURIES

In 1498, when the Portuguese appeared off Kilwa, local opinion was divided. As one anonymous historian wrote,

> some thought that they were good and honest men; but those who knew the truth confirmed that they were corrupt and dishonest persons who had come only to spy out the land in order to seize it.

Both views were extreme. As for seizing the land, the Portuguese were far too few in number to do so. Nevertheless, their possession of firearms was a decisive factor in the taking of Kilwa and Mombasa in 1505, and in their domination of the coast until 1698. In that year the Omani Arabs took the Portuguese Fort Jesus and asserted predominance over all the coast as far as Tungi, just south of the river Ruvuma. It was not wholly effective until about 1827.

The early sixteenth century was a turning point for Ethiopia in a different way. In 1527 Ahmed Grañ ("left-handed," his nickname) refused tribute to the emperor. Grañ's Danakil and Somali warriors, buoyed up by fanaticism and the hope of eternal bliss, but more immediately by the desire for booty, waged war on the Christian empire for thirteen years. By 1541 it was almost lost, but a small detachment under Cristovão da Gama, grandson of the eminent Vasco, saved the situation. Gama was tortured and killed, but the Portuguese artillery won the day. Nevertheless, monasteries and churches had been robbed and looted, and the country reduced to a political and cultural desert.

A Jesuit mission (1555–1632) failed to comprehend either the theology or the ritual of the Ethiopian church, or to conciliate public opinion and accordingly was expelled on a tide of national feeling. Equally less sensitive was the emperor Fasilidas (1632–1667) in his establishment of a fixed capital at Gondar. The medieval emperors had been peripatetic: the whole court and the senior clergy were organized on a basis of perpetual "progresses" throughout the empire. It was this that held it together. Iyasu the Great (1680–1704) was the last effective ruler before the emperor Tewodros II (Theodore, 1855–1868): with the isolation of the court from the people, chaos supervened as the empire crumbled amid murders and court intrigues (see map 75).

Along the eastern African coast in the sixteenth and seventeenth centuries the Portuguese at first attempted to enforce a monopoly of the carrying trade. In this, with all the creeks and marshes of a coast protected by mangrove swamps, they had no hope of success. Trade depends on mutual confidence: in its absence, as the available accounts show, there were profits so minimal as not to justify the lives that were spent. The virtual absence of building on the part of the Swahili is a clear indication of the general sluggishness and malaise that prevailed. The attempts of the Augustinians to evangelize in the seventeenth century had no lasting effect. All their work was swept away when the ivory trade competition between Mombasa and Pate brought the Omani to East Africa at the request of Mombasa.

The Omani installation of local governors and of customs posts along the littoral after the capture of Mombasa in 1698 was inevitably unpopular. The Swahili had invoked the Omani as allies; the latter had remained as conquerors. Local rebellions were not infrequent. Finally, in 1827, Sayyid Said, ruler of Muscat and Zanzibar (1806–1856), asserted Omani power. Zanzibar, he had appreciated, was a more favorable commercial base than Muscat, with its warring hinterland tribes. He moved his court to Zanzibar in 1840. American, British, and French consulates soon followed.

By 1844 caravans set out from Zanzibar inland, bringing slaves and other commodities to the coast. After a long struggle on the part of the British, slaving and then slavery were abolished. An admirable vignette of the period is given in the *Memoirs of an Arabian Princess*, the autobiography of Said's daughter Salmé.

In Mozambique the Portuguese still maintained a tenuous grip on the coast, until they awoke around 1890 to realize that with the "scramble for Africa" other powers would supersede them unless they developed their territories with energy.

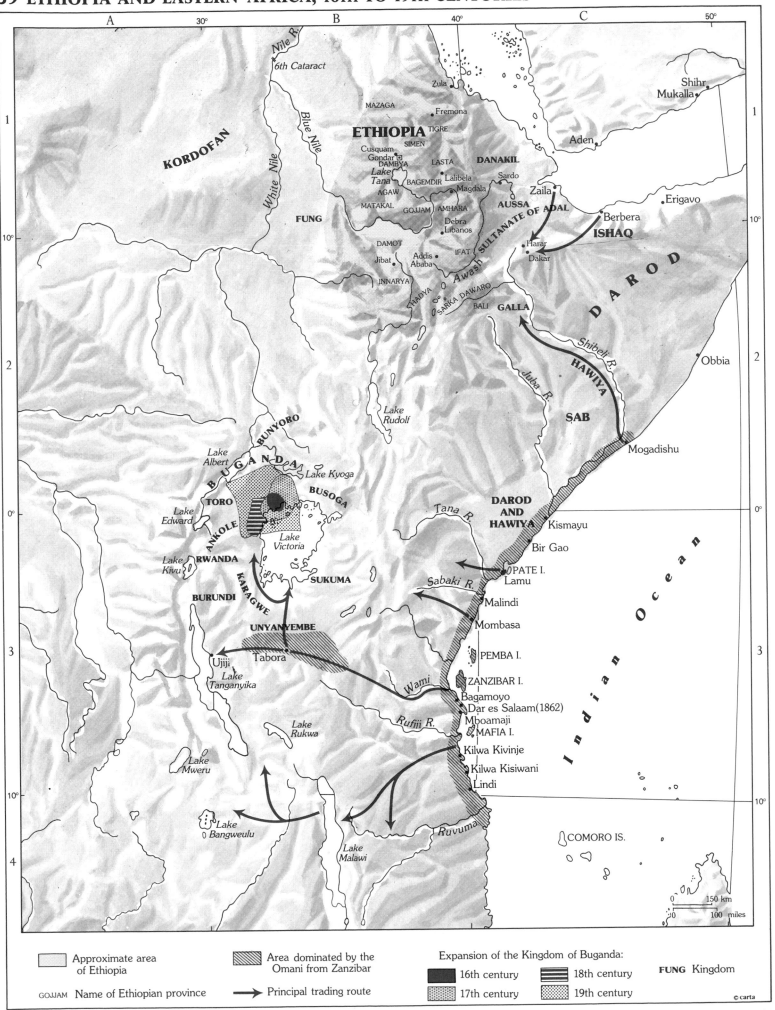

A 30° B 40° C 50°

Nile R.
6th Cataract

KORDOFAN

Blue Nile
White Nile

Zula

MAZAGA
Fremona
ETHIOPIA TIGRE
Cusquam SIMEN
Gondar
DAMBYA LASTA
Lake DANAKIL
Tana BAGEMDIR Lalibela
AGAW Magdala
MATAKAL AUSSA
GOJJAM AMHARA
FUNG Debra SULTANATE OF ADAL
Libanos
DAMOT IFAT
Jibat Addis SARKA DAWARO
Ababa
INNARYA HADYA BALI GALLA

Shir
Mukalla

Aden

Erigavo

Zaila
Berbera **ISHAQ**
Harar
Dakar

DAROD

Awash

Obbia

Shibeli R.
HAWIYA

Juba R.

SAB

BUNYORO
Lake
Albert
BUGANDA Lake Kyoga
TORO BUSOGA
Lake ANKOLE Lake
Edward Victoria
RWANDA
Lake SUKUMA
Kivu
BURUNDI KARAGWE
UNYANYEMBE
Ujiji Tabora
Lake
Tanganyika

Mogadishu

Tana R.

**DAROD
AND
HAWIYA**
Kismayu
Bir Gao
PATE I.
Lamu
Malindi
Sabaki R.
Mombasa
PEMBA I.

ZANZIBAR I.
Bagamoyo
Wami Dar es Salaam (1862)
Mboamaji
Rufiji R. MAFIA I.
Kilwa Kivinje
Kilwa Kisiwani
Lindi

Indian Ocean

Lake
Rukwa

Lake
Mweru

Lake
Bangweulu

Lake
Malawi

Ruvuma

COMORO IS.

0 150 km
0 100 miles

Approximate area
of Ethiopia

Area dominated by the
Omani from Zanzibar

Expansion of the Kingdom of Buganda:

GOJJAM Name of Ethiopian province

Principal trading route

16th century 18th century **FUNG** Kingdom

17th century 19th century

©carta

THE SLAVE TRADE IN THE ATLANTIC AND INDIAN OCEANS, C. 1800

As an institution slavery had deep roots in pre-Christian Europe and in the Middle East as well as in Africa. With the discovery of Guinea in the fifteenth century, Portugal began to import slaves, a practice it maintained even after the formal condemnation on 7 October 1462 by Pius II of the enslavement of Africans.

In the New World, Portugal and Spain first endeavored to use Indians as labor. Finding this system unsatisfactory, in 1517 Charles I (Charles V, Holy Roman emperor), of Spain disregarding papal disapproval, granted letters patent to Spanish settlers to import African slaves into the Caribbean islands and later to the mainland. As sugar cane, and then coffee, were cultivated on Brazilian plantations, the trickle of slaves soon became a flood. In northern America the first African slaves were brought to Virginia in a Dutch vessel. Here growth of the new trade was slower: in 1681 there were only 2,000 slaves in Virginia; there were 59,000 in 1714, and 263,000 by 1754. The greatest increase followed the introduction of cotton, with some 4.5 million slaves held by 1860.

A triangular trade now developed in the Atlantic. To the Slave Coast of Guinea from home ports in Europe came liquor, arms, piece goods, and trinkets with which slaving captains purchased slaves, who were then carried across the ocean closely and cruelly packed; some 20 percent died on the way. In the Americas the ships reloaded with rum, tobacco, and other local products.

In the Indian Ocean the acquisition of slaves by purchase or capture is attested in small numbers from A.D. 50 on. They were known as Habashi (Abyssinians). At the same time Turks and Circassians were being imported into Egypt from southeast Russia and the Caucasus. In Egypt they served the two Mamluk dynasties (map 39, 40) as did the Habashi in Bengal. In the eighteenth century the French East India Company found in Africa a source for labor in Réunion and Ile Morice (later Mauritius), and in the Seychelles. In the nineteenth century Arabs from the Persian Gulf and especially from Oman took slaves for Arabia. By midcentury a prosperous trade was based on Zanzibar, with caravans as far as Lake Malawi and beyond Lake Victoria far into present-day Zaïre. In the Cape local needs for labor were satisfied by imports from Dutch Indonesian possessions, the ancestors of today's Cape Malays.

The fate of the slaves varied greatly. It was first a question of surviving the sea passage. In northern America as in the Cape a distorted Calvinistic theology equated white immigrants with "Israelites" and black slaves with "Canaanites," "hewers of wood and drawers of water." Such color prejudice did not exist so much among the Portuguese and Spaniards or in France, where the practice of intermarriage gave rise to a mulatto class. Similarly, in the Arab lands the beauty of the Circassian, Ethiopian, and Georgian women graced the royal *harems* who provided heirs to thrones. An intermediate class of loyal soldiers and servants, entrusted often with serious responsibilities, emerged from the slave population as well, especially in the eastern lands.

It is estimated that before 1800 more Africans had crossed the Atlantic than European colonists, and that in the Americas they numbered not less than fifteen million. In the seventeenth century the Quakers in Britain and North America, followed in the next century by French rationalists, condemned the brutality and violation of human rights inherent in slavery as an institution. In the United States all the states north of Maryland abolished slavery between 1777 and 1804. In Britain, Lord Grenville's Act of 1807 forbade the slave trade in all British possessions. The struggle for total abolition continued throughout the nineteenth century and continues in an attenuated form today. ☐

60 THE SLAVE TRADE IN THE ATLANTIC AND INDIAN OCEANS, c.1800

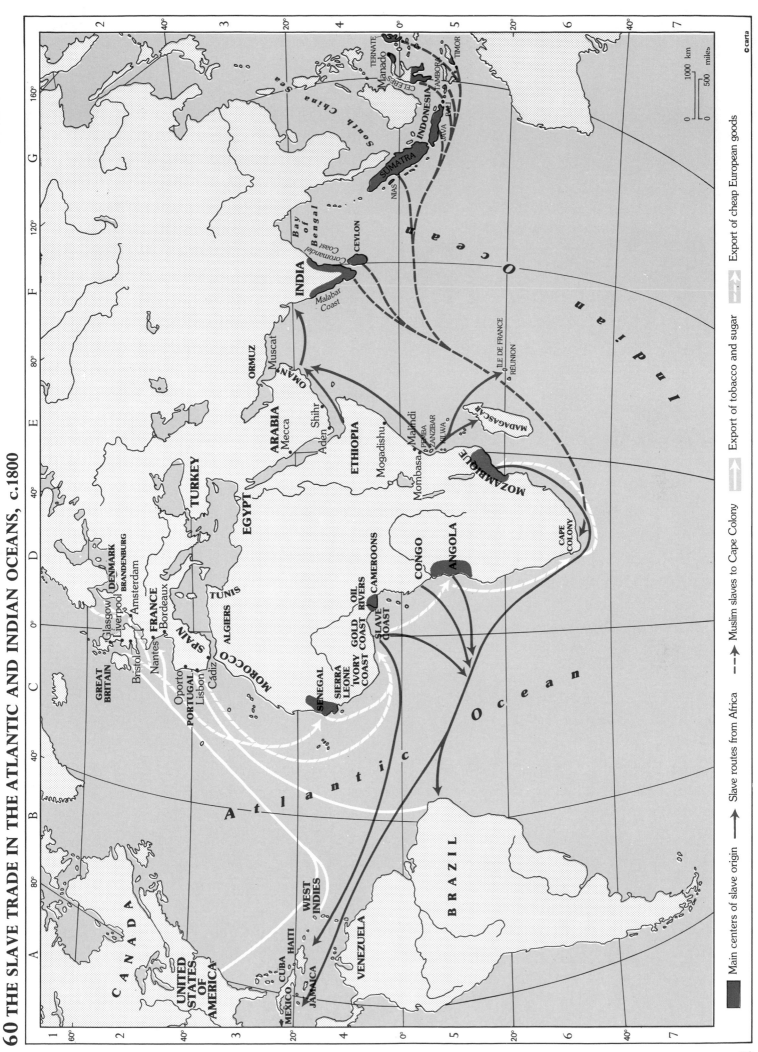

Main centers of slave origin ■   Slave routes from Africa ⟶   Muslim slaves to Cape Colony --→   Export of cheap European goods ⇧

Export of tobacco and sugar ⇧   Export of cheap European goods ⇧

PRINCIPAL AFRICAN STATES AND PEOPLES, C. 1850

A tour of the horizon in the earlier 1800's would have revealed in Africa a remarkable number of individuals who were great by any historical standard: Muhammad Pasha Ali in Egypt (1811–1849); in Algeria Abd el-Kader (Abd al-Qadir) (1832–1847); in western Africa Usman dan Fodio (1803–1817); likewise Shehu Ahmadu Lobo (1818–1845) and al-Hajj Umar (1850–1864); in South Africa Chaka the Zulu (1807–1828); in Madagascar Radama I (1810–1828); and in Zanzibar Sayyid Said, ruler of Muscat in 1806 and in full effective control of Zanzibar from 1827 until 1856. All these men in different ways were founders of what became highly organized states, Tewodros II (1855–1868), a modernizer who for all his weaknesses pulled the ramshackle Ethiopian empire together, appears somewhat later. Only two of the rulers listed here came to power by birth.

Within Africa itself were numerous kingdoms, many of them with sophisticated and evolved constitutions, such as can accurately be described as national monarchies. Only two of these, Sokoto and Ethiopia, can be classed as empires. This was the genius of Usman dan Fodio and Tewodros II, a Muslim and a Christian respectively. In battle the one had consecrated standards for his generals; the other had the *tabot*, that represented both the Ark of the Covenant and the Tomb from which Christ rose from the dead.

Across central Africa, south of the river Zaïre, stretched a number of Bantu kingdoms, none of them touched by Islam or Christianity until the late nineteenth century. In some of these the successors of the Monomotapa preserved a tradition of consulting spirit-mediums. In all the Bantu lands were what are misleadingly called witch doctors: available for consultation, they were ready with rituals to avert disaster, famine, or pestilence, or to promote a good rainfall and successful crops. In some of these the ruler himself was the rainmaker, in others a quasi-hereditary priesthood served that function. Such men were collectors of intelligence, of information, like the oracle of Delphi in ancient Greece and other oracles, great and small. In many such kingdoms there was a well-organized system of local government, of chiefs, subchiefs, and headmen responsible for administering justice and for collecting dues, in a variety of currencies from cattle to cowrie shells or in perishables. Many, too, had trained armies or militias; Dahomey (Abomey) alone enlisted women.

An imperceptible line demarcates the national monarchies and those peoples without a central ruler but subject to a number of different chiefs. The truly national monarchies united all those who spoke a common tongue. Many of these had no central organization, but rather independent chiefdoms. Such were the Sukuma, the Nyamwezi, and the Hehe. Some, like the Ha, had queens. Historically the stage was perhaps transitional, for the Nyamwezi and the Hehe eventually coalesced into monarchies. The most striking example was the creation of a new nation by Chaka the Zulu from a section of the Nguni people, who were remade as new by being married with the widows of their conquered foemen.

There was yet another level, first denominated by the British anthropologist Godfrey Lienhardt as "tribes without heads." Not uncommonly these were quite large linguistic groups such as the Kikuyu or the Masai. The first dwelt in family groups in mountainous regions, the second were transhumant herdsmen living in scattered *manyattas* (low huts) in grassy plains. In such circumstances no need for chiefs arose. An elaborate system of age-grades — of infants, youths, warriors, and elders — provided status, the senior class meeting only if occasion demanded. In all these systems "witch doctors" are found; among the Masai a *laibon*, as it were a principal witch doctor, serves as the overseer of religion and morals, and so a judge within the tribe.

Among all these peoples also, and at all levels, was what can only be described in modern terms as a "welfare state." The tribe took care of the poor, the orphan, the aged, and the traveler, and imposed a set of social rules. These systems were to a large extent dented and fragmented by the colonial regimes that were to follow.

□

MADEIRA

CANARY IS. (Sp.)

MOROCCO
Berbers

Tuareg

EGYPT

KAARTA

AL-HAJJ OMAR

MASSINA
BOURE

GOBIR
KATSINA
GWANDU
KANO
SOKOTO
DAHOMEY
ILORIN
ASHANTI
NUPE
LIBERIA
YORUBA
JUKUN
Ewe
BAMUM
BENIN
Ibo
DUALA
BORNU
Kdoko
MANDARA
ADAMAWA
Sara
MBUM
Tikar
Tikar

WADAI
BULALA
DARFUR
BAGUIRMI

Sidama
ETHIOPIA
Galla
Somali

FERNANDO PO
(Sp.)

Fang

Zaire

Teke

Mongo

Zande
Mangbetu
NYORO
TORO
GANDA
ANKOLE
HAYA
RWANDA
BURUNDI
Sukuma
Nyamwezi
Gogo

Bari
Acholi
Lango
Soga
Suk
Luo
Nandi
Masai
Kikuyu
Kamba
Chagga
Pare
SAMBAA

KONGO

KUBA
LUNDA
MWATA YAMVO

KAZEMBE

Ovimbundu

Bisa

Ngoni
HEHE
Yao

PEMBA I.
ZANZIBAR
MAFIA I.

Swahili

COMORO IS.

Ambo

Herero

Makua

Shona

NDEBELE

Bushmen

GAZI
SWAZI
ZULU
SOTHO
Pondo
Tembu
Xhosa

Hottentots
Griquas

Sakalava
HOVA
Betsimisaraka
Bara

Equator

0   500 km.
0   250 miles

SOKOTO	Empire		*Soga*	People organized under a number of chiefs		British		Portuguese
LIBERIA	Republic		*Mongo*	People without tribal organization		French		Spanish
LUNDA	National monarchy					Omani Arab		Turkish

THE CAPE AND DUTCH SETTLEMENT, 1652 TO 1798

When Jan van Riebeeck arrived at the Cape with fifty Dutch of both sexes in 1652 no one could have foretold that two hundred years later the refreshment station for the Dutch East India Company would have become an Afrikaner nation of two million people. The land was little occupied other than by Khoisan peoples. The Bantu, whose penetration of southern African had remained an historically mysterious process, were still moving southward. The most southerly of the Nguni group, the Xhosa, are recorded in present-day Transkei around 1550, north of the Great Kei River. By 1650 they had reached the Great Fish River, but only in 1775 did they encounter the first Dutch settlers. Thus, the present-day Transvaal, Orange Free State, and Natal, as well as the eastern Cape Province, contained a Bantu population in which there were no outsiders. Other than the Nguni group, Zulu included, there were separate Bantu elements with different linguistic traditions, notably Sotho, Tswana, and Venda. Yet another group, Griqua, formed the nucleus of "Coloured" peoples, descendants of Bantu and Boer.

By 1680 the Cape had six hundred inhabitants. In 1688 their numbers were swelled by three hundred French immigrants fleeing persecution after the revocation of the Edict of Nantes. Along with some Germans these immigrants were speedily absorbed by the Dutch and ceased to form a distinct linguistic community. Their bond was a strict Calvinism, the faith of the "elect" who formed the Afrikaner nation. By 1756 natural increase had brought their number to some five thousand; their boundaries were arid zones in which their cattle could not graze. For the same reason the Bantu cattlemen had not crossed the arid zone. It was when the two parties transgressed these zones that conflict occurred, in the form of the so-called Kaffir Wars (1779–1850).

In 1794 France invaded and seized Holland. On 7 February 1795 the prince of Orange ordered all Dutch overseas possessions to surrender authority to Great Britain, a provisional arrangement that lasted at the Cape until 1803. In this way the conflict that began between Bantu and Boer had a third element added to it.

□

SOUTHERN AFRICA, 1798 TO 1857

In 1814 Holland ceded the Cape Colony to Great Britain for a sum of 6 million pounds. The British took it over in 1815. A flood of new immigrants entered and spread eastward along the coast as far as Port Natal, now Durban. The English language now became mandatory, in administration, law, church, and school. The Anglican missions favored Coloured and Bantu peoples, and in 1834 slavery was finally abolished in all British possessions. All this was as gall to the Boers, who regarded the Coloured and Bantu as of inferior race and incapable of civilization. Continued failure to alleviate their grievances brought about the Great Trek (1836–1837), by which the Boers, with laden ox-wagons, crossed the Orange River and the Drakensberg Mountains, reaching Natal. After several severe struggles with the Zulu (see map 80), the Boers set up a capital at Pietermaritzburg for a Boer state of Natal. The British replied by annexing Natal in 1845. Indomitable, the Boers trekked yet further; and between 1852 and 1854 Britain gave grudging recognition to two Boer republics, the Orange and the Transvaal. A final,

most adventurous, trek was the famous Thirstland trek, which took a small nucleus of Boers into present-day Namibia in 1857.

Among the Bantu also a dramatic change had taken place. In 1807 Chaka, the son of a minor Nguni chief, formed an entirely new tribal grouping which he called *Zulu* (Heaven). At this epoch the Nguni and other southern Bantu had little institutional organization. Chaka established a most severely disciplined military organization of a kind hitherto unknown. By 1828 he had conquered all of Natal, killing old men and children and carrying off marriageable women and young adults. Thus a new nation was generated, with offshoots in Gaza (south Mozambique) and among the still wandering Ndebele. A further party of Nguni migrated northward as far as Lake Malawi, and some of them finally reached the present Tanzania. In the resulting chaos displaced Tswana and Sotho fled, forming separate states, now Botswana and Lesotho. These were made British protectorates in 1884, with Swaziland added in 1885.

□

62 THE CAPE AND DUTCH SETTLEMENT, 1652 TO 1798

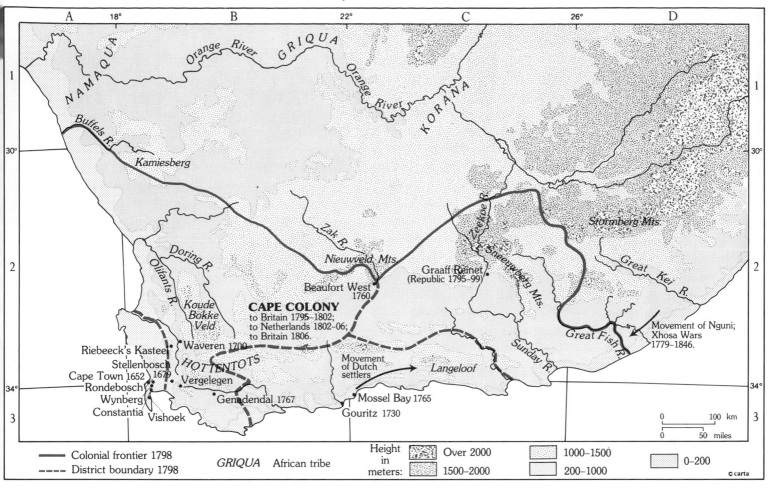

NAMAQUA

Orange River

GRIQUA

Orange River

KORANA

Buffels R.

Kamiesberg

Stormberg Mts

Doring R.

Oliliants R.

Zak R.

Nieuwveld Mts

E. Sneeuwberg Mts

Zeekoe R.

Great Kei R.

Graaff Reinet
(Republic 1795-99)

Beaufort West
1760

Koude
Bokke
Veld

CAPE COLONY
to Britain 1795-1802;
to Netherlands 1802-06;
to Britain 1806.

HOTTENTOTS

Riebeeck's Kasteel
Stellenbosch
1679
Cape Town 1652
Rondebosch
Wynberg
Constantia   Vishoek

Waveren 1700

Vergelegen

Genadendal 1767

Movement
of Dutch
settlers

Langeloof

Sunday R.

Great Fish R.

Movement of Nguni;
Xhosa Wars
1779-1846.

Mossel Bay 1765
Gouritz 1730

0	100 km
0	50 miles

—— Colonial frontier 1798
- - - District boundary 1798

GRIQUA African tribe

Height
in
meters:

	Over 2000		1000-1500
	1500-2000		200-1000

| 0-200 |

© carta

63 SOUTHERN AFRICA, 1798 TO 1857

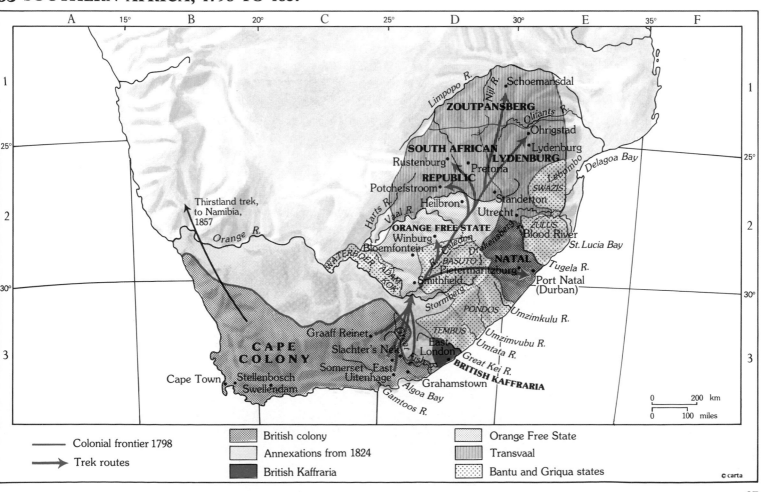

Limpopo R.

Nijl R.

Schoemansdal

ZOUTPANSBERG

Olifants R.

Ohrigstad

SOUTH AFRICAN

Lydenburg

Rustenburg

Pretoria

LYDENBURG

Delagoa Bay

Thirstland trek,
to Namibia,
1857

REPUBLIC

Potchefstroom

Lebombo

SWAZIS

Harts R.

Vaal R.

Heilbron

Standerton

Utrecht

Orange R.

ORANGE FREE STATE

Winburg

Bloemfontein

Coledon R.

Blood River

ZULUS

St. Lucia Bay

WATERBOER
ADAM
KOK

BASUTO

Smithfield

NATAL

Pietermaritzburg

Tugela R.

Port Natal
(Durban)

Stormberg

PONDOS

Umzimkulu R.

CAPE
COLONY

Graaff Reinet

TEMBUS

Umzimvubu R.

Umtata R.

Slachter's Nek

East
London

Great Kei R.

Cape Town

Stellenbosch

Swellendam

Somerset
East

Uitenhage

BRITISH KAFFRARIA

Grahamstown

Algoa Bay

Gamtoos R.

0	200 km
0	100 miles

—— Colonial frontier 1798
→ Trek routes

	British colony		Orange Free State
	Annexations from 1824		Transvaal
	British Kaffraria		Bantu and Griqua states

© carta

THE EXPANSION OF SOUTH AFRICA

In 1857 Britain made Natal a self-governing crown colony. A minority of Boers migrated to the Orange Free State. Britain's aim was not to extend Cape Colony any further than could be helped. In response to challenge, Britain had vacillated, and was now responsible for Cape Colony, British Kaffraria, and Natal. There were two Boer territories. Administrative unity had been fractured and fragmented.

Britain tried to keep out of Boer affairs, but it proved impossible. At once the Boers sought mediation in a conflict with the Sotho. In 1858 governor Sir George Grey proposed federation. The Parliament of the Orange Free State requested "union or alliance" with Cape Colony, but was ignored. Some of the difficulty was resolved when Basutoland was annexed to Cape Colony in 1871.

In 1869 gold was found in commercial quantities in the Transvaal, and in 1870 the first diamonds were mined. Prospectors flocked to Kimberley, Barberton, and Johannesburg. A pastoral community was transformed overnight into an industrial economy with a new population, modern, progressive, and thus antipathetic to the Boer Calvinists, whose ethos was largely seventeenth century.

In 1872 Cape Colony was granted self-government. In Transvaal there was war and anarchy, and the Boers looked to Britain for help. Forty thousand Zulu threatened Natal and Transvaal, and led to war in 1879. Finally, after much hesitation the British government determined to annex Transvaal and, having regard to the great mineral wealth, to ignore Boer insistence on independence. Thus the first Anglo-Boer War broke out in December 1880.

Britain took Bechuanaland (Botswana) and part of Zululand in 1886, Nyasaland (Malawi) in 1889, Southern Rhodesia (Zimbabwe) in 1890, Swaziland in 1893, Pondoland in 1894, and Northern Rhodesia (Zambia) in 1895. The Boer Republics were now encircled, and friction between Boer and Briton led to war. Fewer in number and ill-equipped, the Boers showed themselves masters of guerilla war, and only by a scorched-earth policy did Lord Kitchener overcome them in 1901.

The Peace of Vereeniging (31 May 1901) marked the end of a series of wars. The Boers were given representative government and funds to restock their farms. Britain acquired sovereignty and the gold and diamond fields. On 31 May 1910 the Union of South Africa became a federal state, and on 1 July, a self-governing dominion within the British Empire.

In World War I the South Africans speedily seized German Southwest Africa and put down a German rising in Transvaal. The skill of the German general prevented them taking German East Africa (Tanzania) until 1918. The African National Congress had been founded in 1913; now a new African élite was emerging. The Union drew African labor from the surrounding countries. The pass laws and the Union's refusal to recognize black trade unions were bitterly resented. Africans could not ignore the promise of independence to the French African colonies in 1944, while the independence of Burma, Ceylon, India, Israel, and Pakistan spoke its own lesson.

After 1948 the term *apartheid* — created in 1929 to mean separate black and white development — came to mean Afrikaner dominance in a system with autonomous but economically dependent African states. This the British prime minister Harold Macmillan condemned in his "wind of change" speech in February 1960. The African demonstration and their massacre at Sharpeville on 21 March was the first of a long series. In spite of British attempts at conciliation, after a white plebiscite South Africa withdrew from the British Commonwealth in 1961.

African protest has not diminished and has compelled certain reforms. Riots at Soweto in 1976 forced the government to rescind an order making Afrikaans compulsory in Bantu schools. The Immorality Act (forbidding carnal knowledge between whites and nonwhites), the Native (Urban Areas) Consolidation Act and the Resettlement (Western Areas) Act were repealed. Even the Dutch Reformed Church, the bastion of Afrikanerdom, had to acknowledge racial equality. But deep-rooted bitterness persisted as a result of police brutality, indiscriminate beatings, unexplained deaths of political detainees, lower quality African education, and inferior housing. By 1989, wages for a white remained thirteen times those for a black. The relative poverty of the Bantustans of Transkei, Ciskei, and Bophuthatswana, argues that an end must be made of a system reprehended by every moral and civilized nation. ☐

64 THE EXPANSION OF SOUTH AFRICA, 1857 TO 1881

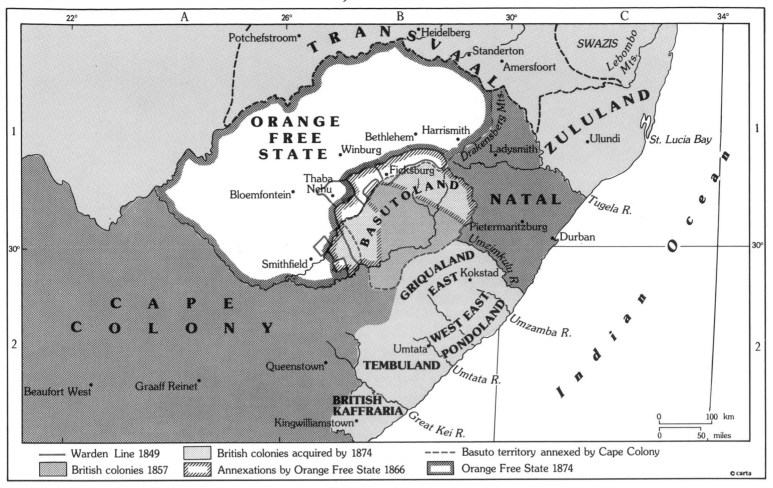

Warden Line 1849

British colonies 1857

British colonies acquired by 1874

Annexations by Orange Free State 1866

Basuto territory annexed by Cape Colony

Orange Free State 1874

© carta

65 SOUTH AFRICA, FROM THE LATE 19TH CENTURY

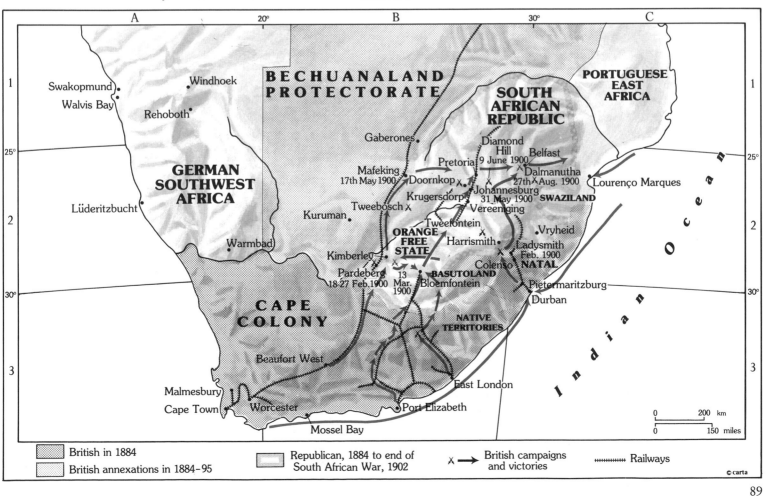

British in 1884

British annexations in 1884-95

Republican, 1884 to end of South African War, 1902

British campaigns and victories

Railways

© carta

CHRISTIAN MISSIONS, FROM THE 16TH CENTURY

The Christian religion is a missionary religion because of the express command of its founder: "Go and make disciples of all nations, baptizing them in the name of the Father and of the Son and the Holy Spirit, and teaching them to obey everything I have commanded you" (Matt. 28:19–20).

Chaplains, usually Franciscans, generally accompanied the Portuguese voyages of the fifteenth century. The church, beleaguered by the Ottoman Turks in northern Africa and the Levant, was unprepared for the great discoveries of the end of the fifteenth century, and then torn by schism in the sixteenth. In the Indian Ocean Franciscans, quickly followed by other religious orders, established themselves in Goa by 1509. By the following year a cathedral had been built from which missionaries went out as far as China and Georgia, and by midcentury to Mozambique. In eastern Africa the first missions were set up in 1596. Goa had given military aid in Ethiopia in 1543, and a mission set up in 1555 made little headway as a result of its unconciliatory attitude to the Ethiopian Coptic Church. It was expelled in 1640. In 1698 the Augustinians similarly were forced to leave Mombasa. In western Africa the earliest missions were eventually abortive. Only in Angola to which the first African bishop was ordained, were any real roots put down — in that case because of the close connection of Catholicism with the royal family.

Not until 1622 did Rome take a new step. A Sacred Congregation for the Propagation of the Faith (commonly called Propaganda) was set up to promote and coordinate missions. A college was established to serve it in 1627. In 1658 the first specifically missionary society, the Société des Missions Etrangères, was established in Paris. Its first article of association spoke categorically of the formation of local clergy in the mission lands. Principally these activities were in lands subject to Portugal and Spain. Among the Orthodox the Greeks lay paralyzed under the Ottoman Turks; the Russians took no part outside their newly occupied territories. Among Protestants, the Danes and Dutch began missionary activity as they secured footholds in Africa and elsewhere; among Anglicans a Society for the Propagation of the Gospel in Foreign Parts was founded in 1701, but during the eighteenth century its principal efforts were directed to the needs of Anglicans in America and the West Indies. Not until the end of that century did other English denominations, such as the Baptist and Methodist, begin to take part. In 1804 a British and Foreign Bible Society was founded, by a committee of Anglicans and Free Churchmen, with the object of making the Bible available in every tongue.

Although the process was not completed until late in the century by what is known as "the scramble for Africa," the nineteenth century as a whole was marked by the advance of imperialism. Thus at different times Belgium, Britain, France, Germany, Italy, Portugal, and Spain carved up Africa, Christian missions sometimes preceding them or following in their wake. Religion apart; the effect of these missions was to bring material skills and knowledge to less evolved peoples, in the same way that earlier missionaries had brought civilization to Europe. This was not without opposition from local rulers or from others with entrenched interests such as the influential *waganga*, the medicine men of East Africa, who are already recorded in the twelfth century. The departure of the colonial powers and the creation of genuinely local churches ruled by African bishops and pastors such as the Société des Missions Entrangères has engendered a greater adaptation of the Christian faith to African cultures. Nevertheless in many areas the ancient gods live on, and in others, long converted to Islam (albeit often syncretically), no headway has been made by the church.

□

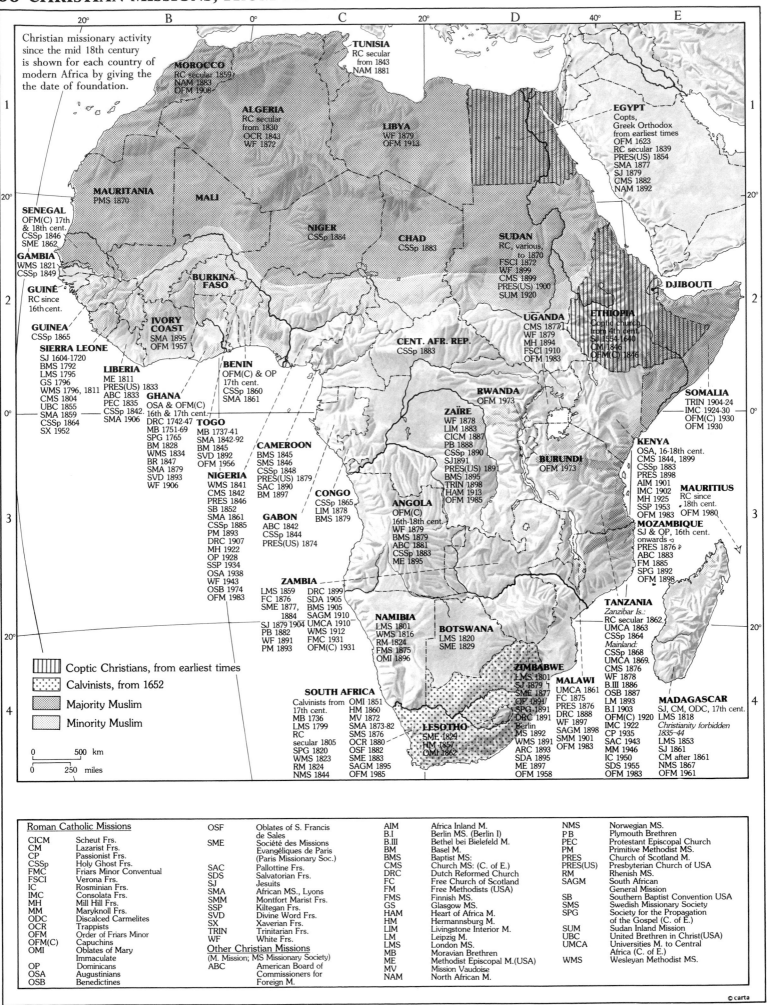

Christian missionary activity since the mid 18th century is shown for each country of modern Africa by giving the the date of foundation.

MOROCCO
RC secular 1859
NAM 1883
OFM 1908

TUNISIA
RC secular from 1843
NAM 1881

ALGERIA
RC secular from 1830
OCR 1843
WF 1872

LIBYA
WF 1879
OFM 1913

EGYPT
Copts, Greek Orthodox from earliest times
OFM 1623
RC secular 1839
PRES(US) 1854
SMA 1877
SJ 1879
CMS 1882
NAM 1892

MAURITANIA
PMS 1870

MALI

SENEGAL
OFM(C) 17th & 18th cent.
CSSp 1846
SME 1862

GAMBIA
WMS 1821
CSSp 1849

GUINÉ
RC since 16th cent.

GUINEA
CSSp 1865

NIGER
CSSp 1884

CHAD
CSSp 1883

SUDAN
RC, various, to 1870
FSCI 1872
WF 1899
CMS 1899
PRES(US) 1900
SUM 1920

BURKINA FASO

SIERRA LEONE
SJ 1604-1720
BMS 1792
LMS 1795
GS 1796
WMS 1796, 1811
CMS 1804
UBC 1855
SMA 1859
CSSp 1864
SX 1952

LIBERIA
ME 1811
PRES(US) 1833
ABC 1833
PEC 1835
CSSp 1842
SMA 1906

IVORY COAST
SMA 1895
OFM 1957

GHANA
OSA & OFM(C) 16th & 17th cent.
DRC 1742-47
MB 1751-69
SPG 1765
BM 1828
WMS 1834
BR 1847
SMA 1879
SVD 1893
WF 1906

TOGO
MB 1737-41
SMA 1842-92
BM 1845
SVD 1892
OFM 1956

BENIN
OFM(C) & OP 17th cent.
CSSp 1860
SMA 1861

CAMEROON
BMS 1845
SMS 1846
CSSp 1848
PRES(US) 1879
SAC 1890
BM 1897

NIGERIA
WMS 1841
CMS 1842
PRES 1846
SB 1852
SMA 1861
CSSp 1885
PM 1893
DRC 1907
MH 1922
OP 1928
SSP 1934
OSA 1938
WF 1943
OSB 1974
OFM 1983

GABON
ABC 1842
CSSp 1844
PRES(US) 1874

CONGO
CSSp 1865
LIM 1878
BMS 1879

CENT. AFR. REP.
CSSp 1883

UGANDA
CMS 1877
WF 1879
MH 1894
FSCI 1910
OFM 1983

RWANDA
OFM 1973

ZAÏRE
WF 1878
LIM 1883
CICM 1887
PB 1888
CSSp 1890
SJ 1891
PRES(US) 1891
BMS 1895
TRIN 1898
HAM 1913
OFM 1985

BURUNDI
OFM 1973

ETHIOPIA
Coptic church from 4th cent.
SJ 1554-1640
OM 1846
OFM(C) 1846

DJIBOUTI

SOMALIA
TRIN 1904-24
IMC 1924-30
OFM(C) 1930
OFM 1930

KENYA
OSA, 16-18th cent.
CMS 1844, 1899
CSSp 1883
PRES 1898
AIM 1901
IMC 1902
MH 1925
SSP 1953
OFM 1983

MAURITIUS
RC since 18th cent.
OFM 1980

ANGOLA
OFM(C) 16th-18th cent.
WF 1879
BMS 1879
ABC 1881
CSSp 1883
ME 1895

MOZAMBIQUE
SJ & OP, 16th cent. onwards
PRES 1876
ABC 1883
FM 1885
SPG 1892
OFM 1898

ZAMBIA
LMS 1859
FC 1876
SME 1877, 1884
SJ 1879 1904
PB 1882
WF 1891
PM 1893
DRC 1899
SDA 1905
BMS 1905
SAGM 1910
UMCA 1910
WMS 1912
FMC 1931

NAMIBIA
LMS 1801
WMS 1816
RM 1824
FMS 1875
OMI 1896

BOTSWANA
LMS 1820
SME 1829

TANZANIA
Zanzibar Is.:
RC secular 1862
UMCA 1863
CSSp 1864
Mainland:
CSSp 1868
UMCA 1869
CMS 1876
WF 1878
B.III 1886
OSB 1887
LM 1893
B.I 1903
OFM(C) 1920
IMC 1922
CP 1935
SAC 1943
MM 1946
IC 1950
SDS 1955
OFM 1983

MADAGASCAR
SJ, CM, ODC, 17th cent.
LMS 1818
Christianity forbidden 1835-44
LMS 1853
SJ 1861
CM after 1861
NMS 1867
OFM 1961

ZIMBABWE
LMS 1801
SJ 1879
SME 1877
CP 1891
SPG 1891
DRC 1891
Berlin MS 1892
WMS 1891
ARC 1893
SDA 1895
ME 1897
OFM 1958

MALAWI
UMCA 1861
FC 1875
PRES 1876
DRC 1888
WF 1897
SAGM 1898
SMM 1901
OFM 1983

SOUTH AFRICA
Calvinists from 17th cent.
MB 1736
LMS 1799
RC secular 1805
SPG 1820
WMS 1823
RM 1824
NMS 1844
OMI 1851
HM 1860
MV 1872
SMA 1873-82
SMS 1876
OCR 1880
OSF 1882
SME 1883
SAGM 1895
OFM 1985

LESOTHO
SME 1829
HM 1857
OMI 1862

Legend

▥	Coptic Christians, from earliest times
▦	Calvinists, from 1652
▓	Majority Muslim
░	Minority Muslim

0 — 500 km
0 — 250 miles

Roman Catholic Missions

CICM	Scheut Frs.
CM	Lazarist Frs.
CP	Passionist Frs.
CSSp	Holy Ghost Frs.
FMC	Friars Minor Conventual
FSCI	Verona Frs.
IC	Rosminian Frs.
IMC	Consolata Frs.
MH	Mill Hill Frs.
MM	Maryknoll Frs.
ODC	Discalced Carmelites
OCR	Trappists
OFM	Order of Friars Minor
OFM(C)	Capuchins
OMI	Oblates of Mary Immaculate
OP	Dominicans
OSA	Augustinians
OSB	Benedictines
OSF	Oblates of S. Francis de Sales
SME	Société des Missions Evangéliques de Paris (Paris Missionary Soc.)
SAC	Pallottine Frs.
SDS	Salvatorian Frs.
SJ	Jesuits
SMA	African MS., Lyons
SMM	Montfort Marist Frs.
SSP	Kiltegan Frs.
SVD	Divine Word Frs.
SX	Xaverian Frs.
TRIN	Trinitarian Frs.
WF	White Frs.

Other Christian Missions
(M. Mission; MS Missionary Society)

ABC	American Board of Commissioners for Foreign M.
AIM	Africa Inland M.
B.I	Berlin MS. (Berlin I)
B.III	Bethel bei Bielefeld M.
BM	Basel M.
BMS	Baptist MS:
CMS	Church MS: (C. of E.)
DRC	Dutch Reformed Church
FC	Free Church of Scotland
FM	Free Methodists (USA)
FMS	Finnish MS.
GS	Glasgow MS.
HAM	Heart of Africa M.
HM	Hermannsburg M.
LIM	Livingstone Interior M.
LM	Leipzig M.
LMS	London MS.
MB	Moravian Brethren
ME	Methodist Episcopal M.(USA)
MV	Mission Vaudoise
NAM	North African M.
NMS	Norwegian MS.
PB	Plymouth Brethren
PEC	Protestant Episcopal Church
PM	Primitive Methodist MS.
PRES	Church of Scotland
PRES(US)	Presbyterian Church of USA
RM	Rhenish MS.
SAGM	South African General Mission
SB	Southern Baptist Convention USA
SMS	Swedish Missionary Society
SPG	Society for the Propagation of the Gospel (C. of E.)
SUM	Sudan Inland Mission
UBC	United Brethren in Christ(USA)
UMCA	Universities M. to Central Africa (C. of E.)
WMS	Wesleyan Methodist MS.

© carta

EUROPEAN EXPLORATION IN AFRICA, 1768 TO 1854

In the age of Enlightenment attention became directed also to geographical discovery. Especially was this encouraged by Sir Joseph Banks, president of the Royal Society from 1778 until 1813. In France this society was paralleled by the Société des Amis des Noirs. In London it was of particular interest to men in the city, commercial magnates and shippers eager to sidestep the Portuguese and Dutch, and to trade in tea, coffee, cocoa, tobacco, sugar, spices, ivory, copal, and whatever other tropical products there might be. As to slaves, Liverpool and Bristol and the western ports dominated that trade. The Association for Promoting the Discovery of the Interior Parts of Africa, founded in 1788, had its French counterpart in Napoleon's Expédition d'Egypte (1798–1801), which was accompanied by three commissions of scholars, absorbed all French resources, and published a giant *Description d'Egypte*. There were nine volumes, four on antiquity, three on modern Egypt, and two on natural history. With nine hundred plates and four thousand drawings, it was the most comprehensive work ever undertaken at that time.

Some earlier work had come from Portuguese sources. Giovanni Battista Ramusio's *Delle Navigationi e Viaggi* (Venice, 1550) describes a Portuguese embassy to Ethiopia in 1520. João de los Santos, *Ethiopia Oriental* (1607), a work by the Portuguese Dominican has a misleading title, for it includes not only Ethiopia but a brilliant survey of the eastern coast of Africa as far as Mozambique. By contrast, two later French writers, Guillaume Delisle (1675–1726) and Jean-Batiste Bourguignon d'Anville (1697–1782), exhibit profound ignorance, even making the Niger flow east from Lake Chad.

The first British traveler of real consequence was a Scot, James Bruce of Kinnaird. He went to Ethiopia in 1768, was received at Court, and saw the source of the Blue Nile. For all his romantic descriptions, his astronomical observations contributed to Ethiopian topography. After various setbacks the Association sent Daniel Houghton to the Gambia and James Watt and Matthew Winterbottom to Futa Jallon and the river Nuñez in 1794. Mungo Park reached Segu in the same year, and the Niger itself in 1796. He confirmed what Houghton had reported, that the Niger flowed west, not east. Contemporaneously, William Browne documented the region of Assyut in 1793–1796. In 1798 Friedrich Hornemann visited Siwa, Augila, and Murzuk for the Association. Unfortunately, his second journey ended with his death from dysentery. The Portuguese Lacerda explored the route from Tete to south of Lake Tanganyika, the first such journey reported since that of Gaspar Bocarro in 1616.

There was much ill luck. In 1805 Mungo Park, this time with the support of the British government, was sent to determine the course of the Nile, and was drowned near Bussa. Disaster also overtook James Tuckey in 1816.

In 1818 Gaspard-Théodore Mollien, a French naval officer, visited Futa Jallon on donkey-back to discover the source of the Gambia and other rivers. Other limited explorations were carried out in that area up to 1844. More important were the explorations carried out by Walter Oudney; Dixon Denham and Hugh Clapperton; René-Auguste Caillé; and Clapperton and Richard and John Lander; these described all western Africa as far as Lake Chad. The course of the Niger was now fully known, while to Caillé fell the honor of being the first to reach the fabled Timbuktu, a journey of great tenacity. The work of adding greater detail to knowledge of western Africa now fell to Richardson, Adolf Overweg, and Heinrich Barth, especially in the field of anthropology.

In eastern Africa, the brothers Antoine-Thomson and Arnaud-Michel d'Abbadie were in Ethiopia from 1837 to 1848 and brought back an important collection of manuscripts as well as commercial knowledge. The journeys of Johann Ludwig Krapf and Johannes Rebmann were primarily missionary in intent, as were David Livingstone's early journeys. Nevertheless they shared with others a perceived commercial and investigative purpose coupled with a scholarly quest for knowledge, such as was the motive of Richard Burton and John Speke on their first journey, from Berbera to Harar and then back to Zaila.

□

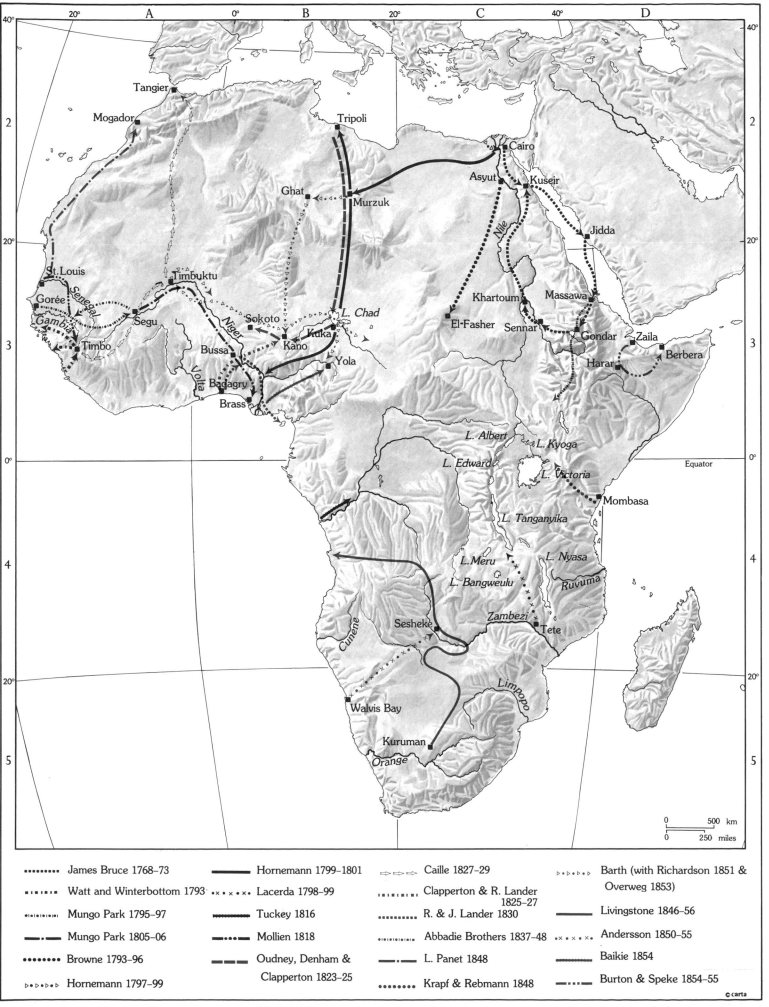

•••••••• James Bruce 1768–73	——— Hornemann 1799–1801	⇨⇨⇨ Caille 1827–29	▷•▷•▷ Barth (with Richardson 1851 & Overweg 1853)
•–••–•• Watt and Winterbottom 1793	•×•×•×• Lacerda 1798–99	•—•—•— Clapperton & R. Lander 1825–27	
•□•□•□ Mungo Park 1795–97	▬▬▬▬ Tuckey 1816	••••••••• R. & J. Lander 1830	——— Livingstone 1846–56
—•—•— Mungo Park 1805–06	•••—••• Mollien 1818	•□•□•□• Abbadie Brothers 1837–48	•×•×•× Andersson 1850–55
•••••••• Browne 1793–96	▬ ▬ ▬ Oudney, Denham & Clapperton 1823–25	—••— L. Panet 1848	═════ Baikie 1854
▷•▷•▷ Hornemann 1797–99		•••••••• Krapf & Rebmann 1848	—••—•• Burton & Speke 1854–55

EUROPEAN EXPLORATION IN AFRICA, 1857 TO 1900

The expeditions of the first half of the century had added greatly not only to geography, but to knowledge of the languages, archaeology, medieval and later history, laws, traditions, manners and customs of the peoples of Africa. For Lord Palmerston it was an invitation to open up trade with Africans. From now on the governments of Belgium, England, France, Germany, Portugal, and the United States showed a lively interest backed by public funds. Among the intrepid and persevering men who became explorers three figures tower over all the rest: Richard Burton, the father of modern anthropology, with a knowledge of twenty-nine languages; David Livingstone, missionary and geographer, eager to open up commerce to make a road for Christianity; and Henry Morton Stanley, a journalist with a scientific and geographical bent. All without exception, both the leaders and the led, were men of exceptional courage in the face of hardship, disease, ignorance, disloyalty, and hostility. Perhaps most remarkable of all was the journey of Livingstone's dead body to the coast, borne — as his epitaph in Westminster Abbey touchingly has it — "by faithful African hands." Without African cooperation, indeed, none of these explorations would have been possible.

In western Africa the conquest of Algeria by France provoked an overtly expansionist policy which aimed at the extension of French sovereignty. By the end of the century exploration, followed by administration backed by military intervention, had joined Algeria to Senegal and then Algeria to the banks of the Zaïre (see maps 79, 85). The German expedition of Nachtigal, from Tripoli as far as Bornu and then back to Khartoum at the expense of the king of Prussia in 1869–1874, was exceptional. Scientific in intention, it was a project that benefited France politically.

Britain, with a developing colony in the Cape (see maps 64, 65), had a primary interest in the south. In 1833 the Cape of Good Hope Association for the Exploration of Central Africa was founded. Expeditions had already gone beyond the boundaries of the colony to the Orange and the Limpopo. Livingstone's first journeys were in 1846–1856, and had taken him to Lake Ngami, to the Zambezi, and to Loanda; and then back via Tete to Quelimane in Mozambique. The knowledge he acquired on these explorations convinced the British government of the utility of his labors, and he was appointed consul at Quelimane. The missionary now wore the uniform of the government servant, and an expedition was fitted out which explored the Zambezi and reached Lake Malawi. Thenceforth until his death in 1873 Livingstone devoted himself to central Africa. His outstanding achievement overshadows other contemporary but more limited expeditions in southern Africa.

The Jesuits had knowledge of the Nile sources at latest by the end of the seventeenth century, but this was not known in England. In the first half of the century some exploration of the Nile had taken place. The first major attempt was that made by Burton and Speke in 1857–1859, during which time Speke reached Lake Victoria. He confirmed that it was the source of the White Nile by a further journey in 1860.

Numerous expeditions — too numerous indeed to show on a single map — followed in which now Italians also participated. The ideas of colonial conquest that had long inspired the French had now percolated to other European nations. Not least was the work of Stanley, a Welshman who took United States citizenship. His luxuriously outfitted expedition in search of Livingstone (who was believed to be lost) was at the expense of the *New York Herald* in 1874–1877. It was a real voyage of exploration, of the Great Lakes and then of the river system of the Zaïre (Congo). Africa was crossed in 999 days. It was this journey that made Léopold of Belgium determined to seize what became the Congo State in 1884. The International Geographical Conference which took place in Brussels in 1884 had motives scarcely disguised by idealism: "to plant the flag of civilization on the soil of Central Africa and to combat the Slave Trade." The "scramble for Africa" had truly begun.

□

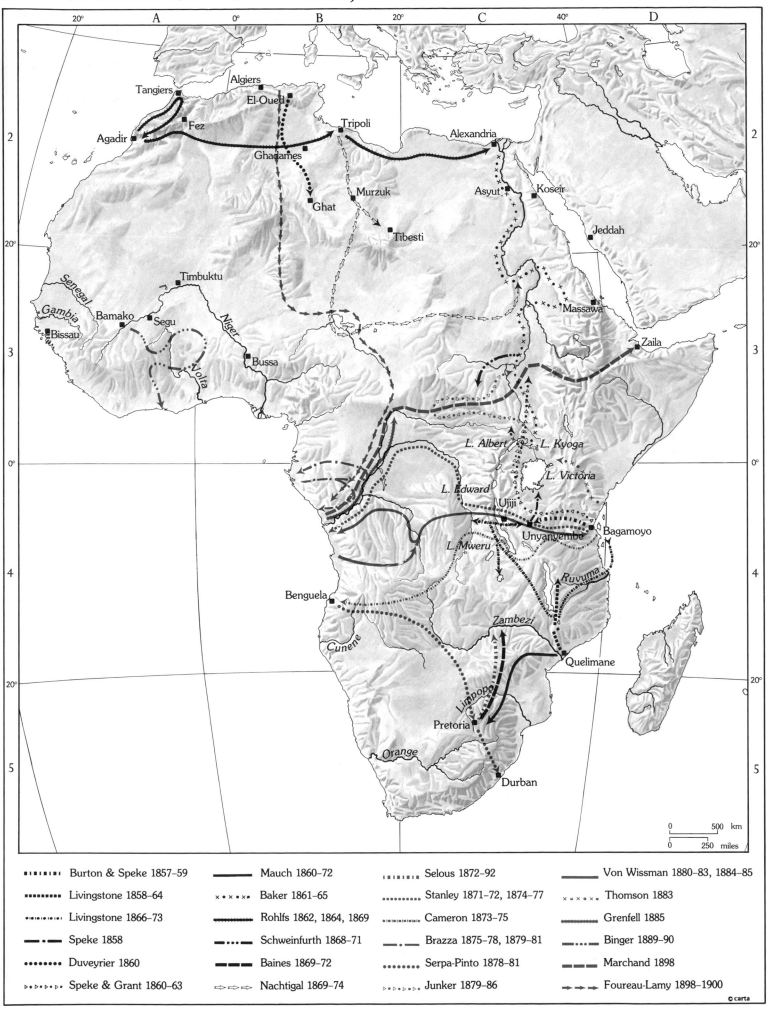

▪▪▪▪▪▪	Burton & Speke 1857–59	——	Mauch 1860–72	▪▪▪▪▪▪	Selous 1872–92	—— Von Wissman 1880–83, 1884–85
▪▪▪▪▪▪	Livingstone 1858–64	×·×·×·	Baker 1861–65	··········	Stanley 1871–72, 1874–77	×·×·×· Thomson 1883
▪▪▪·▪▪	Livingstone 1866–73	▪▪▪▪▪▪	Rohlfs 1862, 1864, 1869	·▪·▪·▪·	Cameron 1873–75	┼┼┼┼┼ Grenfell 1885
—·—·	Speke 1858	——···	Schweinfurth 1868–71	—·—·	Brazza 1875–78, 1879–81	—··— Binger 1889–90
●●●●●●	Duveyrier 1860	━ ━ ━	Baines 1869–72	●●●●●●	Serpa-Pinto 1878–81	▬ ▬ ▬ Marchand 1898
▷▷▷▷▷	Speke & Grant 1860–63	⇨⇨⇨	Nachtigal 1869–74	▷▷▷▷▷	Junker 1879–86	➝➝➝ Foureau-Lamy 1898–1900

© carta

95

EUROPEAN PENETRATION OF AFRICA, c. 1830

Napoleon's Egyptian expedition (1798–1801) is accounted as a series of military and naval disasters, yet Gamal Abdel Nasser's *Philosophy of the Revolution* acclaims it as having "broken the chains of the past." Europe had intruded not only into Egypt but into the crumbling Ottoman Empire. Napoleon's Institute of Egypt, the scholars who accompanied his expedition, had reopened doors closed since 1517. It remained, under khedive Muhammad Ali Pasha (r. 1811–1849), for Egypt to rejuvenate itself. His reforms, if they did little for the peasantry, were accomplished by officers initially recruited from Europe, but now strictly under his control. Thus, ideas percolated but without colonial intervention.

Farther west, Algeria, as Tripolitania and Tunisia, had nominal allegiance to Turkey. Although tribute was paid, the great nomadic tribes were independent in all but name. When France attempted to seize the country in 1830, they took only the seaboard; only after 1841 did conquest begin. Resistance, led by Abd el-Kader, lasted until 1847, but in Algeria the Kabyle held out until 1857, Aurès until 1849, and the southern oases until 1852–1854.

In West Africa France had a trading toehold in Senegal. Portugal had colonies in Guinea, Cape Verde, St. Tomé and Principé, Angola and Mozambique. The Portuguese had intermarried freely, and their progeny enjoyed a quasi-feudal existence. Liberia was a colony for freed slaves, shortly to be enfranchised as a republic by the United States. Apart from the small colonies of Gambia and Sierra Leone, Britain had acquired Cape Colony at the end of the Napoleonic Wars. Except as a refreshment station on the route to India, it was of no particular importance. On the east France maintained, since 1642, small trading settlements in Madagascar. Farther north, along a thin stretch of coast, the red flag of Zanzibar had flown since the fall of Fort Jesus of Mombasa in 1698. The rulers of Zanzibar appointed customs officials; direct intervention by the ruler, Sayyid Said, did not take place until 1827, and it was 1843 or 1844 before the first trading caravans penetrated the interior. He was encouraged by American, British, French, and, later, German consuls. □

EUROPEAN PENETRATION OF AFRICA, c. 1890

By 1890 the whole map of Africa had altered. To the imperial powers were added Germany, Italy, and Spain. True, the Sahara and other large tracts lay unconquered, but hardly any coastland remained free of European control, save the seaboard of Ethiopia. This was disputed with Italy which had proclaimed Eritrea a protectorate, and led to the battle of Adowa and decisive defeat for Italy, which was forced to withdraw this claim in 1896. They recovered it by 1914.

Some fundamental changes occurred. Ottoman Turkey had now virtually disappeared from the northern seaboard save in Egypt, where the khedive ruled as viceroy for the Ottoman sultan. Morocco under its sultan, Liberia under a president, and Orange Free State under a Boer president were the only independent states. The Sudan, free under the khalifa (successor) of the mahdi, was technically in rebellion against Egypt. His rule was terminated shortly by the battle of Omdurman (1896). The dominions of the Sultan of Zanzibar became a British protectorate in 1890.

On the African mainland the Sultan's possessions were split between German East Africa (later Tanganyika) and the Imperial British East Africa Company, which paid the sultan rent for a coastal strip (later Kenya). Portugal had gained nothing, but had consolidated her hold on the interior of Mozambique, agreeing on boundaries with Britain and Germany. The greatest beneficiaries of the scramble, Britain and France, were given formal recognition by the Berlin Act (1885).

It is difficult to assess how the new masters changed the lives of ordinary people. Except in the Cape Colony administrators were few. Only the rudiments of public services had been introduced, and hardly outside the capital cities. However, the long-established lines of commerce had been interrupted. In the new dispensation economic boundaries had been wholly ignored. No less serious, and potentially troublesome was that ethnic boundaries had also been disregarded, and often were no more than lines arbitrarily drawn upon inaccurate maps. □

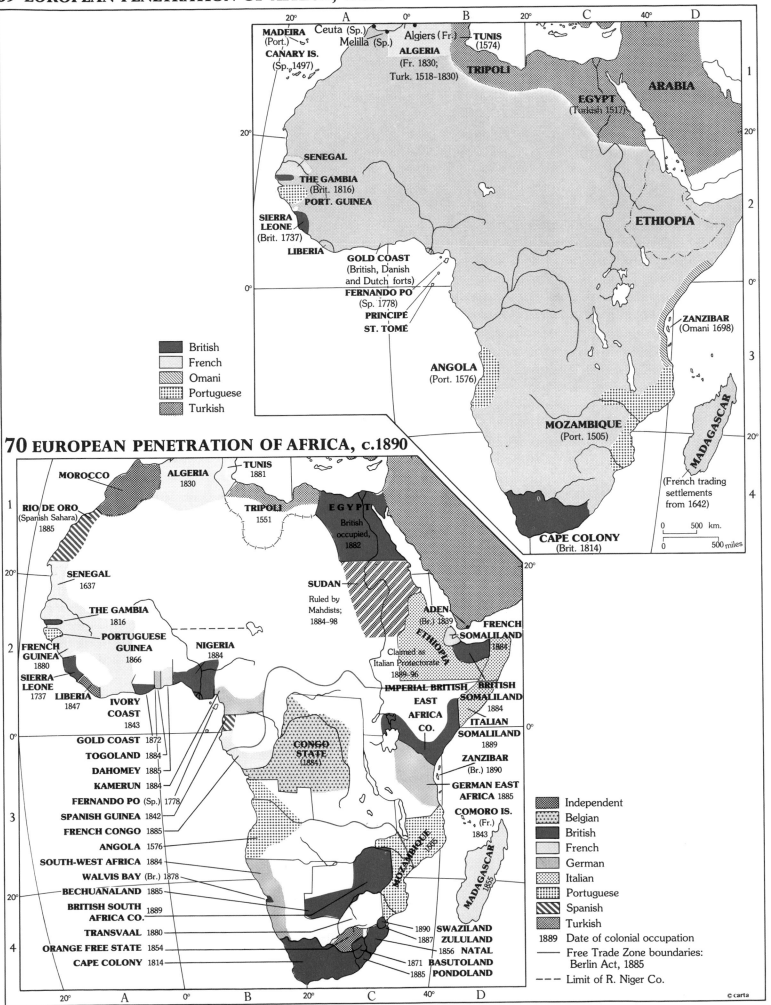

69 EUROPEAN PENETRATION OF AFRICA, c.1830

MADEIRA (Port.)
Ceuta (Sp.)
Melilla (Sp.)
Algiers (Fr.)
TUNIS (1574)
CANARY IS. (Sp. 1497)
ALGERIA (Fr. 1830; Turk. 1518–1830)
TRIPOLI
ARABIA
EGYPT (Turkish 1517)

SENEGAL
THE GAMBIA (Brit. 1816)
PORT. GUINEA
SIERRA LEONE (Brit. 1737)
LIBERIA
GOLD COAST (British, Danish and Dutch forts)
FERNANDO PO (Sp. 1778)
PRINCIPÉ
ST. TOMÉ

ETHIOPIA

ZANZIBAR (Omani 1698)

ANGOLA (Port. 1576)

MOZAMBIQUE (Port. 1505)

MADAGASCAR
(French trading settlements from 1642)

CAPE COLONY (Brit. 1814)

	British
	French
	Omani
	Portuguese
	Turkish

0   500 km.
0   500 miles

70 EUROPEAN PENETRATION OF AFRICA, c.1890

MOROCCO
ALGERIA 1830
TUNIS 1881
RIO DE ORO (Spanish Sahara) 1885
TRIPOLI 1551
EGYPT British occupied, 1882

SENEGAL 1637
THE GAMBIA 1816
PORTUGUESE GUINEA 1866
FRENCH GUINEA 1880
SIERRA LEONE 1737
LIBERIA 1847
IVORY COAST 1843
NIGERIA 1884
SUDAN Ruled by Mahdists; 1884–98
ADEN (Br.) 1839
FRENCH SOMALILAND 1884
ETHIOPIA Claimed as Italian Protectorate 1889–96
IMPERIAL BRITISH EAST AFRICA CO.
BRITISH SOMALILAND 1884
ITALIAN SOMALILAND 1889

GOLD COAST 1872
TOGOLAND 1884
DAHOMEY 1885
KAMERUN 1884
FERNANDO PO (Sp.) 1778
SPANISH GUINEA 1842
FRENCH CONGO 1885
CONGO STATE (1884)
ZANZIBAR (Br.) 1890
GERMAN EAST AFRICA 1885
COMORO IS. (Fr.) 1843

ANGOLA 1576
SOUTH-WEST AFRICA 1884
WALVIS BAY (Br.) 1878
BECHUANALAND 1885
BRITISH SOUTH AFRICA CO.
TRANSVAAL 1880
ORANGE FREE STATE 1854
CAPE COLONY 1814
MOZAMBIQUE
MADAGASCAR 1885

1890 SWAZILAND
1887 ZULULAND
1856 NATAL
1871 BASUTOLAND
1885 PONDOLAND

	Independent
	Belgian
	British
	French
	German
	Italian
	Portuguese
	Spanish
	Turkish

1889 Date of colonial occupation
—— Free Trade Zone boundaries: Berlin Act, 1885
– – – Limit of R. Niger Co.

© carta

97

THE GROWTH OF CITIES IN AFRICA: DAR ES SALAAM

Dar es Salaam is a creation of German imperial times. It has a far older history, however, as a cluster of villages. The principal one was Mjimwema (near the present state house), a fishing village. Finds of Sassanian Islamic pottery show that fishing and agricultural villages existed here by the eighth century A.D. and possibly before. Elaborate Islamic tombs, some destroyed in the 1950s, attest a certain commercial prosperity in the seventeenth and eighteenth centuries. Ruins of a stone mosque at Msasani (fifteenth century?) attest earlier activity.

There are various explanations for Sultan Majid of Zanzibar wishing to build a palace in the land-locked harbor: a caravan terminus, a port, a commercial center, or holiday place. Building began in 1865-1866. The Sultan celebrated his foundation with a dinner for the British, French, German, and United States consuls in September 1867. Dar es Salaam then had a population of nine hundred, including African and Indian traders. Majid died in 1870. His brother and successor, Barghash, had no interest in the project, but others did. In 1877 the British began a road from Dar es Salaam to Mombasa; it had progressed 81 miles by 1881. Thus when the German East African Company set up on the mainland in 1885, it became the German capital, with four or five thousand inhabitants by 1887, with few Germans.

In the 1890s administrative buildings and residences were constructed, with a Catholic cathedral, a Lutheran church, and a casino. Beyond the German quarter an African town grew up, with an Indian trading quarter sandwiched between. The Kariakoo quarter grew out of the Carrier Corps camp built by the British in 1916. They took over the German quarter, and expanded when the Selander Bridge was built in 1930. New quarters — African, Indian, and European — were built following World War II, and when the Korean War precipitated a sisal boom. Today the former "European" quarters, built chiefly for expatriate government officials, have been taken over by their African successors. The number of Indians has lessened since independence in 1961. Today the city contains some 750,000 souls. □

THE GROWTH OF CITIES IN AFRICA: LAGOS

Lagos, capital of Nigeria, and the most important port on Africa's west coast, is a microcosm of the nation in its representative population of Nigerians and foreign traders.

The legendary founder, Ogunfunminire, is said to have been of the Yoruba royal family of Ile-Ife, with the official title Olofin Awogunjoye. There are no written sources or archaeological evidences to date what in origin was a number of fishing villages. The Portuguese are known to have visited the area in 1472; it was certainly a small state capital by 1669. About 1760 Olofin Akinshemoyin formally invited the Portuguese to trade. They brought spirits, tobacco, gunpowder, and other European trade goods in exchange for slaves for export to Brazil. Soon a trade currency of cowries facilitated a sophisticated local commerce, with a barracks capable of holding up to six thousand slaves. By the late eighteenth century the *oba* (ruler) had according to a passing sea-captain,

> rolls of tobacco, boxes of pipes, cases of gin, ankers of brandy, pieces of cloth of In-dian and European manufacture, iron bars, earthenware, a beautiful hand-organ, the bellows of which were bust; two elegant chairs of state, having rich crimson damask covers ... and two expensive sofas.

In 1861 Britain annexed Lagos island following a local dispute, from 1851, on royal succession. In 1859 Lagos had a population of five thousand; by 1880 it had some thirty seven thousand, with administrative buildings and offices, churches, barracks, schools, and a race course. By 1900 the island had a railway terminus linking it with the interior, a busy port, a hospital, electric power, roads, bridges, plans for a new water supply, and a tramway. Government grants had been given for education after 1882, and eventually a university was established. Between 1950 and 1963 the city grew to some 400,000 inhabitants, with new suburbs housing an additional 390,000. Soon the combined population reached over one million.

□

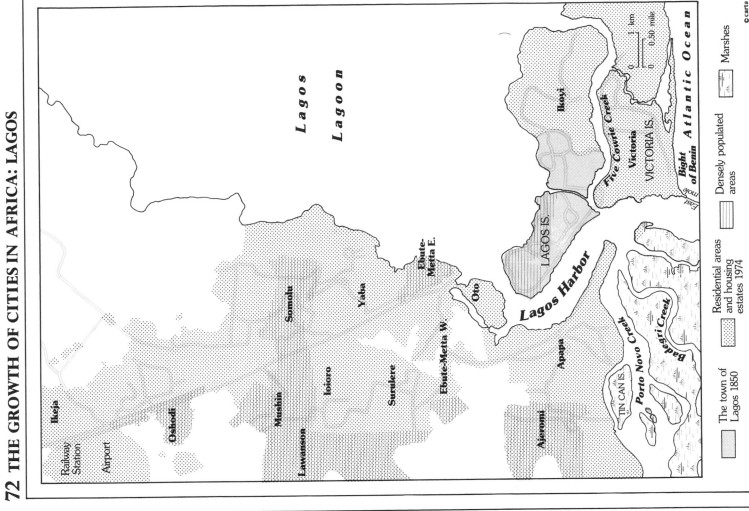

71 THE GROWTH OF CITIES IN AFRICA: DAR ES SALAAM

Indian Ocean

Sisal Estate

Oyster Bay

Msasani

Kawe

Lugalo Barracks

University

Ubungo

Manzese

Mwananyamala

Regent Estate

Kinondoni

Magomeni

Msimbazi Creek

Kigogo

Sea View

Mikocheni

Upanga

Kinondoni

City Center

Ferry

Kivukoni Docks

Harbor

Kurasini

Mtoni

Msimbazi Creek

Mzinga Creek

Kariakoo

Ilala

Keko

Buguruni

Chang'ombe

Mgulani

Kipawa

Airport

Kunduchi

Refinery

Municipal boundary 1970

New boundary

Industrial area

In 1891
In 1916
In 1934
In 1945
In 1969

1 km
0.50 mile

© carta

72 THE GROWTH OF CITIES IN AFRICA: LAGOS

Lagos Lagoon

Railway Station

Airport

Ikeja

Oshodi

Mushin

Lawanson

Somolu

Idioro

Yaba

Surulere

Ebute-Metta W.

Ebute-Metta E.

Oto

Ajeromi

Apapa

Lagos Harbor

LAGOS IS.

Ikoyi

Victoria

VICTORIA IS.

Five Cowrie Creek

East mole

Bight of Benin

Atlantic Ocean

Porto Novo Creek

Badagri Creek

TIN CAN IS.

The town of Lagos 1850

Residential areas and housing estates 1974

Densely populated areas

Marshes

1 km
0.50 mile

© carta

THE GROWTH OF CITIES IN AFRICA: CAPE TOWN

The city of Cape Town (Afrikaans, Kaapstad) is the legislative capital of the Republic of South Africa, and the capital of Cape Province. The "mother city" of South Africa, it did not come into being until the seventeenth century. Initially it was the creation of Jan van Riebeeck, who arrived with the first Dutch settlers in 1652. His intention, however, was to create not a city, but rather a refreshment station that would provide fresh water, meat, and vegetables for vessels passing to and fro between the Netherlands and the Dutch East Indies. The oldest section is in the area south of the Lion's Rump; here the castle lay close to the seashore, dominating the harbor. Between 1938 and 1945, 358 acres were reclaimed from Table Bay, and this made possible the building of the central business area and the Duncan and other docks.

The castle, which was built between 1666 and 1677, contains also the Supreme Court and part of a slave barracks. Some other seventeenth- and eighteenth-century buildings also remain. The Groote Kerk (Great Church) of 1836 replaces earlier buildings. The characteristic "Cape Dutch" gable was in fact introduced by a French architect in 1793, but the former Dutch appearance of the old city has been obscured by modern constructions.

Even in 1840 the city had a population of only about eighty thousand. From quite early times it was divided into quarters, of which the name *Malay quarter*, along with that area's mosque, is a survival. Suburban development began about 1859, and increased following the discovery of diamond fields inland in 1870, and then gold fields in 1886 (see map 74). Further stimulus to building was given by the South African War (1899–1902). The greatest enlargements, with a straggle of suburbs, belong to the twentieth century. They include a town for Coloureds, Mitchell's Plain, and several separate townships for Africans. Coloureds make up more than half of the residents of the city. Afrikaans is the home language of half of all Coloureds, whites, and Asians. A quarter are English speakers, while another quarter is at home in both languages. Among Africans a majority are Xhosa speakers.

□

THE GROWTH OF CITIES IN AFRICA: JOHANNESBURG

Johannesburg is the only great city in the world not built beside a river, a sea, or a lake. When an Australian, George Harrison, discovered gold-bearing quartz in commercial quantities in the area south and southwest of the city in 1886, there was nothing but five farms on the Witwatersrand, a rocky watershed on the Transvaal highveld. It was so named from waterfalls on the north of the ridge. Here were the five farms, of which Randjeslaagte was chosen as the site of the village of Johannesburg. Gold prospecting had begun in the area as long ago as 1852, and by the 1880s several small mines existed in the Transvaal. In the summer and autumn of 1886 several gold-bearing reefs were identified.

There followed a "gold rush" of immigrants eager to enrich themselves. No government could control the flood. A tented camp, named after Veldcornet Johannes Petrus Meyer, was laid out in a military fashion, with the help of a Diggers' Committee, later renamed the Sanitary Committee. This work accounts for the very regular layout of the center of the city and the relative narrowness of the central streets. In 1889 expansion was halted because a type of ore was found of a kind from which it was not known how to extract the gold. After a number of mines had closed down, the cyanide method of extraction was devised, and progress resumed.

By 1896 a majority of the inhabitants were English, and their wish for participation in government was a major factor in the British annexation of the Transvaal in 1900. In addition there were European minority groups — Dutch, French, Germans, Hungarians, Italians, Norwegians, Poles, Swedes, and Swiss, along with Jews from many countries. Thus 30 percent of the city's total population of approximately 1.5 million persons is of European origin, while 60 percent consists of Africans indigenous to southern Africa, and the remainder is made up of Coloureds or Indians. The city has four hundred suburbs, each segregated by color in accordance with the policy of *apartheid*. The city of Soweto, for indigenous Africans only, is twenty six square miles in extent.

□

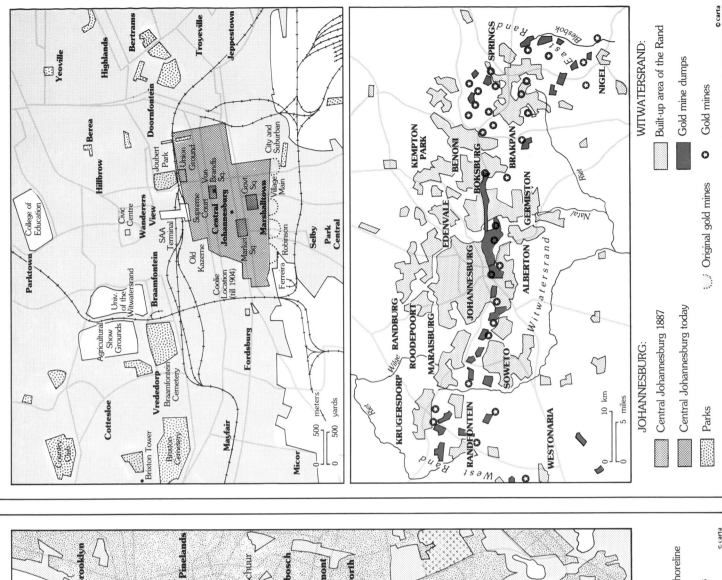

Parktown

Yeoville

Highlands

Bertrams

Troyeville

Jeppestown

Berea

Hillbrow

Doornfontein

College of Education

Wanderers View

Joubert Park

Union Ground

City and Suburban

Civic Centre

Supreme Court

Bands Sq.

Central Johannesburg

Castle Sq.

Village Main

Marshalltown

Braamfontein

SAA Terminal

Old Kazerne

Market Sq.

Robinson

Selby

Park Central

Univ. of the Witwatersrand

Coolie Location (till 1904)

Ferreira

Agricultural Show Grounds

Cottesloe

Vrededorp

Braamfontein Cemetery

Fordsburg

Country Club

Brixton Tower

Brixton Cemetery

Mayfair

Micor

500 meters
500 yards
0

WITWATERSRAND:

Built-up area of the Rand

Gold mine dumps

Gold mines

Original gold mines

SPRINGS

East Rand

Biesbok

NIGEL

KEMPTON PARK

BENONI

BRAKPAN

ROKSBURG

EDENVALE

GERMISTON

RANDBURG

JOHANNESBURG

ALBERTON

ROODEPOORT

MARAISBURG

SOWETO

Witwatersrand

Natal

Riet

Wilge

KRUGERSDORP

RANDFONTEIN

WESTONARIA

West Rand

10 km
5 miles
0

JOHANNESBURG:

Central Johannesburg 1887

Central Johannesburg today

Parks

© carta

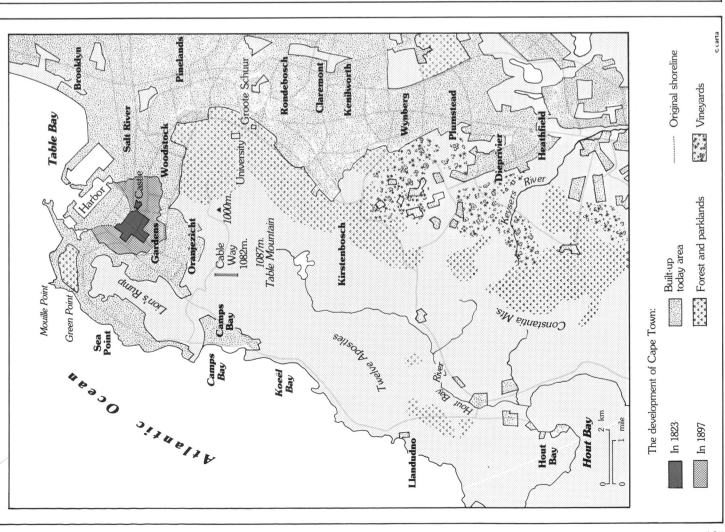

Table Bay

Brooklyn

Pinelands

Salt River

Woodstock

Groote Schuur

Rondebosch

Claremont

Kenilworth

University

Castle

Gardens

Oranjezicht

1000m.

Cable Way
1082m.

1087m.
Table Mountain

Wynberg

Plumstead

Dieprivier

Heathfield

Kirstenbosch

Keysers River

Lion's Rump

Camps Bay

Sea Point

Mouille Point

Green Point

Camps Bay

Koeël Bay

Twelve Apostles

Constantia Mts.

Hout Bay River

Hout Bay

Atlantic Ocean

Llandudno

Hout Bay

The development of Cape Town:

In 1823

In 1897

Built-up today area

Forest and parklands

Original shoreline

Vineyards

2 km
1 mile
0

© carta

101

THE BRITISH EXPEDITION TO ETHIOPIA, 1868

The British expedition to Ethiopia was neither an imperial nor a colonial project. Nothing could have been plainer than the words of the Duke of Buckingham and Chandos, colonial secretary in 1867–1868: "We want no more colonies."

About 1840 Ras Kassa of Kwara, the ruler of a small Amhara chiefdom, embarked on a career of expansion. By 1855 he had acquired all of Amhara and Shoa, and had himself recognized as Emperor Tewodros II. He then turned on the Wollo Gallas, the local people, seized Magdala, and made it his principal stronghold.

In 1860 the British consul, W. C. Plowden, a close friend of Tewodros was ordered by his home government to reside in Massawa. He was mortally wounded by a rebel; his death was avenged by Tewodros. In this action another Englishman, J. T. Bell, lost his life protecting Tewodros. In 1862 Captain C. D. Cameron was sent to Massawa as consul. In October Tewodros sent him home with a letter for Queen Victoria, which the Foreign Office simply laid to one side. The letter asked her to join in war against Islam, a request which, given the large number of Muslims in the British Empire, could hardly be agreed. It is doubtful whether the queen was ever told of it. Cameron returned to Massawa and from there visited Kassala, on the Egyptian frontier. This action, and the failure to receive an answer to his letter, angered Tewodros. In January 1864 he imprisoned Cameron and nineteen others, two Protestant missionaries included.

Britain then sent the Turkish Assyriologist Hormuzd Rassam with a reply to the letter. After some negotiation, his British delegation was allowed to proceed to Kwarata to await the arrival of Cameron and the prisoners. Cameron was shortly freed. A month later the whole party began the return journey to Massawa, but was arbitrarily arrested and imprisoned as hostages. Tewodros then sent another letter to Queen Victoria, asking for British workmen and machinery. Meanwhile, at first the hostages were well treated. Then they were sent to Magdala, put in chains, and half starved.

In the face of such disregard of diplomatic protocol, Britain determined to send a military expedition to free the hostages. Some artisans and machinery were sent, along with a message that they would be handed over to the emperor if the prisoners were released. This offer was ignored. Sir Robert Napier (later first Lord Napier of Magdala) was sent from India with 32,000 men. They landed on 7 January 1868 and marched toward Magdala. Ethiopia had long been restive or in revolt; now Tewodros's army, once over a hundred thousand men, began deserting. There was scarcely enough food for the emperor's immediate followers. He now burned his camp at Debra Tabor and moved to Magdala. His march showed extraordinary resource and engineering skill, and greatly impressed the British. At Arigie, a few miles from Magdala, he ambushed a British advance guard and compelled it to retire.

Early the following morning Tewodros sent messengers to sue for peace. They were told that if he freed all the prisoners and submitted to the queen, he would receive honorable treatment. The prisoners were liberated, and, in accordance with Ethiopian custom, Tewodros sent one thousand cattle and five hundred sheep to show that peace was conceded. Word was sent to him that this offer was accepted, but in the evening he was told that, on the contrary, the gesture had not been understood as a message of peace. Next morning he attempted to flee, but later came back.

That day, 13 April 1868, Magdala was stormed and taken, practically without loss of life on either side. However, when the British reached the imperial tent, they found that the emperor had fallen by his own hand. His object achieved, Napier lost no time in retiring, and left on 18 June 1868. The empress accompanied the British army, but died on the march. Her son Alamayahu was taken to England, because this had been his father's wish.

□

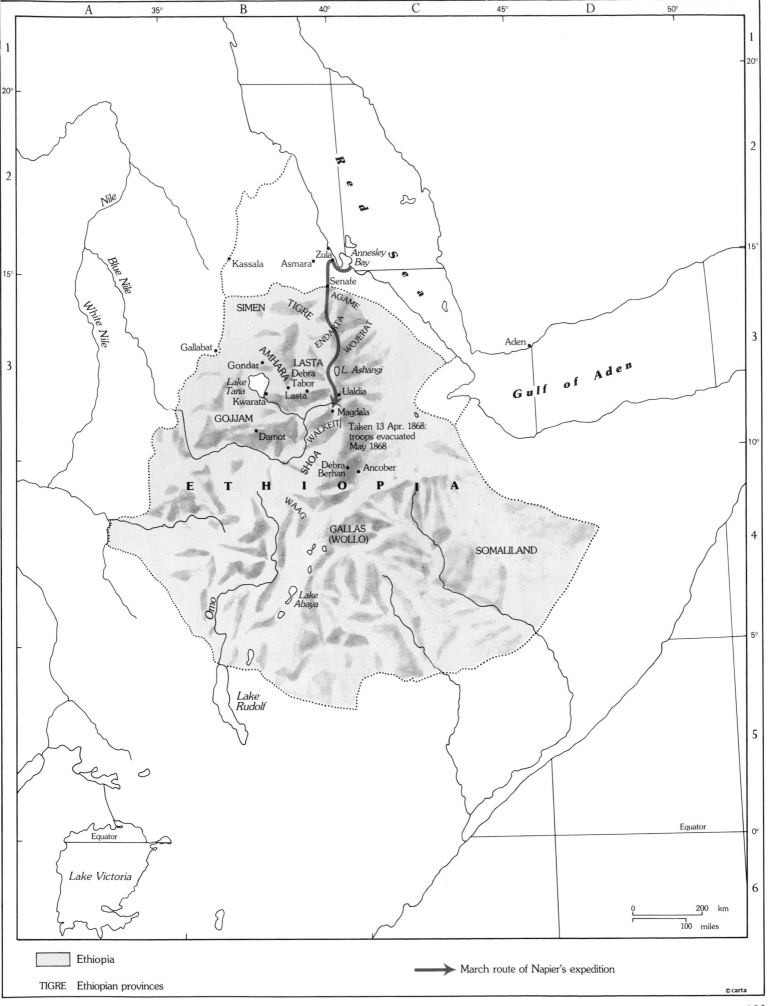

Taken 13 Apr. 1868:
troops evacuated
May 1868

| | Ethiopia |
| TIGRE | Ethiopian provinces |

⟶ March route of Napier's expedition

© carta

THE SUEZ CANAL AND WORLD SHIPPING AFTER 1869

The Suez Canal, 125 miles long, was not the first waterway to connect the Mediterranean with the Red Sea. Around 1800 B.C., under the pharaohs, a canal was built to connect the Nile with Lake Timsah, and this was extended under the Ptolemies to the Red Sea. It silted up, and was cleared by the emperor Trajan, but was again neglected under the Byzantines. The Arabs reopened it in 641–642; after the Portuguese successfully wrested the spice trade from Venice at the end of the fifteenth century, however, the Ottomans filled it up. From then on many writers speculated on the possibility of cutting through the isthmus from Port Said to Suez. Serious study began only after the French occupation of Egypt (1798–1801), but no concession was granted until the khedive (viceroy) of Egypt gave one to Ferdinand de Lesseps in 1854. This made possible the formation of the Suez Canal Company, with a ninety-nine year lease, in 1856.

Construction began in 1859. Climatic difficulties, labor troubles, and a cholera epidemic in 1865 caused the work to take ten years instead of the estimated six. The project included construction of the Sweet Water Canal from the Nile to Suez, and the Abbasiya Canal from the Nile to Port Said, in order to supply drinking water in a desert area. The peasants who were drafted into forced labor worked with picks and baskets, but Europeans later took over, operating steam dredgers and shovels. It was cheaper to flood an area and to dredge it than to dig by hand.

When it was opened by Empress Eugénie in 1869 the channel was 26 feet (8 m) deep, 72 feet (22 m) wide at the bottom, and 190 feet (58 m) wide at the surface. Every sixteen miles passing bays were constructed. Because of the narrowness and tortuous nature of the channel, ships frequently ran aground, and it was necessary to deepen and widen it. By 1967 the minimum width was 179 feet (55 m) and the minimum depth about 40 feet (12 m).

In the first year of the operation of the canal there were 486 transits; by 1966–1967 the number recorded was more than 20,000. An original transit time of forty hours was reduced to thirteen hours by 1939, partly as a result of a transit system of convoys, so that it was no longer necessary for vessels to stop in passing bays.

Following the beginning of the exploitation of oil in the Persian Gulf in 1907, the canal became not only the main artery of communication between east and west, but the main artery of the oil trade. In 1913 this amounted to 291,000 tons; by 1966 it reached 166 million tons. At first 52 percent of the canal shares were held by France and 44 percent by the khedive of Egypt, Ismail Pasha, but the khedive's extravagant habits forced him to sell his shares, which Disraeli acquired for Great Britain. This secured the strategic route to India and the Far East, and was to lead to British domination in Egypt until 1956. The canal was of crucial importance to communications during World War II. In 1956, following the British refusal to finance an additional dam above Aswan, now the Nasser Dam, President Nasser nationalized the canal thirteen years before the end of the concession. This move precipitated war, with France and Britain attacking Egypt, halted largely by United States financial intervention. War with Israel ensued in 1967, when Egypt deliberately sank vessels in the canal in order to deny it to users. It remained closed until 1975. It has declined, however, partly because high-value cargo can be transmitted more economically by aircraft, partly because of the virtual disappearance of the sea passenger trade, and partly because of the development of trade between the countries of the Far East. A further factor has been the development of laden oil tankers for which the canal is too shallow, although such tankers can pass through unladen on their return journey.

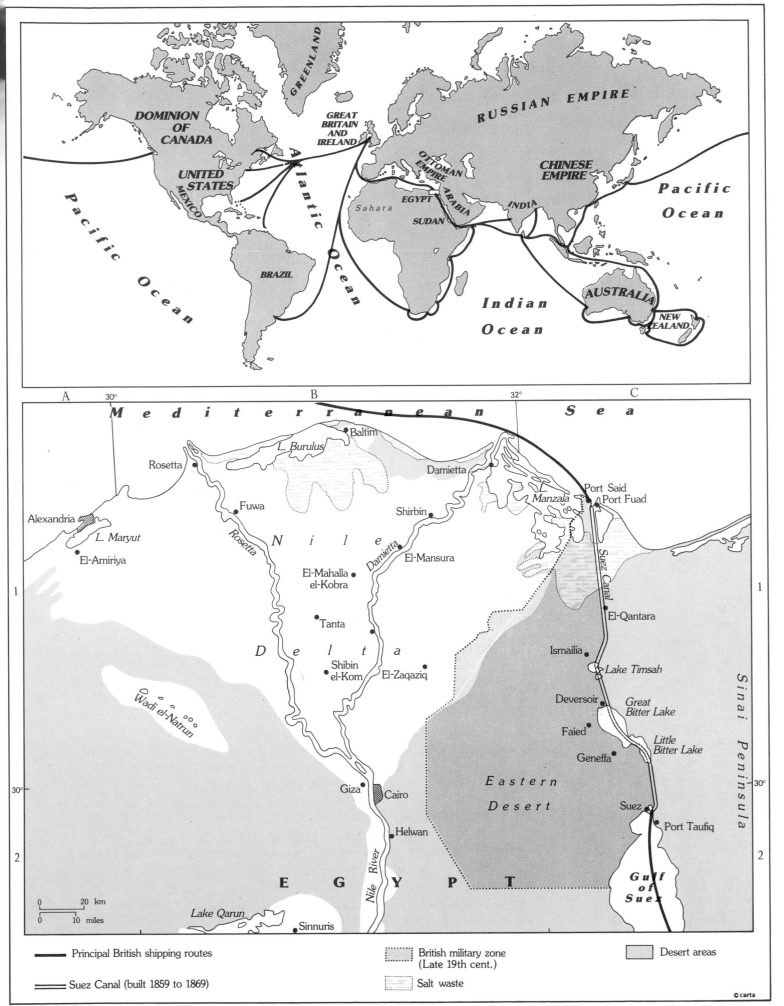

Principal British shipping routes

Suez Canal (built 1859 to 1869)

British military zone (Late 19th cent.)

Salt waste

Desert areas

© carta

THE MERINA EXPANSION IN MADAGASCAR, TO 1861

Radama I, a lively youth of talent and ability, succeeded to the Merina throne in 1810. In the same year the British took Mauritius from the French. Sir Robert Farquhar, a Scot with an instinct for diplomacy and an eye to commerce, was installed as governor. He encouraged Radama's desire to extend his kingdom to the sea, without offending the French trading centers on the east coast of Madagascar. By 1816 Farquhar had made friends with Radama and taken charge of the education of his two brother.

When the Congress of Vienna forbade the slave trade, Radama claimed that he was ruined. Farquhar's treaty of 1817 gave him a subsidy and enabled him to form an army. Within six years the eastern coast was wholly under Radama's control, and shortly the north and southern parts of the island were added as well. Expeditions in 1822 and 1824 took a section of the coast from the Sakalava. In other ways Radama was ahead of his time. He encouraged the London Missionary Society and its schools. By 1824 these had one thousand pupils; by 1828 there were twenty-three hundred, of whom a third were girls. Certain clans had used Arabic script; now Roman script was introduced. By 1827 more than four thousand Malagasy could read and write. A Scottish missionary named Cameron introduced brick making, soap making, and tanning, and taught woodwork, metalwork, and the building of mills. Radama had a handsome palace when he died on 28 July 1828.

A queen, Ranavalona I (1828–1861), succeeded. She was the cat's-paw of a plutocratic oligarchy, and a reaction took place, one determinedly anti-European, anti-Christian and isolationist in outlook. The queen was kept contented by a succession of paramours. The oligarchy enforced slavery by bringing new regions under control. By 1853, however, the old leaders were dying, and power passed into the hands of those who had received a European education. The queen died in 1861, leaving as successor Radama II, a spoiled idealist under whom government rapidly degenerated into anarchy (1861–1863). □

THE MERINA EXPANSION IN MADAGASCAR, TO 1894

In 1863 Radama II was quietly strangled with a silk scarf. Raharo, the prime minister, legitimatized his rule by marrying a member of the royal family, Rasoherina, and proclaiming her queen. A lady of resource, finding that her consort was a brutal drunkard and unfit to wield power, she had him quietly exiled. She then married his brother, Rainilalarivany, and made him prime minister. Of wholly superior character, he was already commander-in-chief and private secretary to the queen. Sadly for him, she died suddenly in 1868, so he put her cousin Ranavalona II on the throne and married her.

The new queen had had a Protestant education, and on 21 February 1869 she and the prime minister were baptized together and took Christian marriage vows. Idols were burned and the "Protestant Sunday" made compulsory — inevitably offending the converts of Catholic missionaries. A legal code was promulgated in 1868, and revised in 1881, on largely European lines, on which government was now modeled.

By slow degrees France steadily succeeded in establishing what has been called a "phantom protectorate," which became to some extent official in 1885. Finally, in 1896, Madagascar was declared a French colony. By now the Merina had nominal authority over the greatest part of the island, only some parts of the west and south being independent. The royal line had in reality failed, and authority rested in the hands of a series of prime ministers who took power as if they were shoguns. Weak at the center, and faced with armed revolts in different parts of the island, Madagascar fell into French hands like a ripe plum. It did not drop without some resistance, however, and a French cruiser shelled Fort Dauphin in 1885. In 1894 the peasantry revolted, and the French took over in the ensuing chaos. □

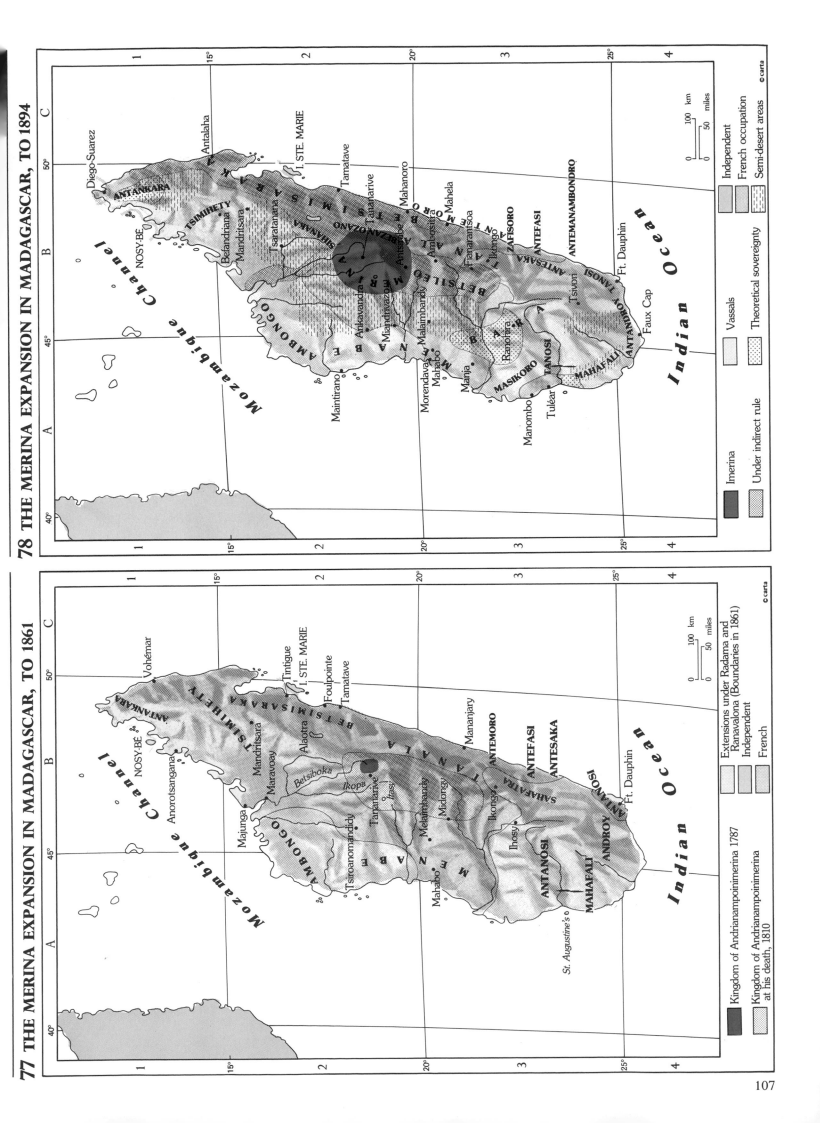

78 THE MERINA EXPANSION IN MADAGASCAR, TO 1894

Antalaha
Diego-Suarez
ANTANKARA
NOSY-BÉ
TSIMIHETY
Betandriana
Mandritsara
Saratanana
I. STE. MARIE
Tamatave
Mahanoro
Mahela
Mahanoro
Tananarive
Antsata
ANTEMANAMBONDRO
ZAFISORO
ANTEFASI
ANTESAKA
ANTEMANAMBONDRO
Ft. Dauphin
Ikongo
Fianarantsoa
Ambasitra
Ankavandra
Miandrivazo
Malaimbandy
Malambandy
Tsivori
ISONDRO
TANOSI
ANTANDROY
Faux Cap
AMBONGO
Mahabo
Morondava
Manja
MASIKORO
TANOSI
Ranohira
MAHAFALI
Manombo
Tuléar
Maintirano

Imerina
Under indirect rule
Vassals
Theoretical sovereignty
Independent
French occupation
Semi-desert areas

Mozambique Channel
Indian Ocean

100 km
50 miles

© carta

77 THE MERINA EXPANSION IN MADAGASCAR, TO 1861

Vohémar
ANTANKARA
NOSY-BÉ
Anorotsangana
TSIMIHETY
Mandritsara
Maravoay
Majunga
AMBONGO
Tsitroanomandidy
Mahabo
ANTANOSI
MAHAFALI
ANDROY
Tintigue
I. STE. MARIE
Foulpointe
Tamatave
Alaotra
BETSIMISARAHETY
Betsiboka
Ikopa
Tananarive
Ifrasi
Melambandy
Midongo
Mananjary
ANTEMORO
ANTEFASI
ANTESAKA
SAHAFATRA
Ikongo
Ihosy
MENABE
St. Augustine's
Ft. Dauphin
ANTANOSI

Kingdom of Andrianampoinimerina 1787
Kingdom of Andrianampoinimerina at his death, 1810
Extensions under Radama and Ranavalona (Boundaries in 1861)
Independent
French

Mozambique Channel
Indian Ocean

100 km
50 miles

© carta

107

PRINCIPAL AFRICAN RESISTANCE TO EUROPEAN PENETRATION

A long period of human history stretches between 1830, when the French first set foot on Algeria, until 1935, when Italy seized the Ethiopian empire, using poison gas as well as aircraft. It was, however, between 1882 and 1914 that the colonial boundaries of Africa were settled, boundaries which have scarcely changed since 1900. Map 70 shows how, by around 1890, Africa had been sliced up between the powers like a badly carved chicken, although the core of the continent was not occupied until the outbreak of World War I. Then only the Republic of Liberia and the Empire of Ethiopia remained independent. The revolutionary change took place with an extraordinary rapidity, during which time each colonial power imprinted on the region it had acquired something of its own national personality, and always its tongue as a second language. These imprints are still markedly visible.

There were various motives for resistance. Economic boundaries had been fractured; ethnic divisions had been ignored; local pride had been affronted; even religion had been contemned. Did the Germans not take dogs into the mosques on a Friday? Did they not have a policy of *Schrecklichkeit*? Were the soldiers not brutal and rapacious? Had not long-established kingdoms such as proud Ashanti been humiliated by the red-faced British? Were not poll taxes — unheard of before, now payable in coin (another innovation!) — forcing men to work for their oppressors? And so on.

Private interests also were threatened. At least in name all the colonial powers were opposed to slavery. In almost all African societies bondage was a recognized institution, and slaves themselves possessed a status recognized in customary law. The *sharia*, the canon law of Islam, reinforced this in Islamic states. In the Congo State, Arab interests, and those of the Swahili, were shattered by the ending of the slave trade; in Zanzibar plantation owners were paupered until they had readjusted themselves, if they could.

Thus were generated economic, social, and political grievances. There was also a less obvious sense of religious humiliation, often hard to define. The missionaries, Catholic and Protestant alike, despised and rejected the old religions by which men and women had regulated their lives for centuries; yet the old rituals, prayers for rain, for fertility, and for the cure of disease, were visibly not without effect in the experience of many. The pure milk of the Gospel was strong medicine, and untried. In Islamic territories, and for certain among the Muslim intelligentsia in West Africa and on the eastern African coast, there were long memories of conflict between Crescent and Cross. In many lands the Crescent had been victorious. In eastern Africa the Islamic religious confraternities quietly went underground, even forming new centers, of which the Mosque College at Lamu is a most notable example. In Sudan the Mahdi's confraternity resisted for fourteen years. There were similar manifestations in West Africa.

In some areas there was a three-cornered contestation. In Egypt modernization of the state and army had been achieved by Muhammad Ali by the recruitment of foreigners from a variety of nations. Even into the 1950s the prevailing culture was French. The British occupation of 1882, declared to be wholly temporary, had — by agreement — to be shared with the French. Friction between the two powers was not lost on the Egyptians, long versed as they were in the labyrinthine intricacies of Mamluk diplomacy and policy.

In southern Africa, Boer and Briton faced one another, and both of these in turn faced the Zulu, a people that had coalesced only in the 1820s (see map 80). The Zulu, on their part, faced other African peoples, and with mutual hostility. These confrontations had not yet been solved even in 1990, when order was still being maintained only by armed force.

These considerations are to a great extent negative. By the mid-twentieth century a new, educated African bourgeoisie was springing up. The African with an education in Europe was now referred to in Ghana as a "been-to." Yet if such Africans were honored at home, as far as Europeans were concerned they were "kept under." The higher reaches of government were inaccessible to them. It was a new humiliation which could only provoke reaction. Julius Nyerere referred to it as "the stigma of colonialism." ☐

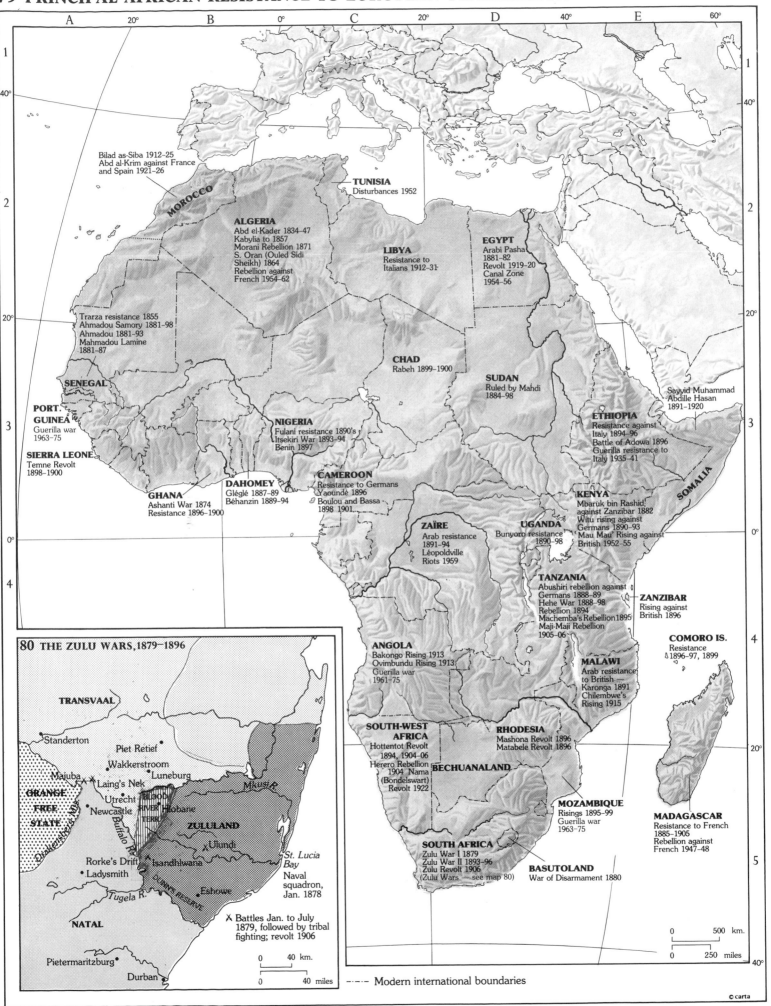

TUNISIA
Disturbances 1952

MOROCCO
Bilad as-Siba 1912–25
Abd al-Krim against France
and Spain 1921–26

ALGERIA
Abd el-Kader 1834–47
Kabylia to 1857
Morani Rebellion 1871
S. Oran (Ouled Sidi
Sheikh) 1864
Rebellion against
French 1954–62

LIBYA
Resistance to
Italians 1912–31

EGYPT
Arabi Pasha
1881–82
Revolt 1919–20
Canal Zone
1954–56

Trarza resistance 1855
Ahmadou Samory 1881–98
Ahmadou 1881–93
Mahmadou Lamine
1881–87

CHAD
Rabeh 1899–1900

SUDAN
Ruled by Mahdi
1884–98

SENEGAL

**PORT.
GUINEA**
Guerilla war
1963–75

Sayyid Muhammad
Abdille Hasan
1891–1920

ETHIOPIA
Resistance against
Italy 1894–96
Battle of Adowa 1896
Guerilla resistance to
Italy 1935–41

SIERRA LEONE
Temne Revolt
1898–1900

NIGERIA
Fulani resistance 1890's
Itsekiri War 1893–94
Benin 1897

DAHOMEY
Gléglé 1887–89
Béhanzin 1889–94

CAMEROON
Resistance to Germans
Yaoundé 1896
Boulou and Bassa
1898 1901

KENYA
Mbarūk bin Rashid
against Zanzibar 1882
Witu rising against
Germans 1890–93
Mau Mau' Rising against
British 1952–55

GHANA
Ashanti War 1874
Resistance 1896–1900

ZAÏRE
Arab resistance
1891–94
Léopoldville
Riots 1959

UGANDA
Bunyoro resistance
1890–98

SOMALIA

TANZANIA
Abushiri rebellion against
Germans 1888–89
Hehe War 1888–98
Rebellion 1894
Machemba's Rebellion 1895
Maji-Maji Rebellion
1905–06

ZANZIBAR
Rising against
British 1896

COMORO IS.
Resistance
1896–97, 1899

ANGOLA
Bakongo Rising 1913
Ovimbundu Rising 1913
Guerilla war
1961–75

MALAWI
Arab resistance
to British —
Karonga 1891
Chilembwe's
Rising 1915

**SOUTH-WEST
AFRICA**
Hottentot Revolt
1894, 1904–06
Herero Rebellion
1904 Nama
(Bondelswart)
Revolt 1922

RHODESIA
Mashona Revolt 1896
Matabele Revolt 1896

BECHUANALAND

MADAGASCAR
Resistance to French
1885–1905
Rebellion against
French 1947–48

MOZAMBIQUE
Risings 1895–99
Guerilla war
1963–75

SOUTH AFRICA
Zulu War I 1879
Zulu War II 1893–96
Zulu Revolt 1906
(Zulu Wars — see map 80)

BASUTOLAND
War of Disarmament 1880

80 THE ZULU WARS, 1879–1896

TRANSVAAL

Standerton

Piet Retief

Wakkerstroom

Majuba
Laing's Nek
Luneburg

**ORANGE
FREE
STATE**

Utrecht

Newcastle

BLOOD
RIVER
TERR.

Hlobane

Mkusia

ZULULAND

Ulundi

Rorke's Drift

Isandhlwana

Ladysmith

Eshowe

St. Lucia
Bay

Naval
squadron,
Jan. 1878

NATAL

Tugela R.

Pietermaritzburg

Durban

X Battles Jan. to July
1879, followed by tribal
fighting; revolt 1906

0   40 km.

0   40 miles

0   500 km.

0   250 miles

– – – – Modern international boundaries

© carta

THE GREAT WAR, 1914–1918: TOGO

When war was declared on 4 August 1914 the governors of the nearest allied colonies had to decide what to do about their German neighbors. At Kamina, Togo had an important radio station communicating with the South Atlantic. It was uncomfortably close for the British to the deep-water port and coaling station of Sierra Leone, strategically important for British communication with the Far East and Australasia.

Militarily Togo was insignificant. The governor had only a police force equipped with rifles dating from the Franco-Prussian War of 1870. He suggested to the British and the French that Togo be regarded as neutral so that Africans should not be demoralized by seeing Europeans fighting each other. Although between them the British and French had only 1738 men against 1500 German police, they were trained soldiers, and possessed artillery. The Allies lost no time before invading Togo from all sides. Lomé was occupied without a shot. The first battles took place along the railway line on 12 August. On 14 August the Allies advanced on the German redoubt of Kamina. They reached it on 24 August, and the Germans promptly blew the radio station up before surrendering unconditionally the following day.

□

THE KAMERUN CAMPAIGN

German Kamerun was larger than Germany, and consisted largely of thick forest. The Germans had three thousand men only, but were able to double that number in the course of eighteen months, and they faced forces many times their number. The principal difficulties of the Allies were the terrain, poor communications, and sickness. At any one time one-fifth of the men might be unfit for battle. In support the Allies claimed that they brought as many as twenty thousand porters into Kamerun.

The principal Allied objective was the deep-water port of Douala, Kamerun's chief external link. It fell on 27 September 1914. Shortly thereafter Port Victoria also fell, followed by the capital, Buéa, on 15 November. Garua, a river port on the Benue, held out until January 1916. The greatest part of the German forces then retreated to their base at Ntem, near Spanish Muni, into which they crossed on 15 February 1916 in order to seek asylum. In the north the German garrison at Mora had fortified a hill outside the town, from which it proved impossible to shift it. It surrendered only when news of the German retreat into Muni was confirmed.

□

THE SOUTH-WEST AFRICA CAMPAIGN

German Southwest Africa, now Namibia, occupied an area larger than France or Spain, but much of it was separated from the Union of South Africa by a wholly barren zone some two hundred miles wide. There are no rivers, and the lack of water limited the possibilities for warfare. On the outbreak of war the Royal Navy bombarded the German installations in Swakopmund and Lüderitz, in order to deny the use of their facilities to German naval forces operating in the South Atlantic. These installations had an added importance because the Ottoman Turks in Palestine could at any time threaten the Suez Canal and make communication difficult between east and west. Even so, substantial numbers of vessels were sunk by the Germans in the region of the Cape (see map 99).

Lüderitz was occupied without German resistance on 15 September 1914, following the landing of a South African force at Port Nolloth on 1 September and the establishment of a third South African base at Upington, on the river Orange. This force defeated the Germans on 22 October It was not until December that General Louis Botha, who had gained distinction in the Anglo-Boer War, could commence serious operations. These were concluded when the German governor surrendered in April 1915.

□

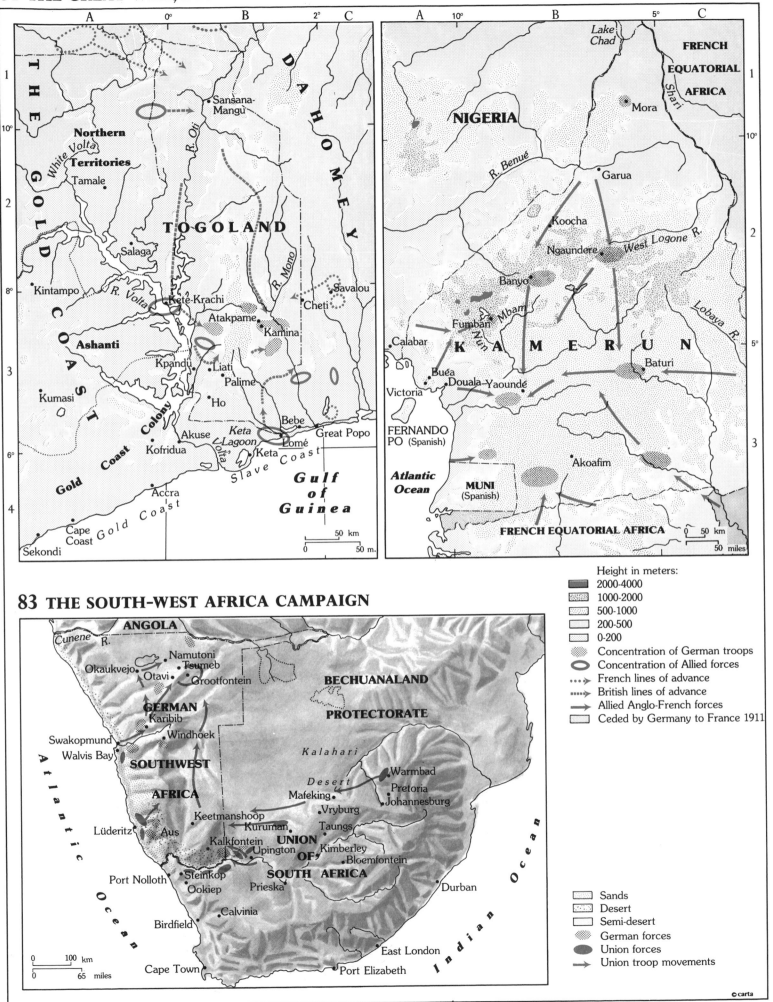

81 THE GREAT WAR, 1914–1918: TOGO

THE GOLD COAST

Northern Territories

Tamale

White Volta

Salaga

Kintampo

R. Volta

Ashanti

Kumasi

Kofridua

Akuse

Gold Coast Colony

Accra

Cape Coast

Sekondi

Gold Coast

Sansana-Mangu

R. Oti

TOGOLAND

DAHOMEY

R. Mono

Keté-Krachi

Atakpame

Kamina

Kpandu

Liati

Palime

Ho

Bebe

Keta Lagoon

Lomé

Keta

Great Popo

Slave Coast

Savalou

Cheti

Gulf of Guinea

50 km
0   50 m.

82 THE KAMERUN CAMPAIGN

Lake Chad

FRENCH EQUATORIAL AFRICA

Shari

NIGERIA

Mora

R. Benué

Garua

Koocha

Ngaundere

West Logone R.

Banyo

Fumban

Mbam

Nun

Calabar

KAMERUN

Buéa

Douala–Yaoundé

Victoria

FERNANDO PO (Spanish)

Atlantic Ocean

MUNI (Spanish)

Baturi

Lobava R.

Akoafim

FRENCH EQUATORIAL AFRICA

0   50 km
50 miles

Height in meters:
- 2000-4000
- 1000-2000
- 500-1000
- 200-500
- 0-200
- Concentration of German troops
- Concentration of Allied forces
- ----▶ French lines of advance
- ----▶ British lines of advance
- ──▶ Allied Anglo-French forces
- Ceded by Germany to France 1911

83 THE SOUTH-WEST AFRICA CAMPAIGN

ANGOLA

Cunene R.

Namutoni

Okaukvejo

Tsumeb

Otavi

Grootfontein

BECHUANALAND

PROTECTORATE

GERMAN

Karibib

Swakopmund

Windhoek

Walvis Bay

Kalahari

Desert

SOUTHWEST

AFRICA

Warmbad

Pretoria

Mafeking

Johannesburg

Vryburg

Lüderitz

Aus

Keetmanshoop

Kuruman

Taungs

Kalkfontein

Upington

UNION OF

Kimberley

Port Nolloth

Steinkop

Ookiep

Prieska

SOUTH AFRICA

Bloemfontein

Calvinia

Durban

Birdfield

East London

Atlantic Ocean

Indian Ocean

Cape Town

Port Elizabeth

0   100 km
0   65 miles

- Sands
- Desert
- Semi-desert
- German forces
- Union forces
- ──▶ Union troop movements

© carta

THE GREAT WAR. 1914–1918: EAST AFRICA

In German East Africa at the outbreak of war the situation was wholly different from that in Togo, Kamerun, and German Southwest Africa. The German colony was commanded by a general of skill, resource, determination, and experience who held down the Allied forces for the entire duration of the war. General Paul von Lettow-Vorbeck was a Prussian aristocrat who had served in China, Southwest Africa, and Kamerun. He arrived in Dar es Salaam in January 1914. With war imminent he could see that the Royal Navy's control of the Indian Ocean made it unlikely that he would receive supplies or reinforcements. His task was to ensure that the colony did not fall into Allied hands or release Allied troops for European battlefields. He had some 250 German officers and NCO's, 2,500 African troops, and 2,200 African armed police. Further, some 3,000 German settlers of military age had had some military training. Enemies — British on the north, Belgians on the west, Portuguese on the south — faced him on all sides.

Initially the British had only a small locally raised force called the King's African Rifles, with British officers. There were three cruisers, but they were no match for the fast German cruiser *Königsberg*, with which the Germans carried out coastal raids. Soon, however, the British were reinforced, and they bombarded Dar es Salaam on 11 July 1915. On land Lettow raided the railway from Mombasa to Nairobi and moved into Uganda, the Belgian Congo, Rhodesia, and Nyasaland. At the end of August 1914 a battalion of the Loyal North Lancashire Regiment arrived along with seven thousand Indian troops. An attempt to land at Tanga was repulsed. The only Allied success was the capture of Bukoba by the Belgians.

After the conquest of German Southwest Africa troops became available for East Africa. General (later Field Marshal) Jan Smuts, who had distinguished himself in the Anglo-Boer War, led British, Indian, Rhodesian, and South African troops who were seasoned in bush fighting.

Taveta and Moshi were taken in March 1916. Smuts now advanced down the river Pangani, while a second force attacked Kondoa- Irangi and the Belgians advanced on Tabora. Lettow was now outflanked and forced to withdraw southward. On 4 September 1916, with support from the Royal Navy, Dar es Salaam fell. At the same time the Belgians took Kigoma and Ujiji. A Rhodesian force had taken Iringa in August; on 19 September the Belgians entered Tabora. The Germans, now split into three groups, could only retire southward.

Smuts retired to South Africa in 1917. He had suffered great losses. Out of fifteen thousand men twelve thousand had to be repatriated on health grounds. They were replaced by Nigerians and newly raised King's African Rifles.

By November 1917 the British had occupied the whole coast as far as the Portuguese borders, and now the Makonde people joined in to harass the Germans. Lettow crossed into Mozambique and eluded the Portuguese forces. He held out there for two months and then reentered German East Africa in order to retreat into Northern Rhodesia, where, on 13 November, he learned of the Armistice. He made his formal surrender in Abercorn on 25 November. There the *askaris* (African troops) who had served under him laid down their arms; the German officers were allowed to retain their swords in honor of the splendid fight they had conducted.

Forty years later General von Lettow-Vorbeck, now an old man, revisited Tanga. The whole populace turned out to greet him, with the sons, daughters, and grandchildren of his old *askaris*. No other German military commander was ever treated with such honor.

□

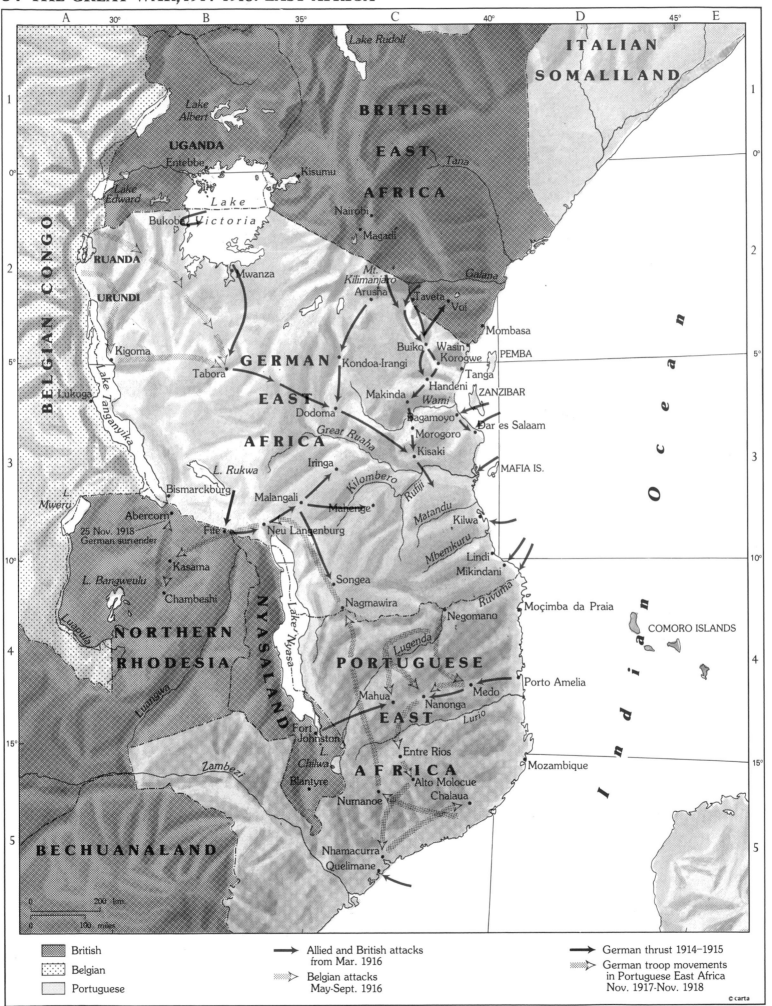

Map legend:

British
Belgian
Portuguese

→ Allied and British attacks from Mar. 1916
⊳ Belgian attacks May-Sept. 1916

→ German thrust 1914–1915
⊳ German troop movements in Portuguese East Africa Nov. 1917-Nov. 1918

© carta

EUROPEAN PREDOMINANCE IN AFRICA, 1914

When war broke out in 1914 only two countries in Africa were independent, Ethiopia and Liberia. Ethiopia was occupied with its own internal troubles under the unsatisfactory emperor Lij Iyasu, who was shortly to embrace Islam; in Liberia a republic with a president was reliant upon the commercial favors of the United States.

France and Britain, the dominant powers in the continent, had consolidated their positions. Belgium and Germany had less large shares. Italy had acquired Libya as recently as 1911 after a brief war with Ottoman Turkey. It had two separate governorates, Tripolitania and Cyrenaica. In Angola and Mozambique the Portuguese, who had had footholds since the fifteenth century, was still developing as a colonial power after intermittent fighting.

Administration was as yet highly uneven. In 1910 the Union of South Africa had become a dominion, with elective parliaments. In British East Africa (later Kenya) a legislative council which had been set up in 1907 was dominated by Europeans. The Belgian Congo had ceased to be the private fief of the king of the Belgians in 1908, and, like most of the rest of the continent, fell under direct European administration. In this political situation — even in Nigeria, where Lord Lugard's policy of indirect rule through local sultans and chiefs provided a model for other territories — the process of devitalization of the traditional forms of government had set in.

Economically, because no colonial power was there as a result of consciously developed planning, there was similar unevenness. It was questionable whether the possession of colonies could be more than marginally profitable. The lust for empire had been an enthusiasm marked by rosy pipe dreams whose financial cost had never been calculated.

□

EUROPEAN PREDOMINANCE IN AFRICA, 1924

At the end of World War I one country, Egypt, had become technically independent: it was recognized as a kingdom on 16 March 1922. The principle of self-determination, formally recognized at the Conference of Paris, made it possible for the former possessions of the German and Ottoman Empires to be carved up among the victors. Thus League of Nations mandates were devised in the Middle East for Lebanon, Syria, Iraq, and Palestine, and in Africa for former Togo, Kamerun, German Southwest Africa, and German East Africa. German Togo was split between Britain and France; Kamerun was split into British Cameroons and French Cameroun; South-West Africa was entrusted to the Union of South Africa; German East Africa became Tanganyika Territory, except for Ruanda-Urundi (taken as a single unit), which was attached to the Belgian Congo.

Under the terms of the mandates each of these powers was responsible for the administration, welfare and development of the native populations until they were able to govern themselves. The Mandatory Powers were thus not given sovereignty. Theoretically they were subject to the League of Nations Permanent Mandates Commission, but this was largely ineffective because no provision had been made to enforce its will. Broadly, however, the provisions were honored, and they served as a first warning that the imperial age was about to draw to its close.

Some additional minor changes may be noted. The Fezzan oasis was now detached from Egypt and transferred to Italian Libya. Apart from the changes of nomenclature already noted, German East Africa now formally became Tanganyika Territory, after the lake on its western border; and, after a bizarre discussion involving the proposal of various quite fanciful names, including "Lululand" (a proposal made by Lord Harcourt, a Liberal peer), British East Africa emerged as Kenya. □

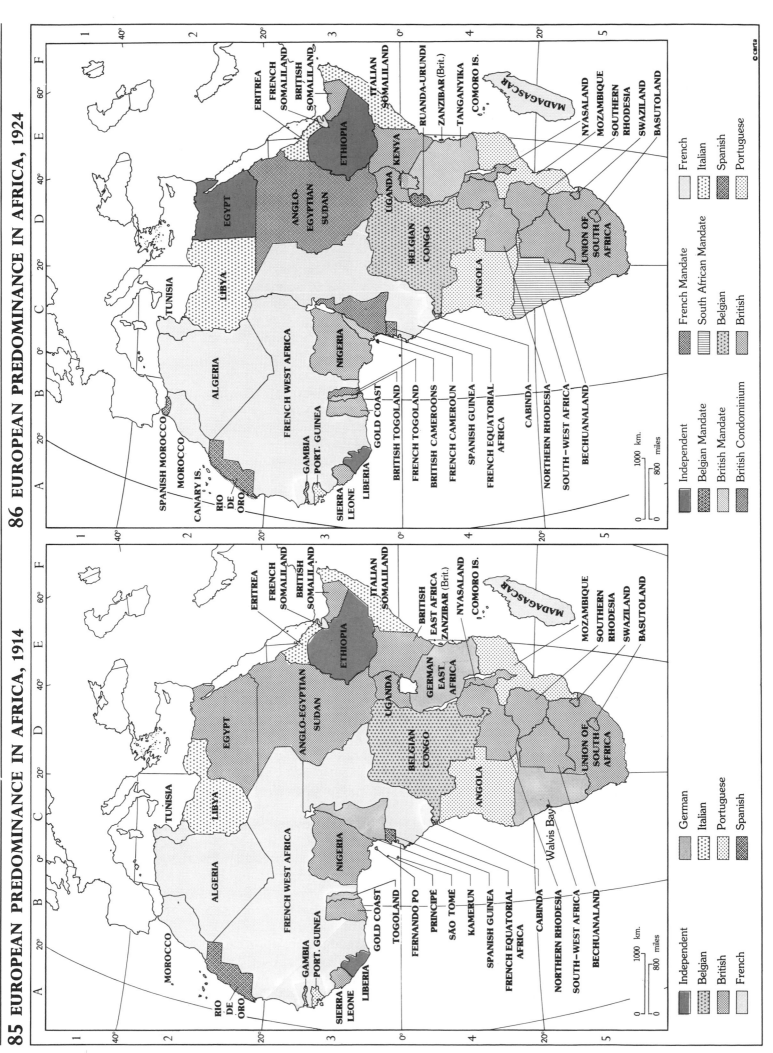

86 EUROPEAN PREDOMINANCE IN AFRICA, 1924

Independent
Belgian Mandate
British Mandate
British Condominium

French Mandate
South African Mandate
Belgian
British

French
Italian
Spanish
Portuguese

SPANISH MOROCCO
MOROCCO
CANARY IS.
RIO DE ORO
TUNISIA
LIBYA
ALGERIA
FRENCH WEST AFRICA
GAMBIA
PORT. GUINEA
SIERRA LEONE
LIBERIA
GOLD COAST
BRITISH TOGOLAND
FRENCH TOGOLAND
BRITISH CAMEROONS
FRENCH CAMEROUN
SPANISH GUINEA
FRENCH EQUATORIAL AFRICA
CABINDA
NORTHERN RHODESIA
SOUTH–WEST AFRICA
BECHUANALAND
NIGERIA
ERITREA
FRENCH SOMALILAND
BRITISH SOMALILAND
ETHIOPIA
ITALIAN SOMALILAND
EGYPT
ANGLO-EGYPTIAN SUDAN
UGANDA
KENYA
BELGIAN CONGO
RUANDA-URUNDI
ZANZIBAR (Brit.)
TANGANYIKA
COMORO IS.
ANGOLA
UNION OF SOUTH AFRICA
NYASALAND
MOZAMBIQUE
SOUTHERN RHODESIA
SWAZILAND
BASUTOLAND
MADAGASCAR

1000 km.
800 miles

85 EUROPEAN PREDOMINANCE IN AFRICA, 1914

Independent
Belgian
British
French

German
Italian
Portuguese
Spanish

MOROCCO
RIO DE ORO
TUNISIA
LIBYA
ALGERIA
FRENCH WEST AFRICA
GAMBIA
PORT. GUINEA
SIERRA LEONE
LIBERIA
GOLD COAST
TOGOLAND
FERNANDO PO
PRINCIPE
SÃO TOMÉ
KAMERUN
SPANISH GUINEA
FRENCH EQUATORIAL AFRICA
CABINDA
NORTHERN RHODESIA
SOUTH–WEST AFRICA
BECHUANALAND
NIGERIA
ERITREA
FRENCH SOMALILAND
BRITISH SOMALILAND
ETHIOPIA
ITALIAN SOMALILAND
EGYPT
ANGLO-EGYPTIAN SUDAN
UGANDA
BELGIAN CONGO
BRITISH EAST AFRICA
GERMAN EAST AFRICA
ZANZIBAR (Brit.)
NYASALAND
COMORO IS.
ANGOLA
Walvis Bay
UNION OF SOUTH AFRICA
MOZAMBIQUE
SOUTHERN RHODESIA
SWAZILAND
BASUTOLAND
MADAGASCAR

1000 km.
800 miles

© carta

115

EUROPEAN PREDOMINANCE IN AFRICA, 1939

The Imperial Conference held in London in October-November 1926 formally recognized the dominion status of the Union of South Africa as well as Canada, Australia, and New Zealand, that is, their position as autonomous communities of equal status with Great Britain. Ethiopia had been seized by Italy in 1936 (see map 88), a conquest that had only two more years to endure in 1939.

By then the various colonial states, protectorates, and mandated territories had acquired a certain legitimacy among African élites, and some concept of nationhood was beginning to emerge. The economic disruption of previous channels of internal trading that had marked the "scramble for Africa" had been replaced by a system of production of raw materials for the colonial powers, whose factories often then returned them to Africa as manufactured goods. In administration the proportion of administrators and ancillaries was slight in relation to the indigenous populations. Nevertheless, new railways and roads linked the areas of export crops and mines; ports and harbors, electric power, and hospitals and schools were developed. In Algeria, Tunisia, Egypt, and the Union of South Africa universities were set up, often primarily serving white settlers. In addition to the local police force, small armies were trained, primarily for local needs, but also as reserves in the case of general war. Governors and administrators had been trained in the hard school of war, and with the military tradition of care for the welfare of troops. While participating in the colonial economic system that the African élite was beginning to see as exploitation, they were nevertheless concerned to improve the lot of the indigenous populations. If the African élite was beginning to demand a share in the administration and control over their own countries, as they now perceived them, there was little thought among them for the rural population, or indeed of actual independence. It was this that war was to change. □

THE ITALIAN INVASION OF ETHIOPIA, 1935–1936

Already in 1882 Italy had acquired a colony in Eritrea; in 1896, following a misunderstanding of the Treaty of Ucciali, it invaded Ethiopia — only to be crushingly defeated at Adowa. The Italian dictator, Mussolini, was pursuing an active colonial policy in Tripolitania, Cyrenaica, Somalia, and Eritrea, and in 1934 was seeking an occasion to avenge the shame of Adowa. A series of frontier incidents culminated in December 1934 at Walwal, a frontier oasis of no particular importance except that both Ethiopia and Italy claimed it, in December 1934. Hostilities began which Britain claimed had been provoked by Italy. In February, Mussolini sent troops to Eritrea and Somalia: in March, Ethiopia requested the protection of the League of Nations, of which she was a member. Both parties agreed to accept arbitration.

While Mussolini continued to send more troops, the League sat on the fence, deciding that neither side was to blame. On 3 October the Italians invaded, using aircraft and poison gas. Ethiopia had one aircraft. Adowa was occupied on 6 October, and by 8 November Makale had been taken along with all of Tigre. Slower progress was made by two columns from Somalia. The League of Nations introduced sanctions, but these were ignored by Austria and Switzerland. The Suez Canal was not closed, nor were sanctions imposed upon oil. On 31 March 1936 the Imperial Ethiopian Army was defeated at Maiceu. On 2 May, following the advice of his council of ministers, the emperor Haile Sellassie left Ethiopia by train in order to keep international negotiations open. He had been defeated not by any lack of courage on the part of his troops, but by lack of modern arms, especially aircraft. These, together with poison gas, the Italians had in plenty.

On 5 May 1936 Marshal Pietro Badoglio entered Addis Ababa and proclaimed Victor Emmanuel III emperor on 9 May. Ethiopian resistance, however, continued in a guerilla movement under Ras Imru and his followers, the Black Lions. Their heroism was rewarded in 1941 (see map 90). □

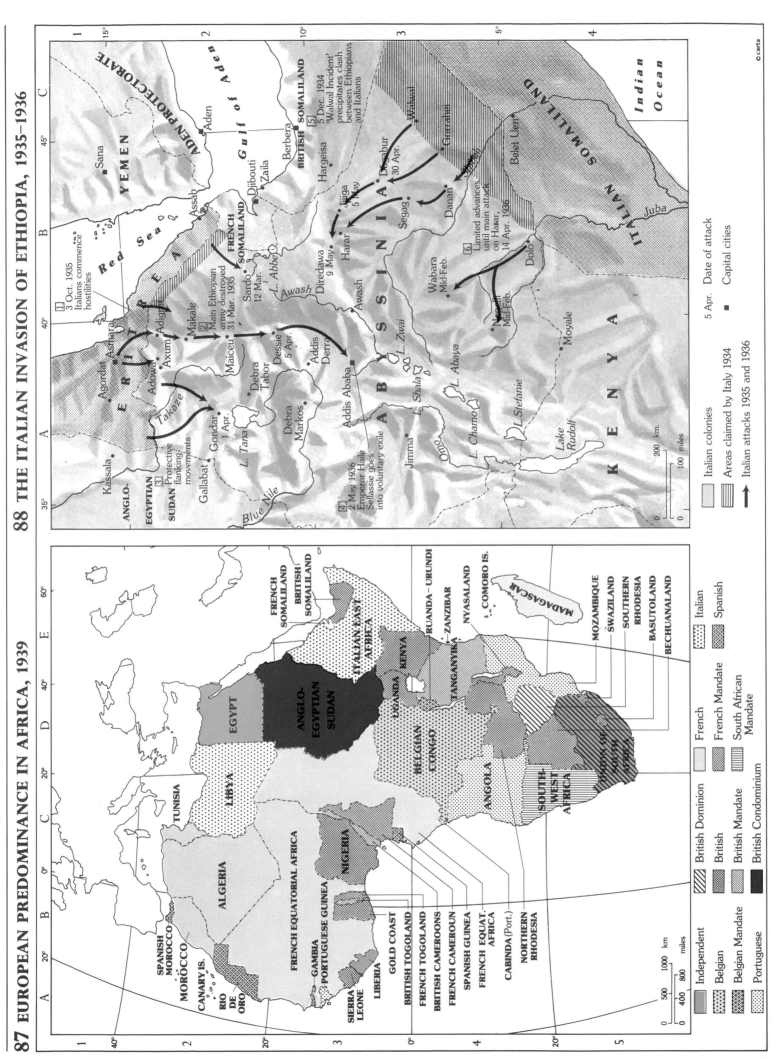

87 EUROPEAN PREDOMINANCE IN AFRICA, 1939

88 THE ITALIAN INVASION OF ETHIOPIA, 1935–1936

Map 87 legend (European Predominance in Africa, 1939):

- Independent
- Belgian
- Belgian Mandate
- Portuguese
- British Dominion
- British
- British Mandate
- British Condominium
- French
- French Mandate
- South African Mandate
- Italian
- Spanish

Labels on map 87: SPANISH MOROCCO, MOROCCO, CANARY IS., RIO DE ORO, ALGERIA, TUNISIA, LIBYA, EGYPT, ANGLO-EGYPTIAN SUDAN, FRENCH EQUATORIAL AFRICA, GAMBIA, PORTUGUESE GUINEA, SIERRA LEONE, LIBERIA, GOLD COAST, BRITISH TOGOLAND, FRENCH TOGOLAND, BRITISH CAMEROONS, FRENCH CAMEROUN, SPANISH GUINEA, FRENCH EQUAT. AFRICA, CABINDA (Port.), NORTHERN RHODESIA, NIGERIA, FRENCH SOMALILAND, BRITISH SOMALILAND, ITALIAN EAST AFRICA, UGANDA, KENYA, BELGIAN CONGO, RUANDA–URUNDI, ZANZIBAR, TANGANYIKA, NYASALAND, COMORO IS., MADAGASCAR, MOZAMBIQUE, SWAZILAND, SOUTHERN RHODESIA, BASUTOLAND, BECHUANALAND, SOUTH-WEST AFRICA, UNION OF SOUTH AFRICA

Map 88 labels (The Italian Invasion of Ethiopia):

- ANGLO-EGYPTIAN SUDAN
- ERITREA
- YEMEN
- ADEN PROTECTORATE
- FRENCH SOMALILAND
- BRITISH SOMALILAND
- ABYSSINIA
- ITALIAN SOMALILAND
- KENYA
- Red Sea
- Gulf of Aden
- Indian Ocean

Places: Sana, Aden, Assab, Asmara, Agordat, Kassala, Adigrat, Makale, Adowa, Axum, Maiceu, Gondar, Gallabat, Debra Tabor, L. Tana, Debra Markos, Blue Nile, Dessie, Addis Derra, Addis Ababa, L. Zwai, L. Shala, L. Abaya, L. Chamo, L. Stefanie, Lake Rudolf, Jimma, Omo, Juba, Belet Uen, Dolo, Neghelli, Wabara, Dagabur, Segag, Gorrahei, Walwal, Harar, Jijiga, Diredawa, Awash, L. Abbe, Sardo, Djibouti, Zaila, Berbera, Hargeisa, Takaze, Awash, Moyale

Annotations:
- ① 3 Oct. 1935 Italians commence hostilities
- ② Main Ethiopian army destroyed 31 Mar. 1935
- ③ Protective flanking movements
- ④ 2 May 1936 Emperor Haile Sellassie goes into voluntary exile
- ⑤ 5 Dec. 1934 'Walwal Incident' precipitates clash between Ethiopians and Italians
- ⑥ Limited advances until main attack on Harar, 14 Apr. 1936

Dates of attack: 12 Mar., 5 Apr., 1 Apr., 9 May, 5 May, 30 Apr., Mid-Feb.

Map 88 legend:

- Italian colonies
- Areas claimed by Italy 1934
- Italian attacks 1935 and 1936
- 5 Apr. Date of attack
- ■ Capital cities

Scale: 0 100 miles / 0 200 km.

c∧carta

117

THE SECOND WORLD WAR: NORTH AFRICA, 1940–1941

Following the fall of France to the Germans, and the British evacuation at Dunkirk on 3 June, on 10 June 1940 Mussolini — jackal-like, as Winston Churchill said — declared war on the Allies. In France he took Nice and Savoy; on 4 July he invaded the Sudan from Ethiopia; in the first half of August he seized British Somaliland; and now he saw before his eyes the glittering mirage of an Italian Egypt and Syria. In fact he had bitten off more than he could chew.

On 3 September Mussolini attacked British forces at Sidi Barrani within the borders of Egypt, but failed to follow up the action. The British recovered Sidi Barrani on 12 December and by 7 February 1941 had driven the Italians out of Cyrenaica. In truth, the Italians had no quarrel with the British, nor stomach for battle, while the British themselves were weakened by the necessary withdrawal of troops to fight in Greece, Crete, East Africa and against Japan. Nevertheless ten Italian divisions had been destroyed, and 130,000 Italian prisoners taken, by only two British divisions.

It was in these circumstances that the German high command sent General Erwin Rommel to take over the fight. He arrived in Africa on 12 February 1941. On 31 March he attacked across fifteen hundred miles of desert. A highly confused battle followed, with successes of a limited kind on both sides. By the end of the year Rommel thought it prudent to retreat in order to build up his resources, while the British forces were further depleted by the necessary withdrawal of British and Australian units to fight Japan in the Far East. Although the British were still able to hold Cyrenaica and had recovered Ethiopia and Somalia (see map 90), it was so far a stalemate. □

THE SECOND WORLD WAR: ETHIOPIA AND SOMALIA, 1941

In spite of the great distance involved, among the responsibilities of the British Middle East command in Cairo was the Horn of Africa. In 1940 the Italian forces had driven the British from Kassala in the Sudan, and overrun Somalia. Very shortly the British were in contact with the Ethiopian guerillas. On 19 January 1941 an offensive was mounted. It recovered Kassala, and was to culminate in the triumphal return of the emperor into Addis Ababa on 5 April. In the north General Platt, after his success at Kassala, had a long-drawn fight for Keren which lasted until 1 April with Asmara falling the following day. At the same time the unit known as Gideon Force, under Major Orde Wingate, in conjunction with Ethiopian guerillas and eight hundred Sudanese, entered Ethiopia across the Blue Nile south of Gallabat and slowly forced his way to the capital. By attacking quickly and often, Wingate deceived the Italians, giving an illusion of superior strength. In their wake the emperor followed. General Platt's northern column finally encircled the duke of Aosta's forces at Amba Alagi on 16 May.

In the south, from bases in Kenya, columns under General A. G. Cunningham, with support from the South African air force, moved up the coast. They included a Nigerian brigade and a South African brigade. They took first Kismayu, and then Mogadishu on 25 February. After a brilliant march across the Ogaden desert they entered Jijiga on 17 March, Diredawa on 29 March, and reached Addis Ababa on 6 April. Throughout all this time the Royal Air Force from Aden and the Sudan was protecting convoys in the Red Sea and attacking the Italian air force. In the south General Cunningham had the support of the South African air force, based in Nairobi.

At the emperor's personal request British advisers now assisted the restoration of orderly government. The recovery of Ethiopia, greatly assisted by the evident unwillingness of the Italians to fight, had been effected in ten weeks. □

89 THE SECOND WORLD WAR: NORTH AFRICA, 1940–1941

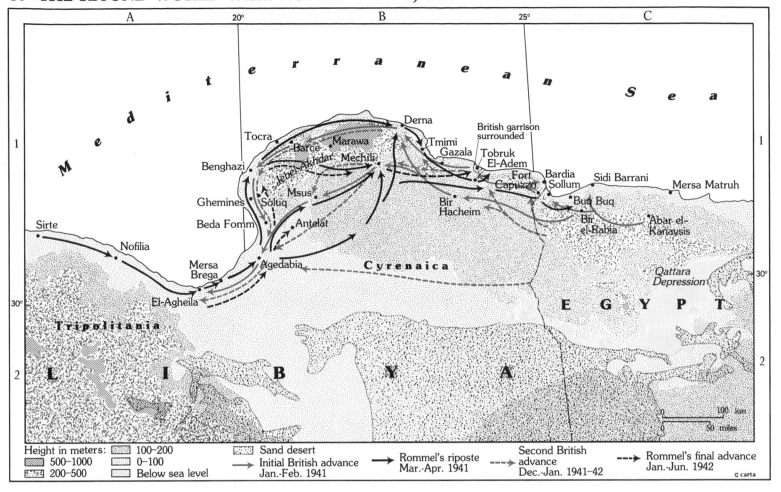

Height in meters:
- 500–1000
- 200–500
- 100–200
- 0–100
- Below sea level

Sand desert

→ Initial British advance Jan.-Feb. 1941

→ Rommel's riposte Mar.-Apr. 1941

⇢ Second British advance Dec.-Jan. 1941–42

⇠ Rommel's final advance Jan.-Jun. 1942

© carta

90 THE SECOND WORLD WAR: ETHIOPIA AND SOMALIA, 1941

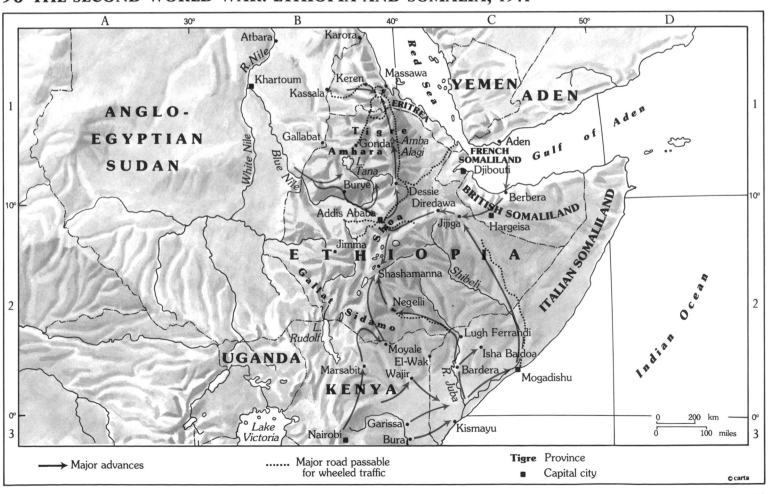

→ Major advances

······ Major road passable for wheeled traffic

Tigre Province

■ Capital city

© carta

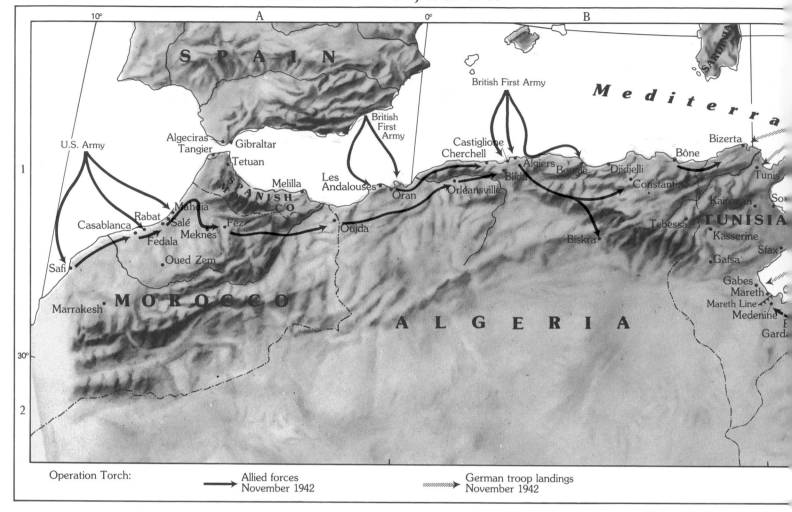

Operation Torch:

→ Allied forces
November 1942

⇛ German troop landings
November 1942

THE SECOND WORLD WAR: NORTH AFRICA, 1942–1943

On 21 January 1942 Rommel began attacks which pushed the British Eighth Army back. Its morale was at a low ebb, and there were misunderstandings between infantry and tank commanders. By 26 June, Rommel had taken Tobruk; ten days later he was near El- Alamein, within fifty miles of Alexandria. Egypt was in a state of panic. Here both Rommel and his opponent, General Claude Auchinleck, paused to regroup. Auchinleck concentrated his forces in a fortress position; Rommel, who had suffered casualties in men and tanks, was dependent upon the gas supplies he had captured from the British. This he was forced to waste, in British attacks on weak Italian units that Rommel was compelled to support. Rommel's

forces were worn out; it was only prudent to retreat. Although it is doubtful that Auchinleck had sufficient strength to attack the Germans decisively, Winston Churchill had him sacked for missing the opportunity.

Auchinleck was now replaced by General (later Field Marshal) Bernard Montgomery. A controversial and flamboyant character, his first care was to restore the morale of the troops. He now began meticulous preparations for an attack, amassing equipment and men. On 23 October, after a long delay that has been criticized, he began the battle of El-Alamein for which he is famous. By 2 November Rommel was left with only thirty-five tanks, and retreat was inevitable.

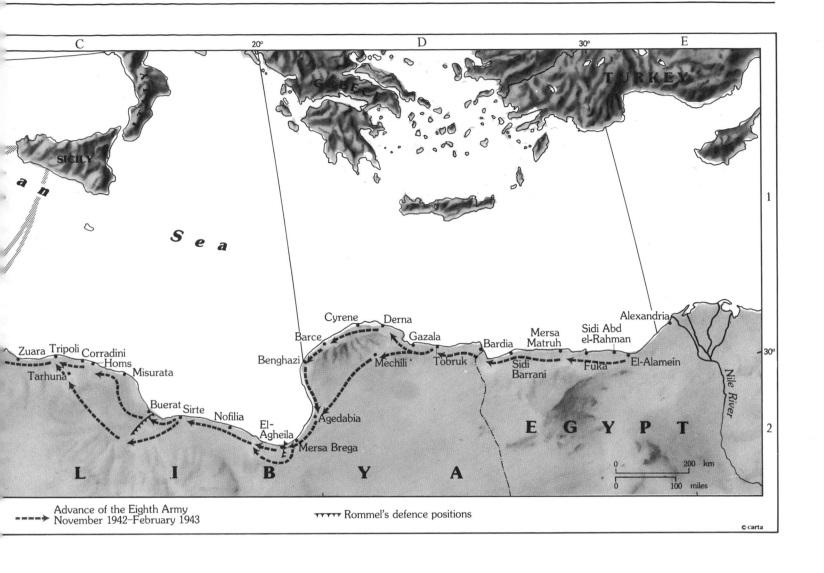

- - - ➤ Advance of the Eighth Army
November 1942–February 1943

ㅜㅜㅜㅜㅜ Rommel's defence positions

This Hitler forbade, but to no effect. The British troops, however, were so exhausted that no effective follow-up was possible.

On 8 November American troops and the British First Army began landings in Morocco and Algeria, as far as the Tunisian border. Some sporadic resistance from Vichy French forces was speedily overcome. The Germans riposted by pouring in tanks and aircraft, and by December had halted the allied advances. By 23 January 1943 Montgomery had entered Tripoli. On 16 February his advance was for a time halted at the Mareth Line, hastily constructed defenses by the Germans at a line of hills on the southeastern Tunisian border. After some difficulty the Mareth Line was penetrated, and slowly British troops edged forward. By 14 April the Germans and Italians were surrounded by the Americans and by the British First and Eighth Armies. After bitter fighting the Axis forces collapsed; on 12 May they surrendered with 250,000 troops. Rommel had already returned to Germany on 12 March. By categorically refusing to allow the evacuation of any of the German or Italian troops, Hitler had denied himself forces which would have been helpful to him in the defense of Sicily and Italy, and had lost aircraft at the time that he was engaged in the struggle for Stalingrad on the Russian front.

In these battles African troops, chiefly from West Africa, had played an important part as lines of communications troops. It was a part which, if not conspicuous, was crucial to the success of operations. African troops came also from Senegal, and crossed the desert under General Leclerc from Chad in a march of great brilliance and daring. Many of them contributed to the Allied victories in Italy which were essential in giving a quietus to the Nazi warlords. □

EUROPEAN PREDOMINANCE IN AFRICA, 1950

In 1950 any man who committed himself to the prediction that by the end of the decade some half of the colonies, protectorates and other states in Africa would be independent would have been regarded as rash. Even in 1951 James Griffiths, British secretary of state for the colonies, predicted that Tanganyika would not be independent until after 1975. Nevertheless, certain signs were plainly visible on the horizon. Outside Africa some mandated territories of the League of Nations had already become independent. Britain had ended its empire in India in 1947, and in 1948 had withdrawn ignominiously from Palestine. Under the United Nations Charter the remaining former mandated territories became United Nations trust territories, with their progress toward ultimate liberation as sovereign states subject to United Nations commissions of inspection. In Africa such were Togo, Cameroons and Cameroun, Ruanda and Burundi, and Tanganyika. As to South-West Africa, the Union of South Africa declined to recognize its new status as a trust territory, and continued to regard it as a mandate. In Eritrea and likewise in Italian Somalia Britain was still in control. Somalia was returned to Italy in 1950 on condition of becoming independent in 1960, while Eritrea was federated with Ethiopia in 1952. In northern Africa Libya had been made independent as a kingdom in 1949. In Egypt — a country which Britain had agreed in 1877 to occupy for only three years, and where bored and listless British forces now lolled along the Suez Canal Zone — the demand for independence swelled. In the northwest and as far as the border of Tunisia and Libya large European settler populations, of French, Italian, and Spanish stock, lived in full confidence that they would not be disturbed. They were to be awakened to reality shortly.

In 1939 some eighty thousand African troops left their homelands for Europe to fight Germany. By 1941 troops from West and East Africa had help oust the Italians from Ethiopia and Somalia. Likewise they had served against Germany, first in North Africa and then in Italy. In the Far East they had seen white men defeated humiliatingly by the Japanese, and then themselves had joined in defeating the same enemy. The Atlantic Charter of 1941 proclaimed "the right of all people to choose the form of government in which they live," and affirmed this with the hope "to see sovereign rights restored to those who have been forcibly deprived of them." To the contrary, Winston Churchill categorically stated that this proclamation did not apply to the African colonies. He was not, he said, going to preside over the dissolution of the British Empire. The crumbling process, however, had already begun, and in 1944 General Charles de Gaulle had outlined at the Brazzaville Conference a series of economic, legal, political, and social reforms which looked forward to political freedom for the territories subject to France, albeit within the framework of a "greater France" rather than one of "self-government."

Other factors however, were at work. A thin trickle of Africans began to issue from secondary schools, and some managed to reach the universities, or took correspondence courses which led to degrees from the University of Fort Hare in South Africa. In the French territories the stream of *évolués* became more numerous. As long ago as the 1920s the Catholic Church had looked forward to the creation of a wholly African clergy, and now the first few priests began to emerge. The soldiers who had seen the world were no longer alone. Literacy too now began to be valued, and inevitably ideas fermented. The cool confidence of the French settlers in the north, and the British settlers in eastern, central, and southern Africa was soon to be upset, although the different regions would be affected at varying times and speeds.

□

SPANISH MOROCCO

TUNISIA

CANARY IS.

MOROCCO

ALGERIA

LIBYA

EGYPT

RIO DE ORO

FRENCH WEST AFRICA

GAMBIA

PORTUGUESE GUINEA

ANGLO-EGYPTIAN SUDAN

ERITREA

FRENCH SOMALILAND

BRITISH SOMALILAND

SIERRA LEONE

NIGERIA

LIBERIA

GOLD COAST

BRITISH CAMEROONS

FRENCH EQUATORIAL AFRICA

ETHIOPIA

BRITISH TOGOLAND

FRENCH CAMEROUN

FRENCH TOGOLAND

ITALIAN SOMALILAND

SPANISH GUINEA

UGANDA

BELGIAN CONGO

KENYA

CABINDA

RUANDA-URUNDI

TANGANYIKA

ZANZIBAR

NYASALAND

COMORO IS.

ANGOLA

NORTHERN RHODESIA

SOUTHERN RHODESIA

MOZAMBIQUE

MADAGASCAR

SOUTH-WEST AFRICA

BECHUANALAND

SWAZILAND

UNION OF SOUTH AFRICA

BASUTOLAND

0   1000 km.

0   500 miles

	Independent		British		French		Portuguese
	Belgian		British Trusteeship		French Trusteeship		South African Mandate
	Belgian Trusteeship		British Dominion		Italian Trusteeship		Spanish

© carta

123

THE DECOLONIZATION OF AFRICA, TO 1960

At the beginning of the decade which began in 1951 Liberia, Morocco, Sudan, Egypt, Ethiopia, and the Union of South Africa were the only independent African states. Libya became independent in that year, while Egypt under treaty was still garrisoned by British troops in the Canal Zone until 1956. By the end of the decade there were but few dependent terriotories, chiefly Algeria and countries in eastern and central Africa. Of these the greater number had been promised an early independence. The year 1960 has been called the Year of Africa, for in it no less than sixteen states became independent. Eleven others followed between 1961 and 1966.

In the states that had been ruled by Great Britain there were few settlers save in Kenya and Southern Rhodesia. The problems of handing over power to indigenous rulers were primarily political and constitutional. In the French territories President de Gaulle offered in 1958 a free choice between complete and immediate independence or autonomy within a Franco-African community. Guinea alone opted for immediate independence, and with it all French aid was terminated, bringing about almost immediate collapse. Belgium was hardly prepared for events, and it was not until 1958, when rioting broke out in Léopoldville, that any thought was given to future independence. The Belgian Congo was given precipitate independence in 1960, without any serious preparation either in terms of the civil service or politically. The result was chaos and civil war (see map 94). Portugal had long pursued a policy of quasi-assimilation of the Portuguese territories and treated them as overseas provinces of Portugal. However much of a facade this may have been, Portugal, as the colonial power that had been in Africa longest, was determined to stay on, and did so until 1975. Likewise South Africa, still maintaining that South-West Africa had mandated status, showed no intention of yielding. In Southern Rhodesia a white majority

of settlers had already attempted in 1922 to gain independence with themselves as masters, and were able to hang on until 1979.

From a constitutional point of view, and even from that of regional and local government, the coming of independence meant but little change for the ordinary African. In the French territories the French ministry of education — by agreement — still controlled education. In Togo, as elsewhere, French-born police could be seen in the streets of the capital. In the former British territories there were formally elected parliaments, and African provincial and district commissioners replaced British ones. In Ghana a district near the capital was still, as a result of popular demand, in the hands of an Englishman. He ruled paternally, in native dress. Economically, whatever colonial masters there had been, the new states were tied to the former metropolitan economy. In Ghana, Guinea, and Mali and later in Tanzania the political leadership proclaimed a socialist or neo-Marxist ideology. In Ghana this was called Nkrumahism. A primary demand was for nationalization, in imitation of Labour Party Britain, which placed businesses, hitherto moderately flourishing, in the hands of men who primarily were politicians, not businessmen. So, by 1966, the income of Ghanaian subsidence farmers had been reduced to one-third of its level at the time of independence, and with inflation at a rate of 66 percent. There were similar manifestations of ineptitude elsewhere, public recognition of which was shifted to some extent by the institution of one-party states, by laws which forebade criticism of the party or the government, and by the nationalization of the press. To take only the Ghanaian example, it was not surprising, when Nkrumah was overthrown in 1966, and his statue — dressed in a Roman toga — cast down by the crowd, that the people of Accra claimed that at last they had gained independence.

□

THE DECOLONIZATION OF AFRICA, TO 1960

| A | | 0° | B | 20° | C | 40° | D | 60° |

MOROCCO
1956

TUNISIA
1956

SPANISH
SAHARA

ALGERIA

LIBYA
1951

U.A.R.
(EGYPT)
1922

MAURITANIA
1960

THE
GAMBIA

SENEGAL
1960

MALI
1960

NIGER
1960

CHAD
1960

SUDAN
1956

ERITREA
1952

FRENCH
SOMALILAND

GUINEA
1958

UPPER
VOLTA
1960

PORT.
GUINEA

SIERRA
LEONE

IVORY
COAST
1960

NIGERIA
1960

ETHIOPIA
1941

SOMALIA
1960

LIBERIA
1847

GHANA
1957

TOGO
1960

DAHOMEY
1960

CAMEROON
1960

CENTRAL
AFRICAN
REPUBLIC
1960

RIO MUNI

GABON
1960

CONGO (Brazzaville)
1960

UGANDA

KENYA

RWANDA
(Belg. Trusteeship)

CABINDA
(Port.)

CONGO
1960

BURUNDI
(Belg. Trusteeship)

ZANZIBAR
(Br. Prot.)

TANGANYIKA

ANGOLA

NYASALAND

COMORO IS.
(Fr.)

NORTHERN
RHODESIA

MOZAMBIQUE

SOUTH-
WEST
AFRICA

SOUTHERN
RHODESIA

MADAGASCAR
1960

BECHUANA-
LAND

SWAZILAND

BASUTOLAND

UNION OF
SOUTH AFRICA
1931

Equator

0   500 km.
0   1000 miles

Independent	British Dominion	South African Mandate
British	French	Spanish
British Trusteeship	Portuguese	1960 Date of independence

© carta

125

PRINCIPAL WARS AND CHANGES IN AFRICA, FROM 1960

The most marked element in African politics since 1960 has been the extent of the influence of the U.S.S.R., compassed initially by Soviet scholarships offered to African youths, who were then trained in Marxist-Leninist theory, strategy and tactics. Often this has been backed by overt armed force, or by means of surrogates from Cuba, and to a lesser extent from East Germany. With the advent of *glasnost* and *perestroika* within the U.S.S.R. itself, and the toppling of the Marxist-Leninist tyrannies in eastern Europe, together with the impoverishment not only of these countries but of the Soviet Union as well, this phase was clearly coming to an end. Ghana's first president, Kwame Nkrumah, had set the tone for African liberation: "Seek ye first the political kingdom and all else will be added unto you." It was a solution that has proved disastrous. Billions of dollars have been spent in grants-in-aid, but it is reckoned by the World Bank that at least half of its projects have failed because of the collapse wrought by bureaucracies, corrupt judiciaries and civil services, and corruption in general reaching from top to bottom. The tide of Marxist-Leninism, so signal a failure in Europe, is still flowing in Africa, and threatens in Zimbabwe, where a "one-party state" is under consideration; in Namibia; and in the proposals for the nationalization of all mines and banks made by the African National Congress in South Africa.

Some of the wars in Africa since 1960 have resulted from the disregard by former colonial powers of ethnic or economic boundaries. In the Sudan the Muslim north and the pagan south were (and are) incompatibles. Morocco, from which Spain had torn the former Spanish Sahara, was attacked by Algeria and Mauritania when the Spanish Sahara was liberated. Border incidents and the insane military ambitions of General Idi Amin drew Tanzania into war. In Ethiopia rival Marxist factions contest each other, the official government in Addis Ababa and the "rebels" in Eritrea. In Zaïre liberation led immediately to civil war, largely because the former colonial power handed over all authority without due preparation and precipitately. In Nigeria the eastern province of Biafra attempted to secede from the Federation, backed, at least so far as propaganda was concerned, by Swiss banking interests, if not by arms and money. Revolutionary interests rather than interests of self-advantage appear to dictate the tortuous policies of Colonel Qaddafi, leading to war in Chad, frontier incidents in Egypt, other interference in the Sudan; not limited to Africa, his projects have included support for the Irish Republican Army (I.R.A.) and a proposal that the Jewish population of Israel should be forcibly deported to Alaska, South America, or — in a recent statement — "anywhere else."

In certain countries, such as Angola, Mozambique, and Zimbabwe, guerilla movements had preceded independence, and had made them difficult to govern. Angola is still torn by factions, while in Zimbabwe the divisions are only superficially healed. More lasting has been the reconciliation between Egypt and Israel, where periods of hostility broken by periods of armed truce were the result of the former colonial power having abandoned Palestine without first settling outstanding political differences.

The population figures given in this map are those of 1975, and should be compared with those of map 100. Africa is not devoid of labor power or of natural resources, but in almost all countries there has been a failure to marshal resources for proper political, social, or other development. Only Africa can save itself by its own exertions.

□

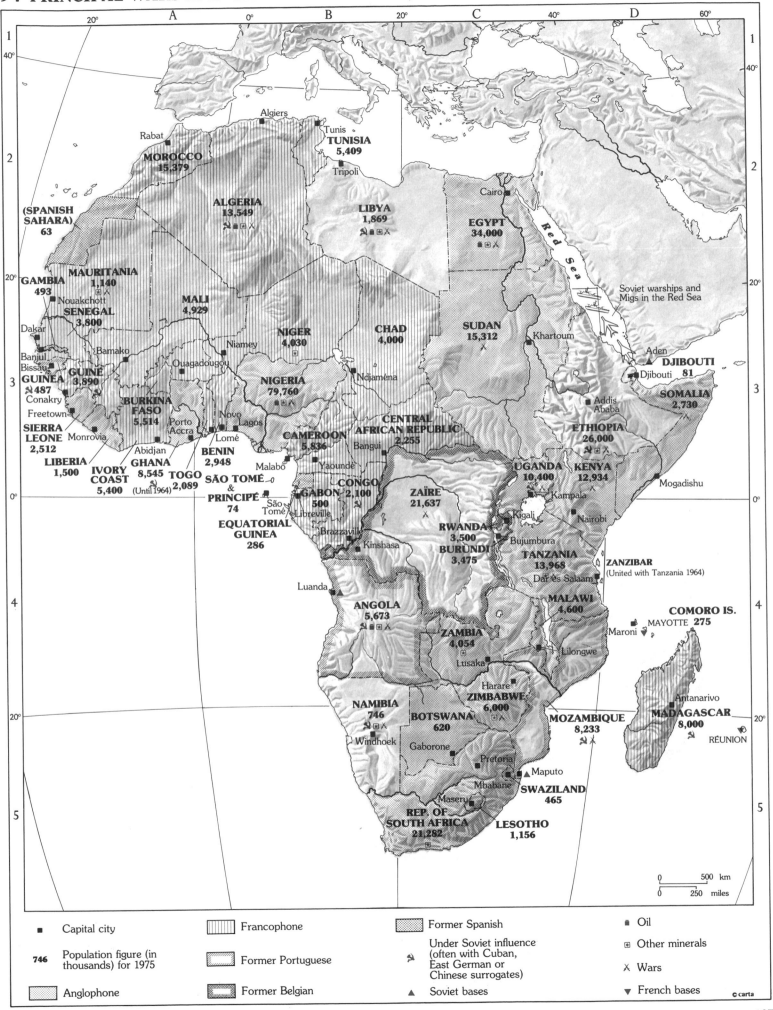

Soviet warships and
Migs in the Red Sea

	Capital city		Francophone		Former Spanish		Oil
746	Population figure (in thousands) for 1975		Former Portuguese		Under Soviet influence (often with Cuban, East German or Chinese surrogates)		Other minerals
	Anglophone		Former Belgian	▲	Soviet bases	X	Wars
						▼	French bases

© carta

THE REPUBLIC OF SOUTH AFRICA, PEOPLES AND LANGUAGES

The Republic of South Africa is a kaleidoscope of peoples and languages. Apart from the official Afrikaans and English, there are nine recognized Bantu languages, two Khoisan languages, and five Indian languages. The Coloureds speak either Afrikaans or English, sometimes both. To these must be added the numeruous other Bantu languages spoken by the neighbors of the Republic and by migrant workers from farther afield in Africa. It is a far from simple linguistic situation.

Many other African countries are marked by a similar linguistic and cultural diversity. In some a temporary solution at least has been achieved by making English, or French, or Portuguese the official language, or at least coequal with another official language. In Ethiopia, Amharic has been pressed upon a population speaking at least twelve different languages. In Kenya and Tanzania the government, colonial as well as independent, have greatly encouraged the use of Swahili in the face of more than one hundred Bantu languages as well as various non-Bantu tongues such as Maasai and Iraqw. It may be noted that Swahili has penetrated far beyond the countries immediately adjacent to Kenya and Tanzania, and indeed as far as Kinshasa on the shores of the Atlantic.

While differing from one another in morphology, the Bantu languages have common grammatical characteristics, so that it is not difficult for the speaker of one language rapidly to acquire a working knowledge of another by noting vocabulary changes. The apparent diversities have an underlying unity; there are no obstacles that cannot be overcome.

Although the word *apartheid* ("separateness") was first used politically in 1943, the practice of segregation in South Africa goes back to the seventeenth century. It is not a phenomenon unique to South Africa. Throughout the former Ottoman Turkish Empire it was practiced in the *millet* system. All those who did not conform to Islam, the state religion, were grouped by religion into separate *millet*s or nations, with domestic laws of their own administered by their religious heads. Both Christians and Jews had such recognition in Egypt and elswhere.

In South Africa *apartheid* in its strictest form forbade the mingling of the races classed as white, black, and Coloured in any public place. This applied to contact on buses and beaches as well as to matters of sport, and in general all social intercourse. From 1948 the policy was enshrined in statutes, in the absence of parliamentary representation, job reservations, and trade union legislation for blacks and Coloureds.

This was all part of the attempt to institutionalize in a formal system one which initially had grown up informally, and which was of itself fundamentally informal. For forty years the practice of *apartheid* has provoked protest both within South Africa and outside. Separate legislative chambers have been created for Coloureds and Indians, but these are still subordinate to the white chambers. *Apartheid* inevitably led to a great sense of inferiority among those affected: one man said: "I wear my skin like a prison uniform." Pass Laws, the Separate Amenities Act, the Group Areas Act, and other restrictive laws have been abolished or relaxed, as have rules relating to sports. Its total abolition has become government policy.

The creation of Bantu homelands and of autonomous black states was an attempt to escape from the dilemma created by total African independence in other lands, not least in neighboring Botswana, Lesotho, and Swaziland. The anti-*apartheid* movements were easily attracted to Communism by Soviet propaganda, or by money. Until recently it was actual and active Soviet policy to promote revolution. In the past several years the Marxist-Leninist states in Europe have visibly crumbled, and Russia itself has opted for democracy. Such profound changes cannot but affect Africa. With the Republic of South Africa poised for the already announced termination of *apartheid* it remains to determine what kind of system can be constructed to meet the exigencies of so many peoples, languages, and cultures. Failure to do so could cause the collapse of the economy, and would involve all South Africa's neighbors whose economies depend upon its prosperity. Whatever may take place in the future, the dismantling of *apartheid* cannot be reversed. ☐

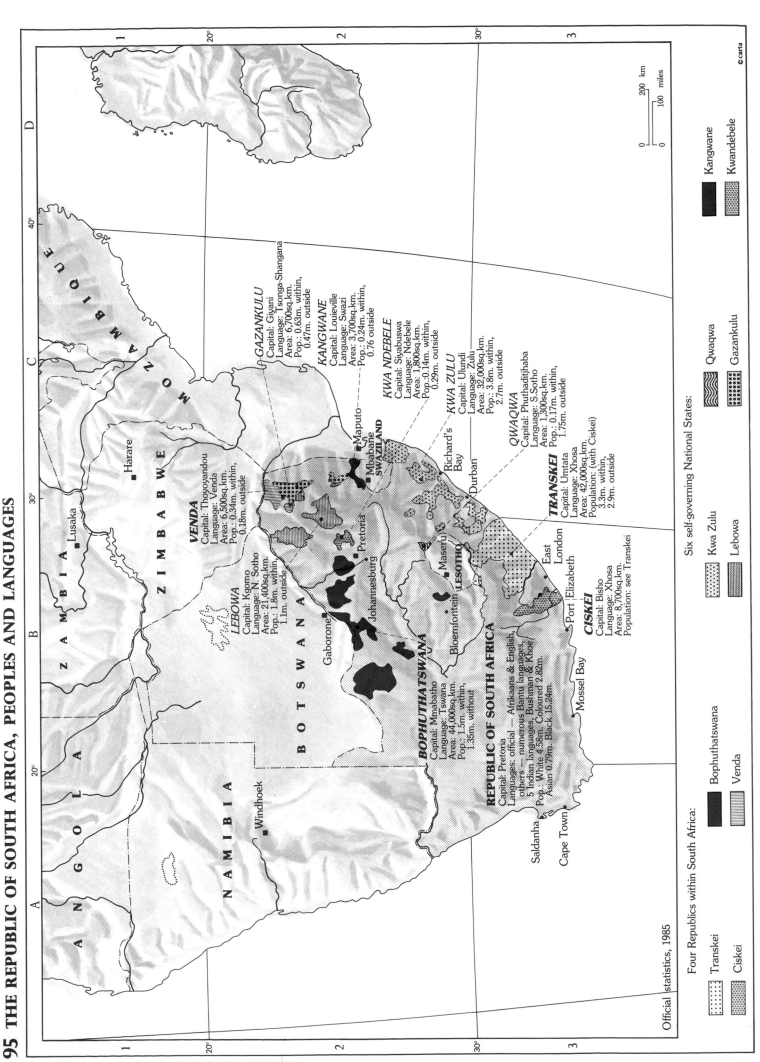

VENDA
Capital: Thoyoyandou
Language: Venda
Area: 6,500sq.km.
Pop.: 0.34m. within,
0.18m. outside

LEBOWA
Capital: Kgomo
Language: N. Sotho
Area: 21,400sq.km.
Pop.: 1.8m. within,
1.1m. outside

GAZANKULU
Capital: Giyani
Language: Tsonga-Shangana
Area: 6,700sq.km.
Pop.: 0.63m. within,
0.47m. outside

KANGWANE
Capital: Louieville
Language: Swazi
Area: 3,700sq.km.
Pop.: 0.24m. within,
0.76 outside

KWA NDEBELE
Capital: Siyabuswa
Language: Ndebele
Area: 1,800sq.km.
Pop.:0.14m. within,
0.29m. outside

KWA ZULU
Capital: Ulundi
Language: Zulu
Area: 32,000sq.km.
Pop.: 3.8m. within,
2.7m. outside

QWAQWA
Capital: Phuthaditjhaba
Language: S.Sotho
Area: 1,300sq.km.
Pop.: 0.17m. within,
1.75m. outside

TRANSKEI
Capital: Umtata
Language: Xhosa
Area: 42,000sq.km.
Population: (with Ciskei)
3.3m. within,
2.9m. outside

CISKEI
Capital: Bisho
Language: Xhosa
Area: 8,700sq.km.
Population: see Transkei

BOPHUTHATSWANA
Capital: Mmabatho
Language: Tswana
Area: 44,000sq.km.
Pop.: 1.5m. within,
1.35m. without

REPUBLIC OF SOUTH AFRICA
Capital: Pretoria
Languages: official — Afrikaans & English,
others — numerous Bantu languages,
5 Indian languages, Bushman & Khoe/
Pop.: White 4.58m. Coloured 2.82m.
Asian 0.79m. Black 15.24m.

Official statistics, 1985

Four Republics within South Africa:

Transkei
Ciskei
Bophuthatswana
Venda

Six self-governing National States:

Kwa Zulu
Lebowa
Qwaqwa
Gazankulu
Kangwane
Kwandebele

MOZAMBIQUE
ZIMBABWE
ZAMBIA
ANGOLA
NAMIBIA
BOTSWANA
SWAZILAND
LESOTHO

Harare
Lusaka
Windhoek
Gaborone
Maputo
Mbabane
Pretoria
Johannesburg
Maseru
Bloemfontein
Richard's Bay
Durban
East London
Port Elizabeth
Mossel Bay
Cape Town
Saldanha

0   100   miles
0   200   km

© carta

129

THE REPUBLIC OF SOUTH AFRICA AND ITS NEIGHBORS, POLITICAL

The Republic of South Africa, like its neighbors is populated principally by Bantu-speakers (see map 95). These populations represent different phases of the expansion of Bantu-speakers throughout southern Africa, a development of the last five hundred years. These people crossed the Great Kei River only in the late eighteenth century, and their tribal genealogies show that before the 1820s they had not formed national groups. The Khoi-San peoples represent a relic of a much earlier population which in all probability was slowly driven south from the latitude of the present Tanzania, where their remains have been found.

The greater part of the population of all these lands is engaged in agriculture and livestock farming, save in the Kalahari Desert, where hunters and gatherers still survive. The most important feature of the region is its mineral wealth. In Zimbabwe gold has been mined since at least the fifth century A.D.; and by 1100 it was being used to make splendid jewelry such as that found at Mapungubwe. Other natural resources are, silver, copper, nickel, coal, chrome ore, tin, iron ore, and cobalt. Zambia has many of these same resources among which copper is preeminent. Angola has oil and diamond deposits, Mozambique coal. The Republic of South Africa, apart from the main industries of gold and diamonds and the ownership or control of other diamond fields besides, has also coal, iron ore, copper, manganese, limestone, and asbestos. Namibia has important reserves of uranium. In Botswana large mines for diamonds and copper-nickel have been opened; it is one of the largest diamond producers in the world. Lesotho also has diamonds, and is prospecting for oil. The whole region thus makes an essential contribution to world economy.

In the organization of the mines of southern Africa, especially in the Republic of South Africa, persons of European descent have played an overwhelming part, although only 18 percent of the population is white. While labor is almost entirely black, very much of it flows into the Republic from outside, even as far away as Malawi and Tanzania. It thus contributes to other economies. In the four independent republics, in each of which there are movements demanding reintegration with the Republic, and in the self-governing dependent homelands, a major proportion of the population is quasi-migratory and engaged in mining and other employments within the Republic.

The rationale of the division of the Republic into what are described as independent republics and dependent homelands has been discussed in Map 95. Uniquely among the people of European descent in Africa, the Afrikaner population of the Republic has long severed all cultural ties with the original Netherlands homeland, and attracted into a new national consciousness the French immigrants who joined them in the seventeenth century. Their position contrasts sharply with that taken by the Portuguese, who intermarried freely with their African neighbors from the fifteenth century on and melted by degrees into the indigenous population. To a lesser degree the same severance of cultural ties with a European homeland may be observed in Kenya and Zimbabwe, and with the acceptance of local nationality. Among the Afrikaners a distinctive cultural tradition has emerged, expressed also in the arts and sciences. In medicine, for example, South African doctors — in spite of their small numbers — have led the world in certain new procedures. The Afrikaner culture is thus by no means what Arnold Toynbee identified as a "fossil civilization." □

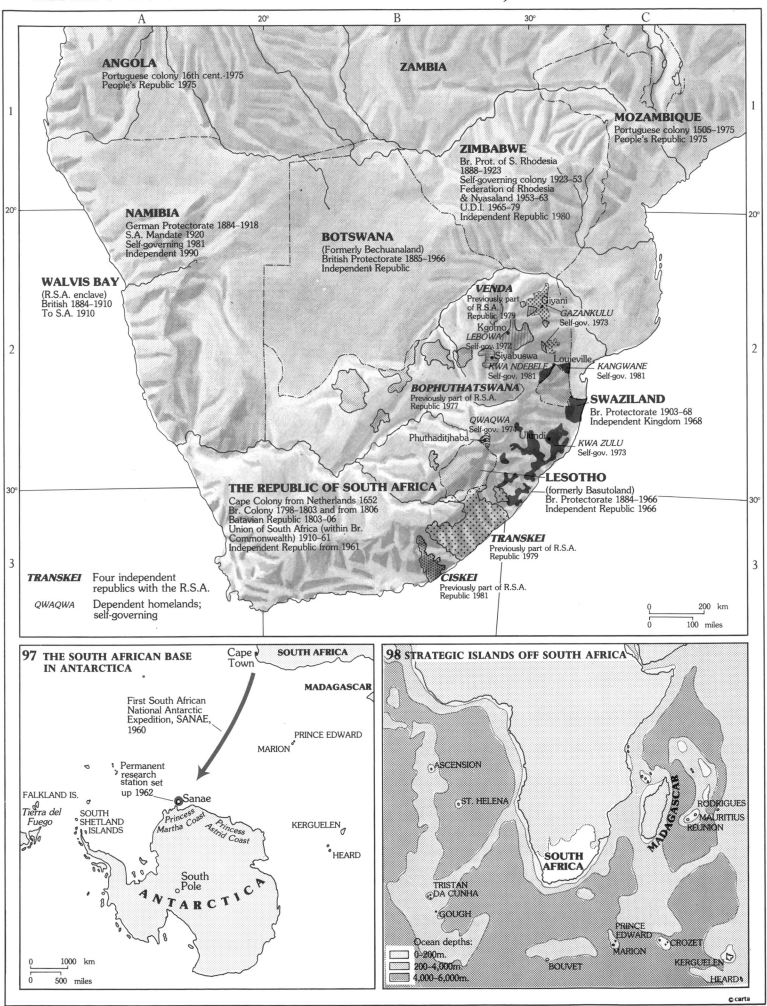

ANGOLA
Portuguese colony 16th cent.-1975
People's Republic 1975

ZAMBIA

MOZAMBIQUE
Portuguese colony 1505–1975
People's Republic 1975

ZIMBABWE
Br. Prot. of S. Rhodesia
1888–1923
Self-governing colony 1923–53
Federation of Rhodesia
& Nyasaland 1953–63
U.D.I. 1965–79
Independent Republic 1980

NAMIBIA
German Protectorate 1884–1918
S.A. Mandate 1920
Self-governing 1981
Independent 1990

BOTSWANA
(Formerly Bechuanaland)
British Protectorate 1885–1966
Independent Republic

WALVIS BAY
(R.S.A. enclave)
British 1884–1910
To S.A. 1910

VENDA
Previously part
of R.S.A.
Republic 1979   Giyani

GAZANKULU
Self-gov. 1973

Kgomo
LEBOWA
Self-gov. 1972
Siyabuswa   Louieville
KWA NDEBELE   *KANGWANE*
Self-gov. 1981   Self-gov. 1981

BOPHUTHATSWANA
Previously part of R.S.A.
Republic 1977

SWAZILAND
Br. Protectorate 1903–68
Independent Kingdom 1968

QWAQWA
Self-gov. 1974   Ulundi
Phuthaditjhaba   *KWA ZULU*
Self-gov. 1973

LESOTHO
(formerly Basutoland)
Br. Protectorate 1884–1966
Independent Republic 1966

THE REPUBLIC OF SOUTH AFRICA
Cape Colony from Netherlands 1652
Br. Colony 1798–1803 and from 1806
Batavian Republic 1803–06
Union of South Africa (within Br.
Commonwealth) 1910–61
Independent Republic from 1961

TRANSKEI
Previously part of R.S.A.
Republic 1979

CISKEI
Previously part of R.S.A.
Republic 1981

TRANSKEI Four independent
republics with the R.S.A.

QWAQWA   Dependent homelands;
self-governing

0   200 km
0   100 miles

Cape
Town   **SOUTH AFRICA**

MADAGASCAR

First South African
National Antarctic
Expedition, SANAE,
1960

PRINCE EDWARD
MARION

Permanent
research
station set
up 1962
FALKLAND IS.   Sanae
Tierra del   Princess
Fuego   Martha Coast   Princess
SOUTH   Astrid Coast
SHETLAND   KERGUELEN
ISLANDS
HEARD

South
Pole
A N T A R C T I C A

0   1000 km
0   500 miles

ASCENSION

ST. HELENA

RODRIGUES
MAURITIUS
REUNION

MADAGASCAR

**SOUTH
AFRICA**

TRISTAN
DA CUNHA

GOUGH

PRINCE
EDWARD
MARION   CROZET

Ocean depths:
0–200m.
200–4,000m.   BOUVET   KERGUELEN
4,000–6,000m.
HEARD

©carta

SOUTHERN AFRICA IN WORLD COMMUNICATION AND STRATEGY

The quantity of the sinkings of naval and merchant vessels illustrate the strategic importance of southern Africa during two world wars. In World War I the Suez Canal (map 76) was threatened by Ottoman Turkey until the British took Jaffa in November 1917 and received the capitulation of Ottoman Turkey in Jerusalem on 9 December. In World War II the canal was closed from 1940 until 1943 because of its vulnerability to air attack by Axis forces. It was closed again from 1956 to 1957 following the Anglo-French attack on Egypt, in defense of their acknowledged rights (according to international law) to its operation. It was closed for a fourth time after the Six-Day War between Egypt and Israel, and was reopened only in 1974. During all four periods southern African waters were the sole means of communication by sea between west and east — a communication with the oil-producing countries of the Persian Gulf, essential to the economies of Europe and the Americas. In the two world wars this was of crucial importance to the Allies, as witness the great number of sinkings not only off South Africa but in the relatively narrow channel between Madagascar and Mozambique. Until 1957 Britain had authority over the naval base of Simonstown. In that year it transferred the base to South Africa, while retaining its use. The only other British bases in Africa during World War II were at Takoradi in Ghana and the magnificent harbor of Kilindini, at Mombasa in Kenya.

Southern African waters contain a number of islands which also are of strategic importance. This was especially the case during the war between Argentina and Britain in the Falkland Islands, when the airfield facilities of Ascension Island were a vital link. Some of these islands — Madagascar, three of the four Comoro Islands, and Mauritius — are independent. Mauritius is a member of the British Commonwealth. Mayotte, the fourth of the Comoro Islands, and Réunion have remained overseas departments of France at their own request.

In the Anglo–South African Wars the Boers were distinguished by their resource and courage as well as by their skill in commando tactics. In World War I, South African troops served not only in South-West Africa and East Africa (maps 83, 84), but also in France. They are particularly remembered for their heroism on the Somme in their defense of Delville Wood, 1 July to 23 October 1916. South African troops served also with distinction in World War II, in which troops from Zimbabwe, then Southern Rhodesia, and from Zambia, then Northern Rhodesia, also served.

In the overall strategic consideration of this vast region one demarche on the part of the Republic of South Africa should not be overlooked. In 1960 the South African government sent the first South African National Antarctic Expedition (SANAE) to the ice cap of the South Pole; a permanent research station, which was of immediate value as a meteorological station, was established in 1962. Research in this region is also of importance because the potential resources of the ice cap, whether in oil or in other minerals, are little known.

□

99 SOUTHERN AFRICA IN WORLD COMMUNICATIONS AND STRATEGY

The sinkings of naval and merchant vessels illustrate South Africa's strategic importance during two World Wars, in the second of which the Suez Canal was closed from 1940 to 1943.

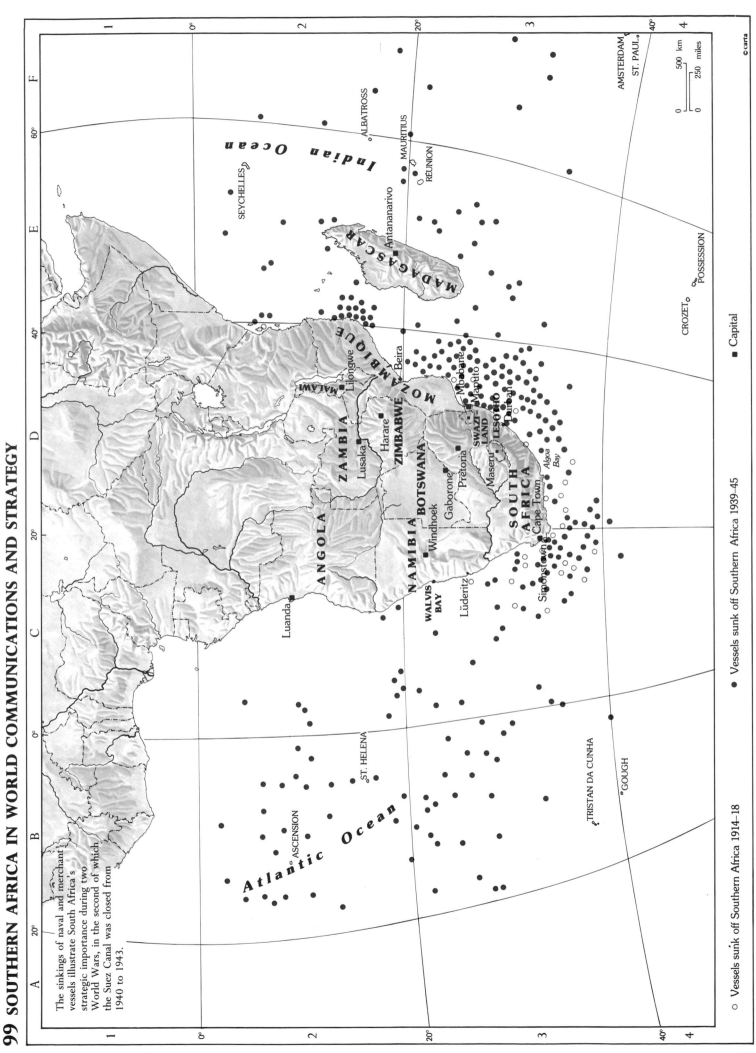

○ Vessels sunk off Southern Africa 1914–18

● Vessels sunk off Southern Africa 1939–45

● Capital

133

AFRICA, POLITICS AND POPULATION, 1990

If in 1799 observers had attempted to predict the course of the French Revolution and its consequences they could not have done so: two hundred years later the future of Africa was equally unpredictable.

Since 1960, the Year of Africa, and the following year, when, in two years, sixteen countries were declared independent, certain distinct trends have been observable. In many countries Marxist or quasi-Marxist political systems have been set up. The stifling of individual human endeavor, the stranglehold of bureaucracy and of one-party states have had the identical consequences that have been suffered in the U.S.S.R. and eastern Europe: of crumbling economies, ever-increasing poverty, and famine. It will be strange if these African efforts, long bolstered by eastern European subventions, do not collapse as their European counterparts have done.

There lurk, too, with ever-increasing pressure, two factors of supreme demographic importance. The first is a population explosion on an unimaginable scale. In Egypt, as in Nigeria, one-half of the population is under twenty-five years of age. A comparison of the population figures for 1975 (map 94) and those for 1989 shows an enormous growth that is virtually unchecked by any form of restraint.

The second demographic factor, with varying severity of incidence from country to country, is the rapid spread of AIDS. Accurate overall statistics are lacking, but some examples are not wanting. Half the troops from Zimbabwe serving in Mozambique are HIV positive. In Uganda one-third of all live births are HIV positive. Incidence of this disease is found to be higher in the better-to-do social grades in the cities than among the more static peasantry. This bodes ill for the future, for it is precisely in these social grades that rests the burden of government, of health and education services, and all the other services that are part of the machinery of every modern state.

Another factor to be taken into account in assessing Africa's future is religion. For this there are no wholly reliable statistics. A great part of the population adheres to ancient traditional beliefs. Large areas (see map 32) have Muslim majorities, compromised often enough by syncretism with the same traditional beliefs. As to Christianity, the missions, so long regarded by some as quasi-agents of colonial powers, have transformed themselves into veritable local churches, with local hierarchies. In Rome, African cardinals sit in council alongside their Asian and European brethren. The upsurge of Islamic fundamentalism which was felt in the 1960s was paralleled in Egypt by a remarkable revival of religious practice among the Copts, particularly of monasticism among the most highly educated. African church leaders participated similarly in the World Council of Churches.

In all matters of politics, economics, health, education, and religion, the choice lies wholly in African hands. Much needs to be done to remedy long-standing griefs and grievances, and nothing can be done by wildcat economics or by multiplying debts. Even if banks or governments write debts off, the managers of the economy will have failed to act with prudence. Progress can only be achieved by the patient building up and reinvestment of resources, not by the application of external emergency aid. The lesson, perhaps, is one which twentieth-century Europe has been very slow to learn. It is that peace and prosperity can only be secured by the recognition of interdependence among neighbors. Peace can be shattered by rogue support for terrorism. The concept of interdependence is the contrary of isolationism. Such a concept of interdependence led Kwame Nkrumah in the early 1960s as far as the concept of an Organization of African Unity. Unfortunately his perception did not go so far as to recognize that Africa, no less than Europe, cannot live as "an island unto itself." □

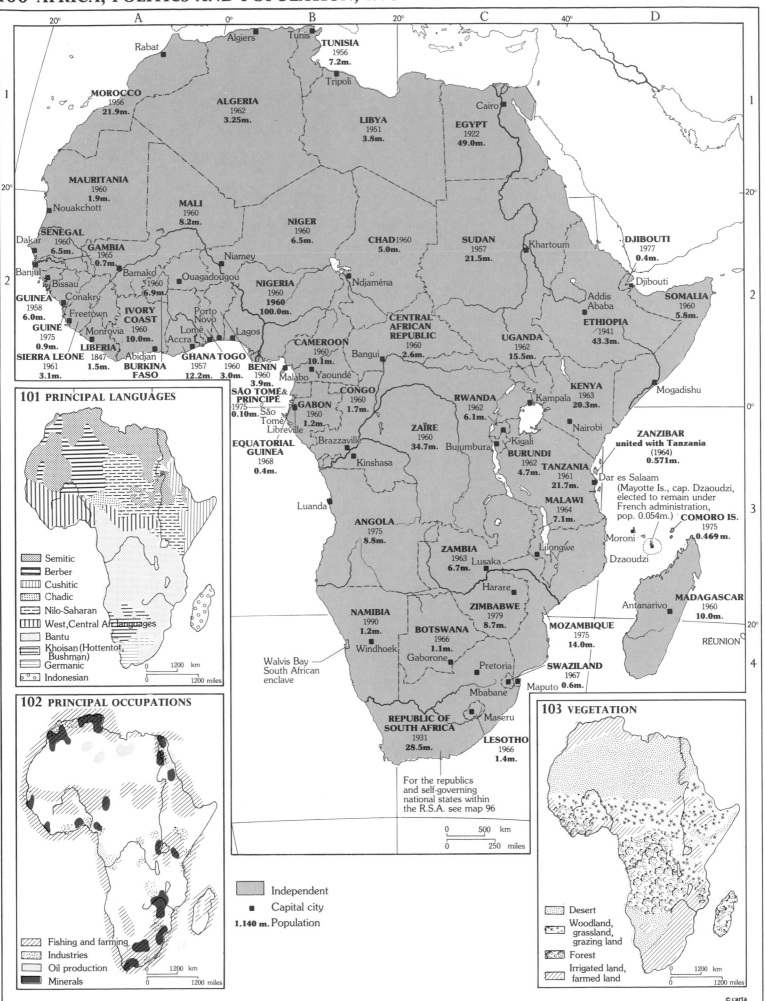

100 AFRICA, POLITICS AND POPULATION, 1990

MOROCCO 1956 21.9m.
TUNISIA 1956 7.2m.
ALGERIA 1962 3.25m.
LIBYA 1951 3.8m.
EGYPT 1922 49.0m.
MAURITANIA 1960 1.9m.
MALI 1960 8.2m.
NIGER 1960 6.5m.
CHAD 1960 5.0m.
SUDAN 1957 21.5m.
DJIBOUTI 1977 0.4m.
SENEGAL 1960 6.5m.
GAMBIA 1965 0.7m.
GUINEA 1958 6.0m.
GUINÉ 1975 0.9m.
SIERRA LEONE 1961 3.1m.
LIBERIA 1847 1.5m.
BURKINA FASO 1960 6.9m.
IVORY COAST 1960 10.0m.
GHANA 1957 12.2m.
TOGO 1960 3.0m.
BENIN 1960 3.9m.
NIGERIA 1960 100.0m.
CAMEROON 1960 10.1m.
CENTRAL AFRICAN REPUBLIC 1960 2.6m.
SOMALIA 1960 5.8m.
ETHIOPIA 1941 43.3m.
UGANDA 1962 15.5m.
KENYA 1963 20.3m.
SÃO TOMÉ & PRINCIPE 1975 0.10m.
GABON 1960 1.2m.
EQUATORIAL GUINEA 1968 0.4m.
CONGO 1960 1.7m.
ZAÏRE 1960 34.7m.
RWANDA 1962 6.1m.
BURUNDI 1962 4.7m.
TANZANIA 1961 21.7m.
ZANZIBAR united with Tanzania (1964) 0.571m.
COMORO IS. 1975 0.469 m.
(Mayotte Is., cap. Dzaoudzi, elected to remain under French administration, pop. 0.054m.)
MALAWI 1964 7.1m.
ANGOLA 1975 8.8m.
ZAMBIA 1963 6.7m.
ZIMBABWE 1979 8.7m.
MOZAMBIQUE 1975 14.0m.
MADAGASCAR 1960 10.0m.
RÉUNION
NAMIBIA 1990 1.2m.
BOTSWANA 1966 1.1m.
SWAZILAND 1967 0.6m.
Walvis Bay South African enclave
REPUBLIC OF SOUTH AFRICA 1931 28.5m.
LESOTHO 1966 1.4m.

For the republics and self-governing national states within the R.S.A. see map 96

0   500   km
0   250   miles

101 PRINCIPAL LANGUAGES

- Semitic
- Berber
- Cushitic
- Chadic
- Nilo-Saharan
- West,Central Afr.languages
- Bantu
- Khoisan (Hottentot, Bushman)
- Germanic
- Indonesian

0   1200   km
0   1200   miles

102 PRINCIPAL OCCUPATIONS

- Fishing and farming
- Industries
- Oil production
- Minerals

0   1200   km
0   1200   miles

Independent
Capital city
1.140 m. Population

103 VEGETATION

- Desert
- Woodland, grassland, grazing land
- Forest
- Irrigated land, farmed land

0   1200   km
0   1200   miles

© carta

135

INDEX

139

GAYLORD S